W9-AUG-125

THE ARCHAEOLOGY
OF ART IN THE
AMERICAN SOUTHWEST

Issues in Southwest Archaeology
Edited by John Kantner

Issues in Southwest Archaeology features volumes that critically evaluate current archaeological research in the U.S. Southwest and Northwest Mexico. Titles investigate pervasive themes both in the archaeology of the region but also in contemporary anthropological inquiry, such as ethnicity, gender, migration, and violence. Authors discuss not only what archaeologists already know about the prehistory of the Southwest, but they also consider issues that impact the practice of archaeology today, including the roles of cultural resource management, oral history, and cultural property rights. Each contribution to the series is ultimately synthetic, comparative, and fully engaged in broader anthropological interests.

Editor John Kantner may be contacted at the following address:
Vice President for Academic and Institutional Advancement
School for Advanced Research
P.O. Box 2188
Santa Fe, NM 87504-2188

Books in the series:
Living Histories: Native Americans and Southwestern Archaeology, by Chip Colwell-Chanthaphonh (2010)

The Archaeology of Art in the American Southwest, by Marit K. Munson (2011)

THE ARCHAEOLOGY
OF ART IN THE
AMERICAN SOUTHWEST

MARIT K. MUNSON

ALTAMIRA PRESS
A Division of Rowman & Littlefield Publishers, Inc.
Lanham • New York • Toronto • Plymouth, UK

Published by AltaMira Press
A division of Rowman & Littlefield Publishers, Inc.
A wholly owned subsidary of The Rowman & Littlefield Publishing Group, Inc.
4501 Forbes Boulevard, Suite 200, Lanham, Maryland 20706
http://www.altamirapress.com

Estover Road, Plymouth PL6 7PY, United Kingdom

British Library Cataloguing in Publication Information Available

Library of Congress Cataloging-in-Publication Data

Munson, Marit K.
  The archaeology of art in the American Southwest / Marit K. Munson.
    p. cm. — (Issues in Southwest archaeology) (Introduction : art and other
practicalities — The problem of art in archaeology — Artists — Audiences —
Images — Aesthetics — The future of art in archaeology)
  Includes bibliographical references and index.
  ISBN 978-0-7591-1077-9 (cloth : alk. paper) — ISBN 978-0-7591-2025-9
(electronic : alk. paper)
  1. Archaeology and art—Southwest, New. 2. Indian art—Southwest, New.
3. Southwest, New—Antiquities. 4. Material culture—Southwest, New. 5. Indians
of North America—Material culture—Southwest, New. I. Title.
  N72.A56M86 2011
  709.79—dc22   2010049878

Printed in the United States of America

CONTENTS

Acknowledgments

IN 2005, JOHN KANTNER ASKED IF I WOULD be interested in contributing something on art and iconography for the series Issues in Southwest Archaeology. Without his prompting, I never would have dared to start such a project. The structure and content of the book owe a great deal to Candace Greene, who has shaped my thinking about anthropology, art, and museums, and to the students in my classes on the anthropology of art at Trent University.

I wrote most of this manuscript while on sabbatical as a visiting research associate at the School for Advanced Research (SAR) in Santa Fe. The SAR is an amazing place to work, with lots of peace and quiet, plus a whole community of marvelous people for interesting conversations and welcome distractions. Many thanks to James Brooks and all of the staff at SAR, to scholars Danny Hoffman, Tim Pauketat, Dean Falk, Wenda Trevathan (Jessie thanks you too), Audra Simpson, and Susan Alt, and to artists Cedar Sherbert and Pat Courtney Gold.

I would like to acknowledge my great debt to the thoughtful, creative, and sometimes provocative work of Patty Crown, Kelley Hays-Gilpin, Jerry Brody, Steve Plog, and Steve Lekson, and Howard Morphy. This manuscript benefited from formal reviews by Michelle Hegmon, John Kantner, and an anonymous reviewer. Many thanks to Wendi Schnaufer and everyone else at AltaMira. I also greatly appreciate the comments and feedback of Linda Cordell, Cam Cocks, Willow Powers, and Wolky Toll. Finally, thanks to Bruce Munson for wanting to know how we recognize the difference between a dog and a cat and to Barbara Munson for reining him in.

Introduction

*[R]ather than fleeing from the word "art," . . . researchers . . .
would benefit from considering the concept. (Morales 2005:70)*

MIMBRES BOWLS ARE KNOWN AND CELEBRATED worldwide as masterpieces of ancient art (figure 1.1). Painted around a thousand years ago, the bowls came to light in the Mimbres Valley of southwestern New Mexico in the early 20th century. They were introduced to the wider world through the work of anthropologist J. Walter Fewkes, who wrote several reports that publicized the amazing images on the newly excavated artifacts—scenes of men and women, of birds and fish, of farming and ceremonies and even human sacrifice. Often dubbed "story bowls," Mimbres ceramics charmed and engaged viewers, tantalizing them with the promise of a glimpse into the past. Today, the bowls' incredible display value is both a blessing and a curse. They are featured in museum exhibits and collections around the world; they inspire contemporary artists. Thanks to contemporary art markets, the bowls also have great monetary value, along with the attendant problems of looting, illegal trade, and forgery (Brody 2005:xvi; Lekson 1992). Mimbres pottery is the quintessential example of ancient Southwestern art.

But what if the Mimbres bowls are not art? While art historians and collectors have readily claimed these bowls as art, many archaeologists are fundamentally uneasy with extending such a concept to 1,000-year-old artifacts, beautiful or not. Archaeologists may use Mimbres images for logos, book covers, and T-shirt designs (Lekson 1992), but we shrink from the implications of calling Mimbres pottery art. How, we worry, can we

Figure 1.1.   This Classic Mimbres black-on-white bowl incorporates mountain sheep heads in the overall layout of the geometric design. Courtesy of the Maxwell Museum of Anthropology, University of New Mexico, 77-67-1a. Photographer unknown.

know what the ancient painters of the Mimbres Valley intended? Were they really artists? How could we possibly understand the emotional or psychological experience of a person viewing or using these bowls a millennium ago? How could the bowls be art if they were actually used to serve food, or to accompany the dead in burial?

These very questions are central to archaeological studies of art, as they reveal a fundamental divide in Western conceptions of art and artifact. Centuries of Western tradition, reaching back to Renaissance Italy, suggest that art is the product of civilization and leisure, not of subsistence farmers. Art, we feel, is "for art's sake," removed from the practical concerns of daily life and intended for the sole purpose of display. The artists who create art are rare geniuses, uniquely insightful individuals who are a far cry from anonymous craftspeople making tools and containers. And art is, we feel certain, painting and sculpture, and perhaps a few other privileged media—not basketry, sandals, or serving bowls. Above all, we believe that art should be beautiful and moving, evoking symbols and expressing complex meanings and truths. When we cannot understand the truths that art tells, we admit our philistine tendencies and turn to connoisseurs and critics for explanations.

What does it mean, in the face of these expectations, to call Mimbres pottery art, or the potters and painters artists? I argue that to name something as art or as artifact has consequences; it shapes the way that we view objects. Calling an object an artifact focuses attention on the practical, the functional, the material, and the assemblage. Applying the term art shifts attention away from these prosaic concerns and toward the aesthetic, the visual, the conceptual, and the individual form. Concerned about the perceived subjectivity of "art," most archaeologists have shied away from the term, focusing solely on the reassuringly material and practical study of artifacts. In doing so, they have rejected potentially powerful lines of inquiry, neglecting the art-like aspects of ancient objects. Rather than fleeing from "art" as a concept, I argue that archaeologists should use this loaded term, letting the powerful associations and assumptions that accompany it frame the ways that we look at ancient objects, the kinds of questions we ask, and, ultimately, what we see.

Framing Mimbres Pottery

The consequences of the labels "art" and "artifact" show clearly in the century of studies of Mimbres ceramics. From the early 20th century to the present day, the status of Mimbres bowls has shifted frequently, from artifact to art and back again. Each shift has had practical consequences in shaping research into Mimbres ceramics, emphasizing different aspects of the same objects.

Smithsonian anthropologist J. Walter Fewkes (1914) first reported on Classic Mimbres black-on-white bowls in the early 20th century, in the context of a standard archaeological report on the prehistory of the Mimbres Valley, in southwestern New Mexico (figure 1.2). The people of the Mimbres Valley painted lively images and striking designs in black paint on white-slipped bowls between about 1000–1150 CE. Fewkes found the designs interesting but initially treated the images as a curiosity, a decorative fillip added to utilitarian pottery.

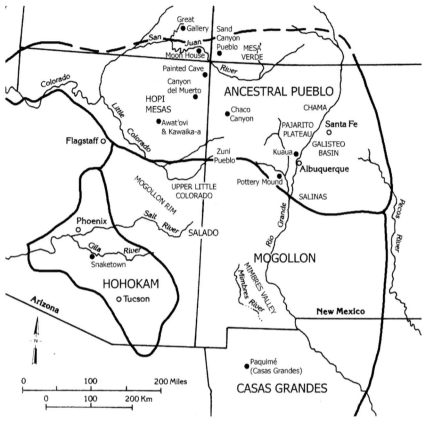

Figure 1.2.   Map of culture areas and major archaeological sites of the Southwest. Drawing by Marit K. Munson.

Fewkes's early publications on Mimbres pottery happened to coincide with the height of the arts and crafts movement and with growing efforts to define a distinctly American identity through art and antiquities (Cumming 1991). The resulting nostalgia for the handmade helped transform early 20th-century Pueblo pottery into art—and created increased interest in the archaeological examples, such as Mimbres pottery, that provided the time depth needed to legitimize early 20th-century Pueblo pottery as a continuation of ancient traditions (Munson 2007). The newfound respect for ancient American art is reflected in Fewkes's statement that "no Southwestern pottery, ancient or modern, surpasses that of the Mimbres, and its naturalistic figures are unexcelled in any pottery from prehistoric North America" (Fewkes 1923:1). Mimbres painters, he wrote, were "great observers [and] clever artists" (Fewkes 1923:4). A year later, Fewkes praised the geometric designs on Mimbres pottery as an important source of inspiration for early 20th-century artists and textile designers—"on account of their strictly American character no less than their great artistic beauty"—adding that "specialists have already begun working on them with this thought in mind" (Fewkes 1924:15).

By the 1930s, the transformation of Mimbres ceramics from artifact to art was well accepted. Glowing reports surfaced of the bowls' reception in Europe as "art [that] was so surprising and superior that savants came again and again, on succeeding days, to look at the craftsmanship of the prehistoric American artists," pronouncing it "unquestionably superior to the Greeks in the field of geometric art" (Jenks 1932:137). With the bowls (or, more precisely, the painting on the bowls) cast as art, the painters were correspondingly elevated to artists, expressing creativity and humor through their work (e.g., Watson 1932). Archaeologist A. V. Kidder (in Cosgrove and Cosgrove 1932:xxi) reflected this newfound interest in the individual artist when he speculated on the origins of Classic Mimbres black-on-white pottery: "All in all, it seems to me that we must attribute this extraordinary fluorescence to the influence of a single potter, whose work was so outstanding that during her lifetime she was able to overcome the conservatism of her contemporaries and found a school of brilliant decorators."

Mimbres ceramics had become, in Stephen Lekson's (1992:114) words, "an isolated artistic miracle," an unlikely pinnacle of civilized achievement in an otherwise unimpressive archaeological region (Lekson 1992:113; also see LeBlanc 2004:3). Indeed, the contrast between such a sophisticated art and relatively "primitive" artifacts and villages gave rise to debates about who or what constituted the "Mimbres culture" (Nelson and Hegmon 2010). Geographically speaking, the Mimbres River's location in southwestern New Mexico suggested that the valley's inhabitants were part of the Mogollon culture (see figure 1.2), one of the "big three" Southwestern archaeological cultures that researchers defined in the 1920s and 1930s (Cordell 1997:164–72). But what was the relationship of the people in the Mimbres Valley with their neighbors to the west, the Hohokam of central and southern Arizona (see Hegmon and Nelson 2007)? And how did the Anasazi (also known as Ancestral Pueblo) people of the northern Southwest fit into the picture?

For a long time, archaeologists believed that the striking black-on-white pottery of the Classic Mimbres period (1000–1150 CE) must somehow be distinct from the relatively unsophisticated Mogollon tradition

(Haury 1936). Perhaps, they proposed, it was the result of Ancestral Pueblo people from the north moving into the Mogollon area and bringing their own pottery traditions (Martin 1975). It was not until the 1980s, when archaeologists began to focus on the pottery as artifacts, that the Mimbres Foundation managed to document continuity in local pottery traditions (LeBlanc 1982, 1983). Gradually, archaeologists' concerns about the aesthetics of the pottery began to diminish, and researchers focused more on dating and other typically archaeological matters.

Since the 1970s, interest in the Mimbres area has exploded, as reflected in a series of shows and art exhibits (Brody et al. 1983; Brody and Swentzell 1996) as well as an astonishing number of research projects drawing on new data from excavations, surveys, and museum collections (see Hegmon 2002; Powell-Marti and Gilman 2006). In one sense, these efforts have successfully brought Mimbres ceramics to a broader audience and are rapidly expanding our understanding of the people and their pottery. At the same time, however, this interest reflects the continued presence of the long-standing divide between art and artifact.

The art side of Mimbres ceramics is represented by a steady stream of work on Mimbres iconography (Moulard 1982; also see Shaffer 2002; Short 1998; Stoffel 1991; Thompson 1999). These studies focus almost exclusively on the images, removing them from their context as if the bowls themselves are an insignificant canvas for master painters (Brody 2005; cf. Moulard 1985). The art approach leads these authors to focus on visual aspects, aesthetic qualities, and the conceptual and metaphorical meanings of the paintings (e.g., Brody et al. 1983; Tanner 1976:140–44). Often, researchers focus on unique images, highlighting the importance of a singular case for their argument.

The other side of the divide, most populated by archaeologists, treats Mimbres ceramics as prosaic artifacts, admirable in appearance but most useful for practical questions of chronology (Scott 1983; Shafer and Brewington 1995), craft specialization (Gilman et al. 1994), regional interaction (Hegmon et al. 1998), the learning process (Crown 2001), and so on (see Hegmon 2002). These artifact studies rely on entire assemblages, collecting masses of data that focus on the materials, technology, and function of the ceramic vessels. Only rarely does a study meaningfully integrate consideration of the imagery or designs on Mimbres bowls with data from the vessels themselves (e.g., Powell-Marti and James 2006), mingling the concerns of art and of artifact.

Art/Artifact

Assumptions about the difference between artifact and art in the Southwest are pervasive, yet few archaeologists are conscious of the effect of these ideas. We need to pay closer attention to the categories of art and artifact—in part, to be clear about our goals as researchers and in part because intentionally moving objects from one category to the other opens up new avenues of research, new questions, and new insights into the lives of the ancient inhabitants of the Southwest.

What Is Art?

Considerations of art and artifact require us to first address fundamental problems of definitions, disciplinary boundaries, and the changing goals of archaeology. In particular, we must begin with a definition of art. As with all definitions, the task is much more difficult than it first appears. As described in chapter 2, art historians, philosophers, and others have struggled with the concept of art from antiquity to the present day (Shiner 2001). Many of these debates are rooted in the nature of art on an existential level: does it exist as an independent entity in the world, or is it created through a culturally mediated process of discovery? Regardless of one's stand on this fundamental question, a brief history of "art" demonstrates that it is an extraordinarily malleable concept, one that has been pushed, pulled, and stretched to encompass an enormous range of objects. Indeed, the history of art is littered with examples of ordinary objects elevated to the status of art, whether Marcel Duchamp's readymade sculptures (Brody 1974), an African mask that Picasso reportedly discovered in a French flea market (Donne 1978), or a pile of tires that Allan Kaprow exhibited in a New York gallery in the early 1960s (Vogel 1988b).

Discovering Ancient Art

The history of art readily shows how definitions of art have expanded over time to engulf countless ancient artifacts, from Upper Paleolithic cave paintings in France to scratched pebbles in southern Africa. As described in chapter 2, the art world has "discovered" these objects as art by singling out their visual properties (Errington 1994): representational imagery (especially of humans), precise bold lines, and appealing combinations of bright or high-contrast colors. In addition to these qualities inherent in the objects themselves, the discovery process is also closely tied to contextual factors. Status as art might rely on actual or purported connections between ancient objects and historically known native artists, on the history of archaeological research in a given area, or on the personal taste of individual collectors.

In the Southwest, as elsewhere, the distinction between art and artifacts is extraordinarily unsystematic, contingent on historical chance, and reflects the whims of art markets more than any inherent qualities of the objects themselves (Munson 2008a). As a result, there is now a tacit century-long history of treating some objects from the prehistoric Southwest primarily as art. This includes Mimbres ceramics (see figure 1.1), first and foremost, but also 14th–16th-century yellowware ceramics from the Hopi area (figures 2.2a, b), rock art of all times and places (figure 1.3), and wall paintings, or kiva murals, of the Pueblo IV period (1325–1600) (see figure 2.1). Other items treated as art include rare and unique figurines and ornaments from Chaco Canyon (figure 1.4), etched shell from Hohokam sites, and pieces with apparent ties to Mesoamerica (figure 1.5). On the opposite end of the spectrum, objects such as stone tools and plainware ceramics (tellingly re-

Figure 1.3.   This often-photographed "star bear" petroglyph is from San Cristobal Pueblo, a Pueblo IV to historic period site in the Galisteo Basin of New Mexico. Photograph by Marit K. Munson.

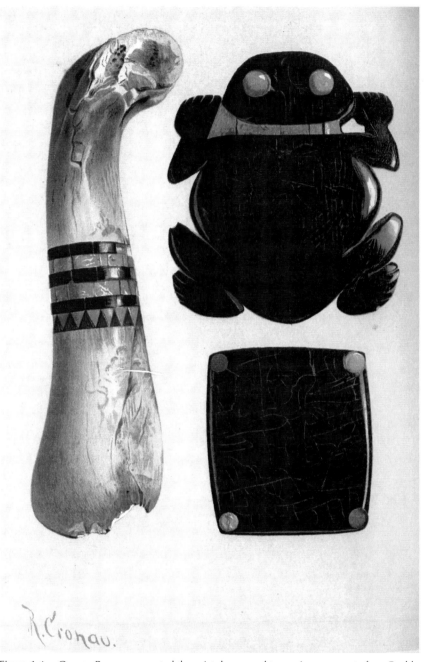

R.Cronau.

Figure 1.4.   George Pepper excavated these jet, bone, and turquoise ornaments from Pueblo Bonito, in Chaco Canyon. From Pepper 1905:plate 26.

Figure 1.5.   A quail effigy jar from Paquimé (Casas Grandes), dating to 1200–1450. Courtesy of the Snite Museum of Art, University of Notre Dame, 2002.68.001.

ferred to as "utilityware") are relegated entirely to the category of artifact. The middle ground is occupied by a large body of objects that are neither completely utilitarian nor so visually appealing or widely known that they have been discovered by the art world.

The Value of "Art" in Archaeology

The problem with categories of art, artifact, and in-between is that they are arbitrary and create bias. Art is used as a term of value. The monetary valuation of art over artifact has material consequences for the archaeological record, in the form of looting and illegal sales (Brody 2005:xvi; Colwell-Chanthaphonh 2004; Gill and Chippindale 1993). In a broader cultural sense, to call something art is to raise it to a higher level than mere artifact (Phillips 2002). To praise an archaeological culture as artistic is to imply its high standing in the world; to deny that a culture produced art is to denigrate its people as uncivilized, not fully human.

Even more significantly, the term "art" comes laden with heavy baggage (Morales 2005:71; Morley 2007:70; Smith 1994:263; Soffer and Conkey 1997:3), most of which can ultimately be traced to ideas that surfaced in Renaissance Europe and became codified in the 18th century. Indeed, archaeologists worldwide share the concern that art "is a useful shorthand term, but one that carries with it inappropriate associations with modern experience and practice" (Smith 1994:263; also see Bradley 2009:4). In fact, the category of art has such strong implications that merely using the word has a strong framing effect, automatically placing an object into a category that begs new kinds of questions about creativity, aesthetics, beauty, meaning, and the like. This can be a heavy load to heap upon an object that was made, used, and experienced a millennium ago, but it is not an entirely undesirable burden. As argued in chapter 2, archaeologists should be able to use that baggage, to harness assumptions about art and use them to expand our research and to ask new questions (Morphy 2005:60).

Where Art and Archaeology Meet

The core chapters of this book outline the assumptions that accompany a shift from artifact to art, then describe potentially productive ways of using those expectations to reframe the picture. Chapters 3 through 6 are titled very simply, with words drawn from the art world that are intended to be a bit provocative in an archaeological context: Artists, Audiences, Images, and Aesthetics. I hope that these terms might prompt archaeologists to look at objects in a different light, remaining empirically grounded but catching a glimpse of artifacts from a new angle. Some of the topics are more archaeologically grounded, requiring little more than a shift in perspective to reassess familiar methods. Others rely on art historical and philosophical work that may seem less pragmatic. As much as possible, the chapters are organized to move from the concrete and familiar to the abstract and speculative. The book draws almost entirely on examples from Southwestern archaeology, which has been my research focus for many years. Nevertheless, the methods and perspectives that I propose should be broadly applicable in other contexts. I have tried to provide enough context and explanation throughout the book to ensure that specialists in other regions or disciplines will be able to engage fully with the ideas presented here.

Artists

Chapters 3 and 4 focus on the social context of artwork, through examination of artists and audiences. Archaeologists have often shied away from using these terms, yet there are numerous studies illustrating different approaches to artists in the past and to the various audiences for their art. Some of our reluctance to discuss artists in the past is rooted, like concerns about the word "art," in uncertainty about the validity of Western concepts in cross-cultural contexts. As described in chapter 3, Western traditions view the artist as a creative genius, tormented by the burden of his (and they are usually male) artistic gift. These ideas began with a cult of celebrity in Renaissance Europe and expanded to encompass van Gogh's madness, the emotions and mental states of Expressionist painters, and the prophetic qualities sometimes attributed to late 20th-century and contemporary artists (Haynes 1997; Shiner 2001). These notions of an artistic personality do not always align well with artists in cultural contexts beyond the West. In the Southwest, numerous ethnographies describe potters, painters, weavers, and other artisans as anonymous, self-effacing, and bound by tradition.

Such contrasting portraits create a real problem when studying ancient artists. On the one hand, potters, weavers, carvers, and other craftspeople are thought of as conformist, conservative, and tradition bound. If true, this seems to negate the role of individual creativity, suggesting that perhaps the Western sense of an artist as a creative genius does not apply. On the other hand, if potters, weavers, carvers, and others truly are artists in the Western sense of rare, unusually skilled, insightful, and creative individuals, this raises a problem for archaeologists. How can we hope to locate and meaningfully discuss a single individual from 500 or 1,000 years ago?

Chapter 3 describes two different archaeological approaches to artists. The first is to focus on matters of the identity and status of artists as a group, with primary consideration given to gender and occasionally age. These studies rely on a variety of direct and indirect lines of evidence, with considerable weight given to ethnographic analogy. The second method is to study artists' products directly. Although most archaeological research has examined how technological variables reflect craft specialization, the same variables can be used, with a shift in perspective, to focus on the artists themselves. The key to doing so, I propose, is an archaeology of artistic practice, built around consideration of the motor skills and cognitive abilities of artists, as reflected in their work.

Two main examples illustrate this approach. The first centers on Steven LeBlanc and others' attribution of Mimbres black-on-white or Hopi yellowware ceramics to individual artists (LeBlanc 2004, 2006; LeBlanc and Henderson 2009), a project that has the potential to provide insights into the place of ancient ceramic artists in society as a whole. This work uses art historical methods based on consistencies within specific motifs, such as rabbits or various geometric designs, cross-checked through supporting archaeological evidence. In this case, identifying the "hand" of the artist involves locating the individual idiosyncrasies that a single artist repeats across multiple painted bowls—a rather subjective method, but one that can perhaps be refined (Russell and Hegmon forthcoming).

The second example draws on Patricia Crown's (1999, 2001, 2002) work on learning and ceramic production. Her approach centers on identifying the inconsistencies in skill level on a single vessel that indicate collaboration between a skilled potter/painter and an unskilled novice. Crown highlights different approaches to collaboration in ceramics from the Mimbres and Hohokam areas, arguing that the two assemblages reflect differing approaches of adults teaching children to form and paint pottery. These varied strategies have implications for the socialization of children, and in particular seem to reflect different ideas about the importance of "correct" production versus creative expression.

Curiously enough, then, the dual focus on collaboration and the hand of the individual leads back to that notion of creative genius that Kidder (in Cosgrove and Cosgrove 1932:xxi) first suggested for Mimbres potters three-quarters of a century ago. That is, the research raises questions about the balance between individual creativity and the constraints of tradition. Although direct study of creativity and tradition in the archaeological record is likely to be quite difficult, some potential avenues of exploration might provide insight into constraining structures and individual agency (David 2004).

Audiences

As with artists, the idea of an audience is seldom evoked directly in archaeological research. Chapter 4 looks at various archaeological studies that allude to the presence of audiences, if not necessarily addressing them directly. Generations of archaeologists have mentioned viewers of art that is fixed in space, such as rock art and kiva murals or other wall paintings. More recently, portable objects like ceramics have been brought into the picture, for qualities of the pottery itself suggest that some bowls were displayed to relatively large audiences at public feasts. Most archaeological studies of audiences focus on artifact style as a form of communication, with an implied, rather than specific, group of viewers. Despite the apparent promise of these studies, however, few examine the social implications of the composition of the audience—and, in particular, how varying access to artwork might relate to secrecy, knowledge, and power.

Archaeology's focus on the material holds great promise for studying viewing contexts and audiences, yet the discipline tends to be disconnected from broader theory concerning audiences. Art history, visual studies, and cultural studies have created a considerable body of work on spectatorship and the gaze, a perspective that highlights audiences' role in constituting that which they view (e.g., Dikovitskaya 2005; Rose 2001). As discussed in chapter 4, the concept of spectatorship offers intriguing avenues to explore, although the lack of material correlates and a general focus on contemporary media provide some serious barriers for archaeological applications.

Archaeologists are perhaps best served by combining the insights of visual studies with a more concrete focus on how artifact characteristics and proxemics affect accessibility for a potential audience. Proxemics, first developed by anthropologist Edward Hall (1966), describes the impact of space and distance on interactions of two or more individuals. Different spatial scales have varying implications for which features or movements are most readily visible to a viewer, from subtle facial expressions to full-body movements. This insight can be extended to art and artifacts as well, considering the ways in which audiences perceive qualities of material objects from various distances or points of view. Studies of the physical characteristics of objects highlight the features that are most relevant in terms of visibility at different scales, from fine infill designs to overall layout, large-scale images, and high-contrast colors.

For portable art, such as pottery, the contexts of viewing must be inferred from the objects' physical characteristics. As discussed in chapter 4, several researchers have been able to use factors such as the size, color, and contrast of decorated ceramic bowls to track changes in the size and composition of gatherings from the Pueblo I period (700–900 CE) through to the protohistoric period (1500–1692). Barbara Mills (2007), in particular, has successfully examined the changing relationships between the physical characteristics of pottery and the size of plazas at three Pueblo IV (1325–1600) villages on the Mogollon Rim in east-central Arizona. Although she does not address the specific composition of the audiences, her research is an important example of how audience size can be inferred from indirect means.

Audience size is reflected even more clearly for art that is fixed in space, such as the kiva murals and rock art mentioned earlier. In most cases, these works of art have distinct viewing contexts that preserve some of the physical relationships of art and audiences. The size of the space is directly relevant for the size of the audience, as an enclosed kiva, or ceremonial room, can accommodate only a limited number of people at any one time.[1]

In addition, the configuration of the space and its use through time also has significant implications for the visual and physical accessibility of the art and, hence, for the audience.

Rock art in the Northern Rio Grande Valley (Munson in press-a, b) illustrates the variability in art's accessibility. The physical layout and position of rock art sites in the region changed greatly from the Pueblo III period (1100–1325) into Pueblo IV (1325–1600), with considerable diversity in the accessibility of the later sites. The different degrees of accessibility in rock art therefore divide individuals from the same village into multiple audiences, which vary greatly in terms of what they are able to create, observe, and overhear. Chapter 4 also discusses the work of Elizabeth Newsome and Kelley Hays-Gilpin (in press) on Ancestral Pueblo murals. They use the spatial context and content of wall paintings to infer changes from the viewing experiences of ritual leaders in the northern Southwest during the Pueblo III period to those of religious societies or sodalities in the aggregated villages of the Pueblo IV world.

Chapter 4 concludes with a consideration of extremely restricted spatial contexts where the "audience" is so limited that the distinction between artist and audience fades away and the two roles merge, such as the pictographs of painted rockshelters in the Northern Rio Grande Valley during the Pueblo IV period (1325–1600). Such cases suggest that the process of producing the art was more important than the final product. In addition, they imply that perhaps the audience was other-than-human—that is, supernatural.

Images

Chapter 5 considers how archaeologists identify and interpret representational imagery. At first glance, this seems straightforward. Images represent things because they bear a resemblance to something in the world; surely it is a simple matter to recognize a picture? As art historian Erwin Panofsky (1955) points out, though, identification and interpretation of images involve multiple levels of inference, requiring increasing degrees of speculation. These levels are amply illustrated with an overview of archaeological work on images in the Southwest, where researchers usually identify figures without specifying what criteria they use. Such interpretations rely on common sense and/or ethnographic data from the historic Pueblos, often with labels drawn directly from specific languages or traditions that may or may not have anything to do with the image in question. As a result, archaeologists are often at cross-purposes, arguing about depictions of katsinas, atlatls, scalps, or the species of fish on Mimbres bowls without any means of determining which identification is the most reasonable.

Disagreements over images may in part be resolved with a combination of cautious documentation and an understanding of what is known as the picture problem (Chippindale 2001): how do artists translate three-dimensional creatures or objects into recognizable two-dimensional form? Although the creative possibilities may seem limitless, research by psychologists and others (Costall 1997; Deregowski 2005) shows that there is a limited number of coherent solutions to the problem. Indeed, artists who wish to create clear and recognizable images usually rely upon canonical perspective (Malafouris 2007), the contour that provides the greatest amount of information about a person or animal's shape. By combining an understanding of the universal factors related to the picture problem with the culturally specific conventions used in depiction, archaeologists are able to better understand modes of representation in the past, leading to more systematic identifications of images. The process of identifying images is illustrated with two different studies, one addressing the puzzle of "guanaco" figurines from Hohokam sites (Chenault and Lindly 2006) and the other examining representations of corn in multiple media across the Southwest (Hays-Gilpin and Hegmon 2005).

The identification of these images raises questions about the continuum in degrees of representation, from realism (however defined) to abstraction. Images of birds, for example, vary widely in the Southwest, from highly detailed pictures of particular species to abstract shapes that vaguely evoke birds or feathers in a general sense. Some of these differences in representation may be related to technical constraints of different media (Schleher and Munson 2010), but in other cases they may reflect the choices of individual artists. Indeed, although it is easy to assume that artists intend to create clear pictures, there are circumstances in which they may embrace ambiguity instead. Katherine Spielmann and her colleagues have argued that late 16th- and 17th-century Pueblo potters in the Rio Grande Valley adopted ambiguous symbols or deliberately obscured images in the early historic period in order to hide meanings from Spanish priests (Mobley-Tanaka 2002; Spielmann et al. 2006).

Chapter 5 concludes with a consideration of aniconicity, or the possibility that artists may have refrained from creating certain kinds of images entirely. Perhaps, as Severin Fowles (2008) has argued, the absence of katsina imagery in some Pueblo IV (1325–1600 CE) contexts reflects a deliberate choice by artists, rather than the absence of katsinas themselves.

Aesthetics

Chapter 6 addresses the final piece of artistic baggage: aesthetics. By this point, the book is on much less familiar ground. The aesthetic experience is, after all, ephemeral and intensely personal, something that does not leave a direct material record and is difficult to describe in words (Berleant 2004; Stecker 2005). However, there are various empirical concepts related to aesthetics that may prove useful for archaeologists interested in trying to understand how ancient people experienced their worlds (Morales 2005). There is, for example, a relatively large body of work in the Southwest that addresses concrete aesthetics, or the specific way in which people in a given time and place value the properties of objects and performances. In addition, anthropologist Jacques Maquet's (1986) concept of the aesthetic locus helps to narrow the focus of inquiry to the areas within a given cultural context where people devoted most of their aesthetic energy and attention. In the Southwest, I suggest, art forms such as Basketmaker basketry, Chacoan turquoise, and ceramics were probably aesthetic loci, along with ritual performance.

Following the work of anthropologist Howard Morphy (1994a, 2005), I argue that we can zero in on the concrete aesthetics of specific contexts in the Southwest by first considering which properties of materials and objects might have potentially been of interest to artists and viewers. In particular, it is important to identify which properties—such as color, sheen, and the like—artists seem to have highlighted through the materials and techniques they chose to use. The resulting set of potentially aesthetic qualities can be further narrowed by looking for consistent associations of different properties with each other, or of properties with particular objects. For example, James Bayman (2002) has identified an apparent association of frog imagery and white marine shell in Hohokam sites, while Stephen Plog (2003) notes a somewhat different pattern of frogs made of jet in the Chacoan world. These properties and associations likely reflect the concrete aesthetics of the people who made and used them. In addition, it may be possible to move into the more speculative realm of the aesthetic experience by considering the relationship between properties, associations of properties, and the contexts within which various objects were used.

Chapter 6 illustrates this method first with several examples of the concrete aesthetics of color and pigment during the Pueblo IV period (1325–1600 CE) in the Rio Grande Valley, when painted rockshelters, brightly colored glazeware ceramics, and speckled effigies reflect an appreciation of multicolored objects. The aesthetic appeal of specific colors is also suggested for the Pueblo II period (900–1100 CE) in the Chaco Canyon area, where Plog (2003) has argued that the color symbolism of black-on-white pottery reflected a preference for blue-greens that are so difficult to produce with natural pigments.

In addition, the work of Patricia Crown and W. H. Wills (2003) on re-painting of Chacoan cylinder jars and rebuilding of kivas in Chaco Canyon suggests that there may have been an aesthetic of renewal that had deep roots in the Southwest. Their work highlights the religious and temporal aspects of renewal; in this way, it is similar to the considerable body of work on replastering and repainting the walls of Pueblo IV kivas (Smith 1952). In addition, some intensely worked rock art sites from the Pueblo IV period show similar focus on renewal and the ritual power of previously existing images (Munson 2003).

Chapter 6 ends on a speculative note, suggesting that it might be worth considering the nonvisual perceptions of experience in the past. Although individuals' responses to properties such as echoes, darkness, or the feel of humid air in an arid environment do not leave material impressions, regular associations of these perceptual properties with particular kinds of art might be a fruitful avenue for additional research in the future.

Intentions

This book is about art and archaeology. It is not an art history, although it draws on the work of art historians. Nor does it provide an overview of ancient Southwestern art,[2] although it does encompass a wide range of media from different times and places. Instead, the book relies heavily on the research of many practicing archaeologists, highlighting studies that I believe are relevant to this business of art in an archaeological context. With a few exceptions, the researchers whose work I emphasize do not explicitly mention art at all. Kathryn Kamp and Patricia Crown focus on learners, not artists, in their studies of socialization in ceramic and textile production (see chapter 3). Nor does Barbara Mills dwell on audiences for decorated ceramics used in public feasts on the Mogollon Rim of Arizona (see chapter 4). Stephen Plog mentions aesthetics only in passing in his examination of color symbolism on black-on-white Chacoan pottery; Patricia Crown and W. H. Wills do not raise the subject at all (see chapter 6).

In presenting other archaeologists' research as studies of art, I recognize that I am adapting and extending the scope and intent of their work. I do not want to put words in their mouths or misrepresent their conclusions. I am, in fact, standing on the shoulders of those who came before, calling

artifacts "art" because I believe that a shift in perspective, wrought by a mi-
nor change in terminology, will affect the way that we approach the past.

In this spirit, I unabashedly refer to textiles (figure 1.6), ceramics,
petroglyphs, carved wooden objects, painted murals, and the like as art.
As chapter 2 outlines, these objects have moved freely back and forth over
time, from artifact to art and back again, depending on a given individual's
interests and the kinds of questions he or she asks. I do not think it does
these objects any great disservice to change categories again, nor does this
mutability distress me. Instead, it reflects the fundamental fact that the

Figure 1.6. One of several textiles recovered from Painted Cave, in northeast Arizona, this
cotton blanket was painted with an elaborate geometric design with an offset quartered layout. Courtesy of the Amerind Foundation, Inc., Dragoon, Arizona. Catalog Number PC/39/36.
Photographer unknown.

terms we use shape the way that we approach our research as archaeologists. To label something "artifact" is to imply that production, technology, and function are of central importance. To label that same object "art" is to shift the focus to artists, aesthetics, iconography, and meaning. Hence, the question of art or artifact is not merely an epistemological or a philosophical one; it is a practical question, a matter of explicit choice with pragmatic consequences. My hope is that examining artifacts as art will reframe some familiar objects, providing a fresh perspective that will lead to new insights into the lives of the ancient people of the American Southwest.

The Problem of Art in Archaeology 2

Art is a category into which some works fit more easily than others: the average painting by Picasso fits, while the average sieve does not. (Morphy 1994b:650)

WHAT IS IT THAT MAKES PICASSO'S PAINTINGS—or even his doodles—art? Why are sieves artifacts? The answers to these questions seem obvious at first. Sieves are functional tools, while oil paintings are not. And Picasso is a famous artist, which accounts for the popularity of his doodles, while the sieve's maker is an anonymous corporation with mechanized production. Yet despite the apparent simplicity of these questions, the answers prove more difficult the more carefully one investigates. What if the sieve is part of a readymade, one of French artist Marcel Duchamp's works of art assembled from found objects? If Picasso painted the exterior of his house a fetching shade of yellow, why doesn't the house become a work of art?

The issue of where to draw the line between art and artifact has been a contentious one for more than a century. Philosophers, art historians, and anthropologists have struggled to understand what art is, focusing considerable attention on defining art as opposed to artifacts, objects, curiosities, crafts, or other similar categories (Gell 1995:27; Morphy and Perkins 2005c; Risatti 2007; Shiner 2001; Vogel 1988a). The problem is especially important to anthropology and the application of the term "art" cross-culturally, for some definitions of art imply that the concept is strictly limited to Western contexts—and even then only from the Renaissance period up to the present day. As described below, this is based on a narrow understanding of art, one which is ethnocentric and excessively limited in scope and utility. Definitions based on descriptions of art's attributes are the most reasonable alternative, although such lists are also plagued with difficulties. Understanding debates about definitions of art is important, though not because they will allow us to settle the question once and for all, sorting objects into categories of art and nonart. Instead, understanding Western notions of art will help to highlight the heavy baggage that comes along with the term—baggage in the form of expectations surrounding artists, audiences, and the images, aesthetics, and meaning of art itself.

As also highlighted in this chapter, the great expectations of "art" have shaped the discovery and consequent "elevation" of some archaeological objects as art, while others have been relegated to mere artifact. This process of "discovering" art is far more subjective than it might first appear and, as discussed below, reflects historical accidents and personal taste as much as any qualities inherent in the objects themselves. The history of archaeological research into art in the Southwest clearly shows the effects of the discovery process, leading to great disparities in the way that different objects are treated. If we are to have an archaeology of art in the ancient Southwest, or any other region of the world, we need to examine our assumptions about which objects are art and which are artifact. In addition, we need to turn some serious and systematic attention to considering which objects might be most amenable to study as art. Although I am not foolhardy enough to create my own definition of art, I do jump into the fray with some deliberately provocative language, hoping to highlight the qualities often present in objects that might reward scrutiny as art.

Art

The English word "art" is derived from the Latin *ars*, referring to skill or, more accurately, "the human ability to make and perform" (Shiner 2001:19). From the Classical world through the Medieval period in Europe, any number of activities and professions fit neatly into this concept of art, including "horse breaking, verse writing, shoemaking, vase painting, or governing" (Shiner 2001:5). This early meaning is reflected in the continued use of phrases such as "the art of war" or the idea that someone has mastered "the art of French cooking."

The roots of modern ideas about art began to emerge among a small group of elites in Renaissance Europe (Shiner 2001:35–56). In contrast to the religious and didactic purposes of Medieval art, Renaissance painting and sculpture was often created for purposes of display (Pocius 1995;

Sparshott 1997). Artists focused a great deal of attention on mimesis, or the mimicry of the subjects in their art. The development of linear perspective, in which lines converging toward a vanishing point create the illusion of depth, made it possible to evoke realistic three-dimensional spaces on flat canvases. Wealthy patrons commissioned portraits for their homes; even paintings with religious subject matter were admired as much for their realism and use of color as for their message. This focus on visual qualities and display value, as opposed to function, foreshadows the divide that still exists today between art and craft, artwork and artifact, artist and artisan/craftsperson (Ingold 2001; Risatti 2007; Shiner 2001; also see Hays-Gilpin 2004:88).

The notion of art as nonfunctional was strengthened greatly through philosopher Immanuel Kant's 18th-century writing on aesthetics. As discussed in chapter 6, Kant's work shifted the meaning of aesthetics away from the senses in general, instead focusing on taste, judgment, and beauty. He proposed that aesthetic judgments are disinterested, in the sense that they are removed from any functional or practical purpose of the object being judged (Berleant 2004; Stecker 2005). This notion of disinterest is critical to definitions of art, for it implies that art objects are discrete works that lack function or purpose beyond the visual—an idea that provides a significant challenge for those who strive to break down the distinction between art and the rest of life (Shiner 2001).

Beginning in the 19th century, European thinkers started to challenge realistic representation as the foundation of art (Shiner 2001), arguing instead that art's primary purpose was to express the artist's inner life, communicating his experiences with the audience.[1] Asserting that the artist's emotions and feelings were more important than mere images allowed greater freedom to play with color, technique, and symbolism; it also shifted attention to the meaning that a piece of art expressed. In search for more authentic emotion and primal meanings, European artists such as Gauguin and Picasso began to derive inspiration from the "primitive" spirit expressed in masks and other objects arriving from colonies in Africa and other parts of the world (Miller 1991; Rubin 1984). Even existing works, such as the *Mona Lisa*, were reinterpreted in light of the new interest in emotional experiences (Boas 1940).

In the 20th century, European and North American artists continued to push the boundaries of art, claiming that art was about significant form rather than meaning or emotion. Formalism, as the movement is known, meant that pure color, the juxtaposition of shapes, and the use of textures were the most important aspects of a work of art. James Whistler's most

famous painting, known colloquially as "Whistler's Mother," is actually titled *Arrangement in Grey and Black #1* because, as the artist asserted, "That's
what it is. To me it is interesting as a picture of my mother; but what can
or ought the public to care about the identity of the portrait?" (quoted in
Anderson 1990:217). Formalism had a significant role in expanding "art"
beyond the boundaries of the European fine art market, for it meant that
art had the potential to exist anywhere and anytime. There was no need
to understand an artist's emotions or messages, or even to worry about
whether or not there was an artist; instead, one merely had to recognize
significant form.

Appropriation and Art beyond the West

Expressionism and formalism opened the door for an assortment of artists, art historians, and collectors, who steadily "discovered" new kinds of
non-Western art through the 20th century (Errington 1998; Myers 2006;
Price 1989; Shiner 2001:270–74): ritual carvings from Pacific Islands, twin
figurines from West Africa, Navajo textiles, Pueblo pottery, and so on.
Over time, all of these objects have been incorporated into Western art
worlds, usually with the addition of qualifying labels such as "primitive,"
"tribal," "ethnic," "souvenir," and "tourist" art (e.g., Graburn 1976; Phillips 2005a). The most recent versions are phrases such as "world art" or
"arts of globalization," terms that have arisen in the context of contemporary concerns with globalization and post-colonialism (Errington 2005;
Venbrux et al. 2006).

As Western art worlds continue "selectively swallowing up the arts
of other cultures" (Morphy and Perkins 2005b:13), the "discovery"
of art in non-Western contexts has raised serious questions about the
character of art as opposed to craft or artifact. Most people still see
incorporation of non-Western objects into Western art institutions as
"elevating" the objects in question. This may be seen as a kind of "posi-
tive ethnocentrism" (Shiner 2001:270), in which raising an object to
the status of fine art avoids the implied insult of calling it craft, or mere
artifact. Overall, though, "this elevation has usually tended to promote
only those things that fit European ideas of fine art, while relegating the
rest to the status of craft" (Shiner 2001:270). The biases apparent in how
others' objects become incorporated into Western art institutions have
led to considerable handwringing about the implications of applying the
word "art" in non-Western contexts (Dutton 2000; Ingold 2001:19–20;
Morphy 2005, 2008).

Many anthropologists worry that "art" is an inherently problematic concept because it "carries such strong evaluative overtones, and . . . is so closely bound up with widely held ideas about the rise and ascendancy of Western civilization" (Ingold 2001:19; also Morphy 1994b:648; 2008:178). Indeed, there is a long history in anthropology of using art as a measuring stick, an indicator by which to rank art-rich and art-poor cultures as more or less advanced (see Coote 2005; also Ekholm 1959:79). The converse was also used to determine what was—and was not—art. In the U.S. Southwest, for example, late 19th-century Pueblo painting was not considered fine art because, in the evolutionary framework of the time, "the fine arts were, by moral and ethical definition, the products of civilizations, and the Pueblos were not classified . . . as civilized" (Brody 1991:12). Even today, museums worldwide often treat non-Western art as chronologically remote, as if it represents the earliest (most primitive) stages of human evolution, regardless of when the items in question were actually produced (Errington 1998).

In addition, many anthropologists believe that the term "art" has little or no meaning cross-culturally, a view often expressed through the claim that a given culture has "no word for art" (Hardin 1988; Maquet 1986:66; cf. Perkins 2006). For example, Bruce Hucko's book (1996) on contemporary art programs in Tewa Pueblo schools in northern New Mexico is called *Where There Is No Name for Art*. However, the lack of a "name" for art does not mean that the children whose work is featured in the book are incapable of producing art—for indeed, the works are expressive, charming, and full of creativity—but rather that their *approach* to art, or their concept of art, is different from that implied by the word in English. Highlighting the differences in Tewa versus Western understandings of art is a far cry from claiming that art does not exist for the Pueblo people. As several researchers have pointed out, the apparent lack of a single vocabulary word need not imply that art or any other subject—kinship, religion, second cousins on one's mother's side, and so on—do not exist (Anderson 1992; Davies 2000:202; Morales 2005:66–68; Morphy and Perkins 2005b:13; also see Dutton 2000). Indeed, as Kelley Hays-Gilpin and Michelle Hegmon (2005:108, note 1) have noted, reserving the concept of art for Western contexts alone is both "inconvenient and ethnocentric."

Defining Art in a Post-Modern World

Art in the present day encompasses an enormous and ever-expanding range of objects, media, performances, and concepts, to the extent that "today you can call virtually anything 'art' and get away with it" (Shiner 2001:3). For those who seek to create meaningful definitions of art, this diversity has proven an enormous challenge (see Renfrew 1994:265; Stecker 2000, 2003; Svasek 2007). As a specialist in folk art wrote, one difficulty of defining art stems from the fact that there are "too many different kinds of art created under too many different circumstances" (Congdon 1987:96). The range of specialists who have entered into the fray is equally varied, from philosophers and art critics to artists, anthropologists, and sociologists to folklorists and interdisciplinary scholars (e.g., Alexander 2003:1–6; Anderson 1992; Becker 1982; Boas 1955 [1927]; Carroll 2000; Danto 1988; Dark 1978; Davies 2000; d'Azevedo 1958; Dutton 2000; Gell 1996; Goldstein 1994; Novitz 1998; Perkins 2006; Pocius 1995; Stecker 2000, 2003; Weitz 1956).

The core problem of trying to define art boils down to this: Does art have an essential nature, or is it entirely about the cultural and historical context within which it is encountered? In short, does art exist, or is it created? These debates about art are interesting and useful in understanding both the nature of art (if it does, indeed, have an essential nature) and the limits of Western constructs (if, indeed, art is a culturally constructed category). The debate is not one that we will be able to solve; it strikes at philosophical questions of being and essence, the nature of knowledge, and the ways that people think, experience, and construct their worlds (Mortensen 1997). Happily, anthropologist Howard Morphy offers a way to make some sense of the multitude of positions on art itself. In a general overview of the anthropology of art, Morphy (1994b) points out that the many competing conceptualizations of art generally reflect one of three basic kinds of definitions: art by intent, art by institution, and art by attribute.[2]

Art by Intent

Definitions of art by intent put the onus on artists, who are essentially authorized to decide what is or is not art by declaring their intentions in making an object (Morphy 1994b). In a practical sense, this means that any item (performance/concept/expression) that an artist intends as art is indeed art, regardless of its appearance, aesthetic appeal, materials, or any other qualities (Danto 1988; Dutton 2009:167–72). This type of definition is an attempt to encompass changes wrought in the Western art world when artists challenge the status quo, such as Marcel Duchamp's presentation of mass-produced "readymade" objects as sculptures. Duchamp's most infamous piece, from 1917, was a urinal signed with the fictitious name R. Mutt and titled *Fountain* (Naumann 1999). His motivation was, in part, to challenge the notion of art as skilled creation, replacing it instead with the artist's concept. Although his work was greeted with an uproar at the time, the piece has since been absorbed into the canon of Western art history.

In order for definitions of art by intent to be useful, it is necessary to determine who is (or is not) an artist and to understand his or her intentions. This therefore shifts the problem from defining art to defining the artist (see chapter 3), an exercise that can be relatively straightforward within the context of commercial art galleries, collectors, and art museums, where contemporary and historic artists are expected to express their intentions and explain their artwork. Understanding the intention to create an object as a work of art is more difficult when artists do not express their goals in a permanently recorded form or are not culturally recognized as artists. Nevertheless, some authors have proposed that definitions of art by intent are relevant in at least some archaeological contexts (e.g., Taylor 1994:250).

Art by Institution

Definitions of art by institution shift the focus from the artist to institutions that specialize in art, such as galleries, art museums, fine art auction houses, or similar settings (Morphy 1994b:651). In a broader sense, these definitions draw on the notion of an "art world," which encompasses the entire context within which discourse and transactions surrounding art take place (Becker 1982; Danto 1964; Dickie 1974). Institutional definitions are, like art by intent, well suited to contemporary art that pushes boundaries. As art historian Susan Vogel (1988b:11) summarizes the situation,

> Because today the forms and materials of art are frequently the same as those of non-art objects, the setting or context in which art is displayed may be its most evident defining characteristic. A pile of tires in a museum is to be viewed as art, whereas the same pile in a gas station is clearly not.

By default, institutional definitions of art rely upon the expertise and taste of curators and collectors within the art world, who serve as gatekeepers deciding which objects are allowed into sanctioned spaces. The pieces that they admit become "like members of an exclusive club" (Morphy 1994b:651), while the rest are consigned to mere artifact (see Vogel 1988a).

Definitions of art by intent and art by institution require the presence of recognized artists or art institutions, such as museums and galleries, which were relatively rare outside European traditions prior to the modern era (cf. Gell 1995; Kreps 2003). Despite the apparent lack of parallels between artists and institutions in the Western world and beyond the West, these definitions are still critical to the history of non-Western objects as art. They empower anyone recognized as an artist to declare what is art and, most importantly, provide the space, both physically and conceptually, for a wide range of items to be "discovered" as art (Gell 1996; Morphy 2008; Shiner 2001:270–74; Vogel 1988a).

Art by Attribute

The third approach, defining art by attribute, marks an attempt to create a culturally neutral definition, one that is relevant cross-culturally rather than being tied to a particular time or place (Morphy 1994b). Also known as substantive definitions, definitions of art by attribute center on lists of qualities or traits that are thought to characterize what is—and is not—art (Morphy 2008:179). Each author focuses on different criteria, but these definitions tend to coalesce around a specific set of traits (e.g., Anderson 1992; Berleant 2004:3; Dutton 2000; Hays-Gilpin and Hegmon 2005:108, note 1; Novitz 1998; Weitz 1956). Art:

- is created by human hands,
- involves unusual skill in production,
- is made within a stylistic or formal tradition (whether adhering to tradition or reacting against it),
- is capable of evoking an aesthetic experience,[3]
- conveys meaning, and
- is judged, critiqued, or appreciated (i.e., it is public to some degree).

Definitions of art by attribute imply that art exists in the world, waiting to be discovered, regardless of whether it was or was not seen as art within its original cultural context. Such definitions also offer an air of objectivity and simplicity. One compares an object to a check list of attributes, concluding art or not-art based on how much of the list applies. In practice, though, none of the lists seems entirely satisfying. Different criteria are more or less applicable to different objects (Gaut 2000), so that applying them stringently results in excluding some items that surely seem art-like and including others that do not. This, Morphy (2005:60) and others argue, is because art is "a ragbag category," a fuzzy set with vague boundaries. Objects at the core of the body of works of art, like Michelangelo's *David* and paintings by van

Gogh, are accepted without question. Objects far beyond art, like the average sieve or metate, are equally noncontroversial. It is, however, "at the margins [that] the category is highly contested" (Morphy 2008:171).

The problem is that what falls in the core or at the margins of "art" varies considerably in the views of different people. Despite the many attempts to create formal definitions of art, researchers and lay people alike often unwittingly echo Supreme Court Justice Potter Stewart's 1964 sentiment about obscenity: we may not know what art is, but we know it when we see it. The process of "intuitive recognition" (Morphy 2008:171) is powerful, but it also results in wildly varied sets of art versus artifact in different times and places.

What Became Art from the Ancient Southwest?

When anthropologist Shelly Errington (1994, 1998) examined the concept of art in late 20th-century import businesses in California, she found that "what became authentic primitive art" was bound up in a complicated web of ideas about civilization, progress, authenticity, and the primitive. Dealers bought, promoted, and sold one kind of widget, all the while working to "discover" the next little-known traditional artifact that would become art. The continual process of "discovery" constantly expanded the realm of art, in ways that were both patterned and arbitrary. On a practical level, objects being collected as art needed to be durable and of a suitable size for transport and display. On more conceptual grounds, dealers focused on objects that they found visually appealing and that were made of art-like or highly valued materials, such as paint, silver, or gold. Although Errington (1994) emphasized the common threads that tie together many different kinds of objects treated as art, it is clear that the "discovery" of art is also influenced by arbitrary decisions and historical accidents (Bradley 2009:11–12; Munson 2008a).

In a recent survey, I examined the question of what became art in the ancient Southwest (Munson 2008a), considering the many different factors that affect which objects from archaeological contexts are presented as art and which as artifact. To do so, I looked through 55 publications that explicitly focus on ancient Southwestern objects as art. The survey was based mostly on exhibit catalogs from art shows, either in fine art or natural history museums, and on overviews of native arts of North America. I collected basic information about every picture in these volumes, whether a photograph or line drawing, ultimately amassing just under 800 images of archaeological objects displayed as art.

I found that these sources promote Southwestern ceramics as art far more than any other kind of object. In fact, nearly 70 percent of all of the artwork was ceramics. Not surprisingly, Classic Mimbres black-on-white pottery was the most frequent type, constituting 30 percent of all of the ceramics. Other ceramic wares and types were also featured as art, although they were usually presented with a generic identification, such as "painted Anasazi pottery" or "black-on-white bowl." Most of the non-Mimbres ceramics were Ancestral Pueblo/Anasazi, although a token Hohokam jar was often included.

Beyond ceramics, entire categories of art are usually represented by a relatively small number of objects and images. Mesa Verde cliff dwellings, for example, are typically featured as Ancestral Pueblo architecture. Although these images are sometimes used to provide a sense of context for the lives of ancient Southwesterners, the architecture is often presented as an art form in its own right, complete with discussions of three-dimensional form, line, and the interplay of sun and shadow. Murals and wall paintings are usually represented by protohistoric kiva murals from Pottery Mound, in the Rio Grande Valley, and Awat'ovi, near modern Hopi Pueblo. Jewelry and figurines are more mixed, with examples from multiple locations around the Southwest illustrating materials from turquoise and jet to carved shell and stone. Other objects that might seem obvious possibilities as art are relatively infrequent in publications of prehistoric Southwestern art. Petroglyphs and pictographs, despite the convenient phrase "rock art," are seldom included, and textiles and basketry are also poorly represented. Ground stone is almost never discussed as art, while flaked stone is completely unrepresented, save some occasional vague references to Clovis or Folsom projectile points (9500–8000 BCE), from the Paleoindian period.

What qualities of ancient Southwestern objects contribute to the evaluation of these items as art or artifact? Iconicity seems to be one of the most critical factors. Objects and images that represent people, first and foremost, or animals are most likely to be treated as art. This is in large part because imagery evokes the need for art historical approaches, such as studies of style, iconography, and meaning. In addition, as discussed in chapter 5, we humans seem to have an innate predilection for representations (Brody 1991:33). Mimbres ceramics are the quintessential example, for their charming images of human figures captivate today's viewer. The elaborate kiva murals from the Pueblo IV period (1325–1600 CE) are also widely celebrated (figure 2.1). Overall display value is a notable factor in many examples of archaeological art. Of all the Jeddito yellowware, it is "the most spectacular" Sikyatki-style ceramics (Hays-Gilpin and LeBlanc

Figure 2.1.   A kiva mural from Pottery Mound, in the central Rio Grande Valley, shows cur-
vilinear Sikyatki-style designs above a human figure with raised arms. Drawing by Marit K.
Munson, after Hibben (1975:fig. 38) and Crotty (2007:95).

2007:124) that are displayed as art (figures 2.2a, b). The same is true of
objects made of rare and brightly colored materials, such as turquoise, shell,
and jet.

Artifacts that have direct parallels in Western art history also tend to
be treated as art. Carved and painted three-dimensional objects, such as
figurines or effigies, can readily be treated as sculpture (Walt 1978); paintings on walls, in the form of kiva murals (Brody 1974), have an artistic
parallel in Renaissance frescos. Rock art is an interesting case because it
arguably has parallels to wall painting, yet it is often conceived of as akin to
graffiti—a marginal art form at best in contemporary Western art worlds.
Still, rock art is frequently discussed in art historical terms in the Southwest, probably simply because the phrase includes the word "art."[4] Acid-
etched shells from the Hohokam area are also sometimes recognized as art
(Jernigan 1978:85), in part because acid etching is a familiar technique in
the art world.

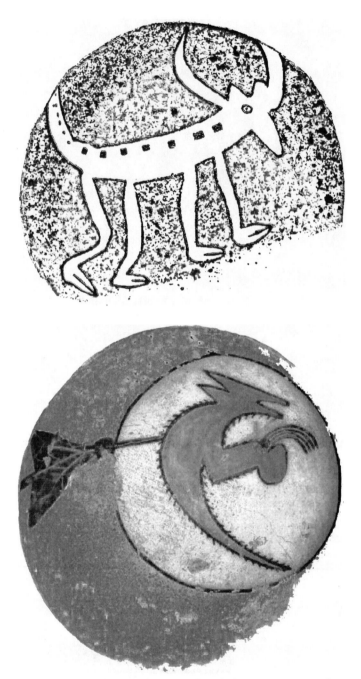

Figure 2.2 Animals painted on Sikyatki polychrome ceramics include a horned creature with cloven hooves (above) and a probable badger (below). Both images show the use of spatter painting to create negative designs. Drawings by Marit K. Munson, of vessels in the collection of the National Museum of Natural History (a, A155,473; b, A155,484).

In addition to the properties of artifacts themselves, external factors have a major influence on what became prehistoric art (Bradley 2009:1–25). Indeed, a whole host of geographic and historic factors are implicated in the widespread acceptance of Ancestral Pueblo and Mimbres pottery as art—and in the relative neglect of objects from Paquimé and the Hohokam region (cf., LeBlanc 2006:149, note 17; Munson 2008a). Anthropologist J. Walter Fewkes's connection to the Smithsonian Institution and the Bureau of American Ethnology made possible his late 19th-century fieldwork near Hopi Pueblo, and later in the Mimbres Valley. The publication of his results in widely distributed government-sponsored series helped bring about broad exposure for both Hopi yellowware and Mimbres black-on-white. In contrast, the striking polychrome pottery from Paquimé (Casas Grandes) was neglected as art until fairly recently (figure 2.3) (Stuhr 2002), despite relatively early publications (e.g., Chapman 1923; Hough 1923). This is probably due, in large part, to language differences, ethnocentrism, and nationalism that hampered research and collaboration among Mexican and American archaeologists.

The history of collections also affects what was discovered as art in the Southwest. For example, relatively few examples of objects from Chaco Canyon are published and celebrated as art. Even the striking painted wooden objects excavated from several rooms at the Great House of Chetro Ketl have primarily been described and discussed strictly as artifacts (Vivian et al. 1978). This probably reflects the fact that most objects from Chaco were recovered by archaeologists and are held by natural history museums (figure 2.4), which are not usually considered the natural habitat of works of art (Errington 1998; Morphy 2008:chap. 8). As a consequence, relatively few pieces from Chaco have been given the institutional stamp of approval from fine art museums, galleries, or exhibits.

Once an object is "discovered" as art, it becomes accepted into the art historical canon, to be shown again and again as a masterpiece (see Davis 1993:327). Images of the Great Gallery pictographs from southeast Utah commonly stand in for rock paintings across the entire Southwest. The paintings are undoubtedly striking, even moving, to a modern viewer, yet they represent just one single example of Southwestern rock art traditions more characterized by variability than unity. The Mesa Verde architecture mentioned earlier is a similar case, where a few striking cliff dwellings are given primacy over all other forms of Southwestern architecture.

The canonization of particular objects also leads to a kind of guilt by association, where the aura of art transfers from an acknowledged masterpiece to less visually appealing examples of the same kind of item.

Figure 2.3.   A polychrome effigy jar from Paquimé shows a seated male smoking. Courtesy of the Snite Museum of Art, University of Notre Dame, 1993.092.003.

Just as Picasso's casual doodles are revered, the vast majority of Mimbres black-on-white bowls are also treated as art. The most detailed and narrative human images initially drew viewer's attention, but once the "story" bowls became art, the geometric bowls were brought into the category

Figure 2.4.   Shell and turquoise mosaic pieces from Chaco Canyon are displayed as part of an exhibit at the Maxwell Museum of Anthropology. Courtesy of the Maxwell Museum of Anthropology, University of New Mexico, 192_1_1183. Photographer unknown.

as well. Even relatively poorly made Mimbres vessels are displayed as artwork, regardless of their individual merit as aesthetically pleasing, skillfully produced, creative pieces (e.g., LeBlanc 2004). The converse applies to White Mountain redware (figure 2.5), a series of polychrome vessels from east-central Arizona. Their images, designs, and color combination in the Pueblo IV period are arguably as striking as many Mimbres bowls, but because the White Mountain redware vessels are not part of the established canon, they are seldom displayed as art.

Finally, there is also a clear bias toward objects that help establish a historical trajectory for more recent artwork. Numerous art historians and anthropologists have emphasized continuities in artwork from the area around Hopi Pueblo. Late 14th-century Sikyatki polychrome ceramics, and related Hopi yellowware pottery, are lauded as providing the inspiration for the work of Nampeyo, a famous Hopi potter at the turn of the last century (Colton and Colton 1943), and now for her descendants into the 21st century (Blair and Blair 1999). Similarly, protohistoric kiva murals from the Hopi area sites of Awat'ovi and Kawaika-a are recognized as a point of reference for the work of Hopi painter Michael Kabotie and

Figure 2.5.   Pinedale polychrome is one of several types categorized as White Mountain red-ware. Courtesy of the Snite Museum of Art, University of Notre Dame, 1998.016.007.

others. In the Rio Grande Valley, San Ildefonso Pueblo potters Maria and Julian Martinez were inspired in the early 1900s by the Mimbres bowls of previous millennia, as are many artists active today (Brody 2005:184–89; LeBlanc 2004). The Hohokam etched shells mentioned earlier are frequently cited as the earliest known example of etching worldwide, a quirk that cements their status as art by appealing to the desire to document historical trajectories of techniques and styles (Jernigan 1978:85).

A History of Art in Archaeology

The curious thing about art and archaeology, in the Southwest or elsewhere, is that the vast majority of objects canonized as works of art were "discovered" as such by art collectors or art historians (e.g., see Brody 1991:1–19; Vincent 1995). In fact, when it comes to discussing art, archaeologists have abdicated. Few address the subject directly, seldom venturing further than terms such as style, design, craft, craftsman, or perhaps artisan (e.g., papers in Conkey and Hastorf 1990; Conkey et al. 1997). When archaeologists do mention art, it is often as part of an argument against applying the term to prehistoric visual and material imagery (Aldhouse-Green 2004; Conkey 1987; Soffer and Conkey 1997:2–3; Tomášková 1997; White 1992). Even archaeologists who openly discuss art or who recognize the aesthetically pleasing aspects of ancient objects remain hesitant about the notion of art. Colin Renfrew, for example, argues that the term art is "highly culture-specific" and has "very little usefulness" for archaeology (1994:264–66).

This unwillingness to engage art is based in part on concerns that focusing on form over function strips away the context of the objects, removing works of art from the realm of anthropology (see Errington 2005; Morphy 2008; Phillips 1994; Tomášková 1997:270). In fact, Richard Bradley (2009:20) suggests that objects lacking provenance, such as those obtained by looting, are more likely to be transformed into art because their lack of contextual information forces observers to focus on the only available details—the visual and aesthetic properties of the objects. In addition, there is a widespread perception that studying art means relying on individual judgment and good taste, an approach that seems unacceptably subjective to archaeologists trained in scientific modes of thought (see Ekholm 1959; Lekson 1992:112; Whitley 2001). The long-standing equation of science with objectivity and art with subjectivity results in what art historian J. J. Brody (2005:xv) calls a "foolish fear of art," leaving archaeologists unwilling to even broach the subject.[5] This is unnecessarily limiting; art historians have a lot to offer to studies of art (e.g., Brody 1991, 2005; Newsome and Hays-Gilpin in press; Phillips 1994), but so do—or should—archaeologists.

Archaeologists have not always been afraid of art. When archaeology was a younger discipline, art was, in fact, "a central component of the humanistic tradition of archaeology" (Snead 2001:160). Much of this early work was focused on descriptions of different art forms (Chapman 1917a; Fewkes 1923) and understanding the evolution of art styles (Chapman 1916, 1917b). Even into the early 20th century, archaeologists tried to tie modes of representation into stages of cultural evolution, documenting presumed progress from naturalistic images of animals and people (hunter-gatherers) to abstract images (agriculturalists) to sophisticated representations (advanced civilizations, such as the Maya, Egyptians, and so on) (Taylor 1994; also see Ekholm 1959).

As evolutionary approaches fell out of favor, culture historians began to focus on identifying prehistoric cultures and tracking their movements and histories (Trigger 2006). In the Southwest, Alfred Kroeber's (1916) ceramic seriation at Zuni Pueblo helped demonstrate the chronological significance of different ceramic styles, an observation that was given great practical significance through Nels Nelson's and A. V. Kidder's pioneering work on stratigraphic excavations in the Northern Rio Grande Valley (see Cordell 1997:158–61). Kidder was also interested in the spatial distribution of different artifact types, as well as their chronological change. His 1924 volume *An Introduction to the Study of Southwestern Archaeology* was the first attempt at culture-historical synthesis in the United States (Trigger 2006). Others joined him in the attempt to document the time and space of the three major Southwestern archaeological cultures—the Anasazi (now usually referred to as Ancestral Pueblo), the Hohokam, and the Mogollon (see figure 1.2)—codified in the late 1920s and early 1930s through the Pecos Conference and the work of Winifred and Harold Gladwin, among others (Cordell 1997:164–72).

Culture-historical archaeology had several important implications for the study of archaeological art. For one thing, archaeologists focused primarily on artifact typologies as they were relevant for regional chronology. This put the emphasis on form only to the extent that it reflected time; unique or nontemporally significant objects were largely ignored. In addition, explanations of change centered on migrations first, based on the assumption that native North Americans were tradition-bound and slow to change. Diffusion was "only grudgingly admitted to indicate creativity on the part of North American Indians" (Trigger 2006:288). This reluctance created tension between the notion of craft (artifact) as characterized by static tradition versus art as reflecting individual creativity (chapter 3) (also see Shiner 2001; Smith 1962).

As North American archaeologists grew frustrated with diffusion and migration as explanations, they shifted their focus more toward human behavior (Trigger 2006). Drawing on ideas from the social sciences, archaeologists tried to understand cultural and social systems from the inside, seeking explanations based in function or process. For example, when Walter Taylor (1948) published a study comparing designs on baskets from the San Juan Anasazi in the Four Corners region to baskets from the state of Coahuila, in northern Mexico, he argued that varying uses of symmetry reflected fundamental differences in how different ethnic groups saw the world. These synchronic studies looked at art as a fully integrated part of culture as a whole.

Processual archaeologists, in their attempts to understand diachronic change, adopted evolutionist, behavioral, and ecologically grounded approaches. Lewis Binford and others took a positivist stance, arguing that archaeologists had just as much ability to reconstruct social organization or religious activities as they did economic activities. In doing so, they implied that art was part of what was knowable about the past, often adding a box labeled "art" to diagrams of cultural systems. In practice, however, art was often dismissed as insignificant for purposes of adaptation to the environment. In fact, style, often used as a kind of code word for art, was explicitly defined in opposition to function (Conkey 2006; Trigger 2006:396).

Nevertheless, processual archaeology's indifference to art did not mean that art-like objects were neglected entirely. In fact, studies such as the "ceramic sociology" of the early 1970s are a good example of how the art that interested archaeologists in the early 20th century cycled around to become artifact once again. The ceramic sociologists looked at designs as a means of measuring social relations within and among communities (e.g., Hill 1970; Longacre 1970), using ceramic designs as interchangeable units of analysis. The content of the design or image was not important; what mattered was the order in the designs' distribution that would reveal social patterns. Dorothy Washburn's extensive work on the symmetry of design structures is similarly positivist and artifact based, proposing that different structures used to generate symmetry reflect underlying cognitive differences (Washburn 1977, 1978). Although these studies arguably focused on artwork, form became, in practice, epiphenomenal—"a mere decorative or aesthetic veneer" (Morphy and Perkins 2005b:22) that social scientists could safely ignore.

Information exchange theory and the debates about active and passive style, which arose in the late 1970s and 1980s, helped to shift the mode of analysis from artifacts to art by calling attention to the specifics of objects' form and content (see overviews in Conkey 2006; Hegmon 1992; Plog 1983). Studies of ceramic designs focused on the symbolic functions of style, highlighting the active role of designs in communication with others (e.g., Graves 1982; Hegmon 1986; Plog 1980). Rock art researchers, too, began to study the information potential of petroglyphs, arguing that their placement relative to trails and other archaeological features reflected attempts to communicate with others (Grant 1978; Hartley 1992; Olsen 1985; Rohn 1989).

Archaeologists' quantitative, generalizing approaches to art began to shift somewhat toward the end of the 20th century, as post-processual and other post-modern approaches made it more acceptable to pursue culturally specific details (Trigger 2006:456). Subjects that had been pushed to the fringe of processual archaeology became more prominent, including cosmology, religious beliefs, art as expression, and aesthetics (see Morphy and Perkins 2005b:10). In addition, archaeologists began highlighting the multiplicity of symbolic meanings in material culture, calling into question the subjective nature of the archaeological record and their own role in creating the past (Trigger 2006:444ff). Ethnoarchaeological work also helped to demonstrate that artifacts played an active role in creating and contesting social relations, rather than being passive reflections of social organization. In the Southwest, Margaret Ann Hardin's (1991) work at Zuni demonstrated that different design styles were associated with different teachers in the Pueblo's high school pottery program, while Lydia Wyckoff's (1985) study of art at Hopi Pueblo showed that children's drawings and pottery designs reflected the views of different political factions.

At present, archaeologists working in the Southwest reflect a multitude of approaches to art, or art-like objects. There are numerous descriptive studies that provide overviews of particular media, including kiva murals (Crotty 1995; Dutton 1963; Hibben 1975; Smith 1952), rock art (Schaafsma 1980, 1992b), textiles (Kent 1983a; Teague 1998; Webster 1997), jewelry (Jernigan 1978), basketry (Morris and Burgh 1941), and ceramics (Peckham 1990). Studies of style as indicators of migration and group interaction are still going strong (Crotty 2007; Eckert 2007; Hays-Gilpin and LeBlanc 2007; Schaafsma 2007), as is research into art as communication (Crown 1994; Hartley 1992) and studies of symmetry and cognition (Lindauer and Zaslow 1994; Washburn and Webster 2006). More recent trends are reflected in work on structure and agency (Hegmon and Kulow 2005) and cultural metaphor (Ortman 2000; Sekaquaptewa and Washburn 2004). Approaches aligned with art history, such as iconographic interpretation, continue as well (Schaafsma 2002; VanPool 2009). Perhaps the most promising, to me, are numerous studies focused on cross-media comparison (Hays-Gilpin 2002; Schaafsma 2007; Webster 2008; Webster et al. 2006).

This is merely a brief sketch of contemporary archaeological research on art in the Southwest. A more complete overview is provided in chapters 3 through 6, which focus on specific concepts related to art. For now, suffice it to say that the current state of research suggests that although archaeologists have often shown a fear of art, there is increasing attention to art in archaeology, both in the Southwest and in the broader discipline (e.g., Bradley 2009; Domingo Sanz et al. 2008; Heyd and Clegg 2005).

Susceptible to Treatment as Art

Despite increasing openness to art as an archaeological subject, one major problem still remains: how can one study art, in the Southwest or elsewhere, if it is so difficult to determine what is—and is not—art in the archaeological record? Instead of focusing on the question of art versus artifact, we should accept the idea that art objects "are not necessarily different in kind from other objects. Rather they possess features that, because of their properties, intensity, and interrelationships, render such objects particularly effective" (Berleant 2004:35) as art. This then shifts our perspective to the more pragmatic question of how framing ancient objects as art changes our approach to the past. We could hypothetically ask art-like questions or apply art-like methods to any number of objects, but surely some are more likely than others to reward such scrutiny (Gell 2005:233). Neither ash deposits nor butchered bones are, to me, very convincing as art.[6] These prosaic materials seem unlikely to yield many new insights if treated as art. A carved stone frog, on the other hand, might do exactly that.

Where, then, do we draw the line? How might we recognize objects that could productively be treated as art? I propose that we should focus our attention on objects that:

- appear to have particular potential to be laden with meaning.
- are made with a level of skill or care that distinguishes them from the ordinary.
- evoke a sense of playfulness on the part of the artist, the viewer, or both.
- show signs of individuality or originality in their production.
- draw a viewer's attention through striking color, shape, or rhythm.

Note that these qualities do not define art per se. Instead, they are intended as loose guidelines that highlight the kinds of objects that might usefully be *treated* as art. As listed above, these qualities are vague and open to interpretation. They are also couched in language that deliberately avoids the vocabulary most common in debates about defining art. I have done this intentionally, as I wish to keep the list open, inclusive, and suggestive rather than prescriptive.

The important thing about this list is that it can provoke archaeologists to consider *the ways in which an object is art-like*. Instead of relying on the historical vagaries of promoters or fashions, as led to the definition of Sikyatki polychromes or Classic Mimbres black-on-white pottery as art, archaeologists can approach objects in a more methodical manner, asking themselves whether or not treating an object as art may lead to new insights. If a worked piece of stone has none of the qualities mentioned above, it is likely that many of the art-focused methods discussed in this volume will not be very productive. If, on the other hand, the researcher is struck by the banded colors or extraordinary skill in flaking the tool, then perhaps a shift in perspective will lead to different questions and new insights.

In the remainder of this book, I will refer to a wide range of objects as art. In doing so, I make a claim not about the object's essential nature, but about its susceptibility to study as art. This, in turn, implies that the object's creators might readily be considered artists, rather than merely potters or painters or weavers. In calling them artists, I suggest that we might focus on their individuality and their collaboration with others, perhaps even pushing the issue far enough to address the relationship between individual creativity and the constraining factors of tradition. I also use the term art to highlight the ways in which artists' creations are perceived and appreciated by an audience, whether of the artists' peers, of distant strangers, or even of supernatural beings. Calling objects art also draws attention to images, and in particular to the ways that we interpret pictures as a window into the past. Identifying images is not as straightforward as merely recognizing depictions, though, for artists make many choices about subject matter, the best way to represent a given subject, and when ambiguous images are appropriate—or even when to refrain from depicting a subject. Finally, art brings with it implications of aesthetics, that sense of the beautiful or the moving aspects of viewing a work of art. This is among the most difficult of art-related concepts to apply in the deep past, but it offers the potential to bridge the gulf of time by providing an appreciation of the sensory experiences of the ancient peoples of the Southwest.

Artists 3

ARCHAEOLOGISTS HAVE SPILLED A CONSIDERABLE amount of ink on potters, painters, weavers, and other craftspeople in the ancient Southwest, studying specialization, modes of production, technological and individual style, and even socialization and the learning process. Despite all of this attention, though, archaeologists have shied away from applying the word "artist" to these past practitioners. This notable reluctance is centered in contemporary popular notions about artists, which create a picture of the artist as an individual who is considerably different from other people—eccentric, insightful, even self-destructive or mad. This image forms a sharp contrast with the ethnographic record of Pueblo potters and other native artists in the Southwest (and in other cultural contexts worldwide), where artists are portrayed as anonymous, self-effacing craftspeople no different from their peers and neighbors. As a result, many archaeologists are uncomfortable discussing artists in the past.

There are, however, numerous archaeological studies in the Southwest that touch on the identity of ancient craftspeople and artisans, whether through direct evidence of human bodies and tools, or indirect evidence of imagery, analogy, and the like. I believe that calling these individuals artists helps to shift the focus of attention from relatively dry discussions of craft specialization in ceramic production to a consideration of the role of the individual artist in the past. In particular, focusing on artistic practice—what an artist does—provides a solid foundation for examining questions about the relationship of the individual to a work of art. As discussed below, the idiosyncrasies or quirks in an individual's work may make it possible to identify the "hand" of the individual artist across multiple works of art, as in Steven LeBlanc's work with Classic Mimbres black-on-white and Hopi yellowware pottery. Ironically, the focus on individual artistic practice also calls attention to cooperation among multiple artists on a single work of art, as shown by Patricia Crown's work on collaboration between skilled potters and novices. Finally, these studies of the individual and of collaboration highlight some of the tensions between individual creativity and tradition in middle-range societies (Smith 1962:1167).

The Artist

Contemporary Western thought lionizes artists as unique individuals, unusually skilled creative geniuses who are set apart from the rest of society (Haynes 1997). This notion creates considerable problems for Southwestern archaeologists, as it appears to directly contradict ethnographic depictions of artists in the Pueblo Southwest, as well as cross-cultural studies of artists worldwide.

Artists in the West

Contemporary Western ideas about the nature of artists are, like current definitions of art, in large part a legacy of Renaissance thinking. In Classical Greece and Rome, and through the Medieval period, artists were considered nothing more than skilled workers, who might occasionally be recognized for their unusual skill but did not possess any special status (Haynes 1997:102; Shiner 2001). One might admire the work of an artisan/artist, but there was "a strong aristocratic prejudice against all manual production or performance for pay no matter how intelligent, skilled, or inspired it might be" (Shiner 2001:23). Many artists, in fact, were anonymous. In Medieval Europe, artists were not given credit for being particularly creative or even talented. They were, instead, considered conduits for divine inspiration (Haynes 1997:57; cf. Shiner 2001:31).

Notions of the artist began to shift in Renaissance Europe, especially in Italy, as ideas about the nature of art and of artistic inspiration reflected an increasingly secular understanding of the world (Baxandall 1972:1–27; Haynes 1997:103–6). Religious subject matter gave way to portrait painting in the 15th century and artists began to sign their work. Individual artists gained status, with the best known traveling to take commissions or accepting appointments as court artists (Shiner 2001:40–42). A cult of celebrity grew up around master painters and sculptors, with corresponding interest in the personal histories of individual artists. The newfound interest in individual artists is reflected in the first work of art history, Vasari's

(1991 [1550]) *Lives of the Artists*, which recounts the stories of Botticelli and other recognized masters. Despite these gains in status, there was little sense of artists as autonomous—or even particularly unique—individuals (Barker et al. 1999). Artists were constrained by contracts that often specified materials, subject matter, and color, yet there is no evidence that these limits were seen as an affront to an individual artist's sense of creativity (Shiner 2001).

It was not until the second half of the 18th century that the divide between artists and artisans became a great gulf (Shiner 2001:99–129). Ideas of genius and freedom became associated with artists, who were considered original, inspired, imaginative, and creative in a godlike sense. Genius was seen as "irregular, wild, untamable, a devouring fire" (Shiner 2001:112), a defining quality limited to a few unusual individuals. Artisans, in contrast, were thought of as rule-bound, mechanically skilled, but limited by practical factors.

Portraits of artists as individual geniuses have persisted since the 18th century, even as they gained additional layers of meaning (Haynes 1997). Art took on a spiritual patina in the 19th century, with the role of artist cast as a vocation or calling. Artists began to see themselves as a separate, special subculture, inhabiting "a singular world of beauty and spiritual value within an uncomprehending, commercial society" (Shiner 2001:199). The emphasis on autonomy and individuality gave rise to the idea of art as the expression of an artist's unique thoughts and feelings. Indeed, the struggles of van Gogh and other artists suggested that torment and turmoil were a crucial part of the artistic personality (Gedo 1996; Jamison 1996). Despite numerous 20th-century attempts to reunite ideas of art/craft and artist/artisan (Shiner 2001:157–86), the distinction between artists and other individuals has remained a fundamental divide in Western thought to the present day. As Deborah Haynes (1997) discusses, multiple overlapping narratives of the artist are in play today, from the artist as prophetic healer to the eccentric outsider.[1]

Artists beyond the West

When anthropologists and art historians initially sought artists in non-Western contexts, they often searched, wittingly or not, for Western stereotypes: a skilled individual, probably male, who is creative, out of the ordinary, egocentric, self-promoting, and visionary. Such individuals proved difficult to find. Instead, researchers described countless examples of art created by apparently anonymous and non-self-aggrandizing individuals, often working cooperatively, who were considered little different from the rest of society (e.g., Anderson 1989:84–103; Babcock 1993; Gerbrands 1969:70).

The apparent anonymity of many non-Western artists was particularly troublesome to anthropologists and art historians who had a difficult time reconciling the idea of art produced without obvious artists (Driscoll-Engelstad 1996; Kasfir 2000; Vogel 1999). The lack of signatures on art did not necessarily mean that the works were anonymous, though, as the authorship of many, if not most, works of art within a given village or region would have been recognized by the local inhabitants (Bunzel 1929:64–65; Guthe 1925:78; Stanislawski and Stanislawski 1978; cf. Brody 2005:99). Indeed, researchers came to realize that signatures were unnecessary in most cultures until and unless they were demanded by outside market forces (Babcock 1995; Colwell-Chanthaphonh 2008; Ewers 1981; Ritzenthaler 1979; Warner 1986; cf. LeBlanc and Henderson 2009:109).

The position and status of artists beyond the West have also proven contentious. Many researchers insist that artists are, by definition, distinct from the everyday individual, whether revered as heroes (Gell 1998:39) or tolerated as eccentrics (Blocker 1994:148). On the other hand, an ideology of anonymity would suggest that artists are no different from their peers. This notion appealed greatly to anthropologists in the early 20th century, who romanticized the value of honest craftsmanship and wrote with great nostalgia of the days when everyone was an artist (Halseth 1926). This line of thinking tied in neatly to primitivist myths that endowed noble savages with inherent artistic sensibilities and talents (see Errington 1998; Hays-Gilpin 1996).

Primitivist thinking aside, anthropological and art historical research around the world has actually documented great variation in artists' status and position (see Anderson 1989:88–91, 96–103; Berlo 1993). Although formal studies of artists are still relatively rare, sociologist John Anson Warner (1986) has suggested that how artists are culturally recognized and valued is related to the collective or individual orientation of each society. His work suggests that artists in individually oriented societies seem more likely to self-aggrandize, to innovate, and to promote their own unique artistic creations (Warner 1986). Men's art from some 19th-century Plains tribes provides a good example, for men created and displayed artwork primarily to proclaim and celebrate their individual accomplishments in warfare (Greene 2001). Women in some Plains groups achieved similar ends through public vows relating to quillworking (Marriott 1982).

In contrast, more collectively oriented cultures, such as the Pueblo people of the Southwest, are thought to downplay recognition of artists (Benedict 1961; Guthe 1925). It seems that artists oriented to the good of the group may be more constrained by tradition, less likely to innovate, and likely to make only small changes when they do innovate (Warner 1986). Anthropologist J. Walter Fewkes faced this conservatism at Hopi Pueblo in 1899–1900 when he tried to commission paintings of supernatural beings known as katsinas. He eventually found four individuals who agreed to paint the pictures, but they were subject to criticism from other Hopi and reportedly were accused of witchcraft (Fewkes 1903:14). Whether or not the story is true (Munson 2006), its persistence points out the potential negative repercussions for individuals who might be perceived as acting too independently (also see Wade 1986). Anthropologist Ruth Bunzel's (1929) work with Pueblo potters in the 1920s shows another facet of collective orientation, as she found that potters were typically unwilling to critique the work of others. This avoidance provides a means of avoiding social conflict in small groups where face-to-face contact is inevitable (also see Shostak 1993 on the !Kung San).[2]

The Ancient Southwestern Artist

The many well-known examples of Pueblo artists at the turn of the 20th century, discussed above, provide the default model of artifact production for archaeologists working in the Southwest. The general assumption is one of craftspeople guided by conservatism and long-standing tradition. As a result, most archaeologists are reluctant to refer to the people who shaped turquoise beads, painted ceramics, or wove textiles as artists. To do so seems to imply that the individual fits into the Western mold of a creative, nonconforming individual. With few exceptions (Brody 2005:101; LeBlanc 2006; Meyers 2007), archaeologists sidestep these problematic associations by avoiding the word "artist" entirely. Instead, they refer to artisans or craftsmen, or adopt media-specific terms such as potter, weaver, and so on.

Despite discomfort with the word "artist," archaeologists have in fact been quite successful in identifying the individuals or groups of individuals who made art in the ancient Southwest. There have been some attempts to use skeletal evidence to provide information about the tasks in which a specific individual was engaged during his or her life (Kamp 2001), whether through remodeling of bone or exposure to substances such as the lead used in preparing paint for glazeware vessels. Recent studies have examined the physical characteristics of the individuals producing art (e.g., Bagwell 2002; Stinson 2004). For example, Kathryn Kamp (2001) has analyzed the metrics of fingerprints on figurines and pottery from 12th- to mid-13th-century Sinagua sites of central Arizona. The width between the lines of individual fingerprints indicates that adults made most of the full-sized vessels, though children made many of the clay figurines as well as some of the pots in the sample. Various authors have also speculated about the size of the final product being related to the age or gender of the producers. Julia Meyers (2007:105) and others have proposed that the small handprints in the plaster on some kiva walls may mean that women or children were the ones who periodically refreshed the surface, while Clara Lee Tanner (1976:46) implies that unusually small baskets may have been made by beginners.[3]

The presence of tool kits or raw materials may suggest a direct connection between an individual artist and his or her medium. Across the Southwest, potter's tool kits are most frequently found with adult female burials (e.g., Crotty 1983; Herr and Stinson 2005; Mills and Crown 1995; Shafer 1985). A small number of children's graves in the Mimbres area also include potter's tool kits (Crown 1999). Whether these specific children were potters or not, the presence of the kits suggests that the tools were considered appropriate for children. Tools associated with weaving have been found in burials at the late prehistoric site of Hawikku, near Zuni Pueblo (Howell 1995). A spinning kit associated with a woman at Canyon Creek Ruin in east-central Arizona suggests that at least some women were spinners in the 1300s (Haury 1934). Spindle whorls at various Hohokam sites were often associated with female burials, though some specific kinds of spindle whorls were found with both males and females (Hays-Gilpin 2000:106). Basketmaking materials were found in some female Basketmaker period graves in Canyon del Muerto (Odegaard and Hays-Gilpin 2002).

The many different tools and raw materials found in ancient burials highlight some of the difficulties, though, in tying particular individuals to specific media. The Hawikku burials included a wide range of tools and raw materials used in craft production, such as polishing stones, weaving tools, paint-grinding stones, abraders, raw clay, hammerstones, bone needles and awls, and pigments (Howell 1995:table 1). Many of these items could be useful when working in a variety of media. Bone awls, for example, might be used for textile production, basketry, or hide working (see Hays-Gilpin 2000:107). Pigments are even more versatile, being implicated in everything from mural painting and pictographs to body paint, dry-painting, and even food preparation. The differential distribution of pigments and pigment-stained mortars in burials across the Southwest is intriguing (Neitzel 2000), but ultimately difficult to interpret in terms of artistic practice.

Imagery of artists may also provide a rare glimpse into the identity of ancient artists. Mimbres bowls appear to show a woman painting pottery and a man weaving at an upright loom (figure 3.1) (Moulard 1984). Narrative imagery is quite unusual in the Southwest, though, and there are no other known examples that may show artists at work. Nevertheless,

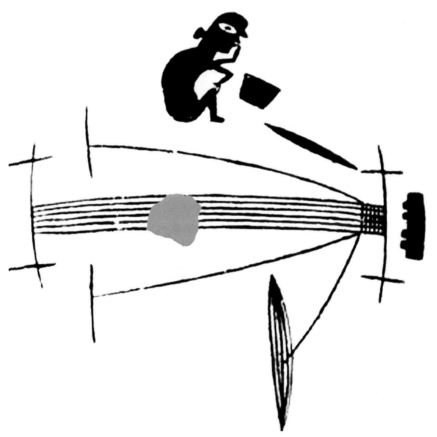

Figure 3.1.   An image from a Mimbres bowl appears to show a low stool (far right) at the base of a vertical loom and a person with a masculine hair knot sitting off to the side. The gray blotch in the middle is a missing piece of the bowl. Drawing by Marit K. Munson, based on Moulard (1984:plate 3).

the depiction of specific subjects has been at the center of many arguments about the identity of artists, most infamously regarding the painters of Mimbres black-on-white ceramics. Art historian J. J. Brody (1977:116) once suggested that paintings of apparent ceremonies likely meant that men painted Mimbres pots, apparently based on assumptions that men were more likely to be participants in ceremonies. He has since tempered his opinion somewhat (Brody 2005:100–1). Michelle Hegmon and Wenda Trevathan (1996) used similar logic to propose that men who lacked direct experience with birthing may have painted anatomically inaccurate images of human birth on Mimbres pottery. The furor that their assertion provoked centered mostly on the misidentification of a crack in a pot as part of the image painted on it (Espenshade 1997; LeBlanc 1997; Shaffer et al. 1997; see Hegmon and Trevathan 1997 for their response). The larger issues, such as consideration of a painter's choices about how to represent birth (see chapter 5), were mostly ignored.

Above all, discussions of the identity of artists in the ancient Southwest draw most heavily on the ethnographic record, usually of the historic Pueblos. Prehistoric potters are widely assumed to have been female (e.g., Brody 1983:76, 1991:42, 2005:101; LeBlanc 2006:109; Tanner 1976; Wright 2005:301), based primarily on historical data showing that women were the primary potters among the Pueblo people prior to the existence of a cash economy (see Mills and Crown 1995). The ethnographic record also provides supporting evidence regarding the age of potters (Brody 2005:102; Crown 1999:28–29) and the possibility that men did some painting on pottery (Brody 2005:101). In addition, researchers have drawn on analogy in commenting on the presumed gender and age of artists producing Ancestral Pueblo kiva murals (Hays-Gilpin and LeBlanc 2007:128–29; Meyers 2007:fig. 3.2), rock art in Mimbres and Ancestral Pueblo contexts (Brody 1991:42, 2005:100–1), and textiles across the Southwest (Hays-Gilpin 2000:106; Teague 1998:161–67), among many other media.

Cross-cultural regularities may also provide some insight into artists' gender and age. Surveys of artistic production worldwide suggest that men most often work with hard materials, like metal, stone, and wood, while women work with soft materials, such as clay and fibers (Anderson 1989:85–88; Cohodas and DeMott 1985; Linton 1941; Teilhet 1978). They also suggest that men typically create representational or naturalistic images, while women are restricted to angular, geometric shapes.

Generalizations about gender roles and art are perhaps more stereotypical than thoroughly researched, and some of their conclusions are quaint at best (Hays-Gilpin 2004). Nevertheless, they do highlight a useful observation about gender differences, whatever is at their core: Women and men often use different design styles on different media (Linton 1941:43). When styles differ across media within the same temporal and spatial context, they can be described as partitioned (or partitive) design styles (DeBoer 1991). This seems to be the case with Basketmaker III artwork (400–700 CE), which shows two different design styles (Hays-Gilpin 1995). One style is geometric, with small elements in rotational symmetry; the other is representational or uses geometrics arranged in patterns with translational and bilateral symmetry. These different Basketmaker III design styles appear to be partitioned by gender, with various lines of evidence linking the former style to women, the latter to men.

The partitioning visible in Basketmaker III art was replaced by a more pervasive style by the early Pueblo III period, around 1100–1200 (Hays-Gilpin 1995; also see Christensen 1994). Pervasive style shows considerable overlap that cuts across a wide range of media (DeBoer 1991). In the Pueblo III Southwest, objects as varied as rock art and pottery, Hohokam etched shell, painted wood from Chaco Canyon, and textiles across central Arizona and northern Mexico all shared a unified style. This widespread style may have been based in textile designs and was probably related to the larger community, rather than one gender or another (see Neitzel in press).

The significance of partitive versus pervasive styles is threefold. First, the distinction has implications for the rate of change in art. Partitive styles are more likely to undergo rapid change, while pervasive styles remain more stable (Hays-Gilpin 2000:95). Second, the distinction has broad implications for differences in social organization and ideology. Finally, and most relevant to this chapter, partitive styles imply the presence of multiple, probably mutually exclusive groups of artists (Hays-Gilpin 2004:102–5), in large part because of the difficulties in mastering the skills needed for different design styles (Munson 2002). In fact, dramatic differences in the structure of textile designs around 1000 CE led Kate Peck Kent (1983b:133) to suggest that the changes might reflect a switch from women doing nonloom weaving to men weaving on looms. Different groups of artists are most often assumed to reflect masculine versus feminine gender roles, but as Hays-Gilpin (2000:95) points out, it is also possible that partitive styles might reflect other distinctions, such as secular versus religious functions or other social differences within a group.

As always, reliance on analogy and cross-cultural regularities calls for caution in its application. Although Southwestern archaeologists often think of rock art as a masculine medium and textiles and pottery as feminine art forms, there are also numerous counterexamples—of men and women making stone tools, of men weaving on looms, and of women weaving nonloom textiles or using belt looms (Hays-Gilpin 2000:93, 95).

Artistic Practice

In addition to studies of artists' identities, archaeologists have long focused on artistic practice, in various guises (see Stark 2006:20–23). Recently, several researchers have begun to consider evidence for how artists learn to create art (Crown 1999, 2001, 2002; Kamp 2001), a process that is more complicated than it may appear at first glance. Indeed, creating works of art involves skills on both a physical and a conceptual level, a combination that Tim Ingold (2001:20) refers to as "both practical knowledge and knowledgeable practice." No one is born knowing how to create art, any more than we are born knowing how to walk, cook, or carry on a conversation. Acquiring artistic skills requires both time and opportunity. Skill (or lack thereof) has material consequences that are readily visible in the archaeological record (Minar and Crown 2001).

Motor Skills

Creating art is a physical process that requires appropriate motor skills. Just as a child must learn how to grip a crayon in order to draw, artists in all media need to master a certain level of strength, control, and coordination in order to create their art (Laszlo and Broderick 1985). Fine motor skills are required for most artistic practice in the Southwest, such as painting pottery, flaking stone, carving wood, or spinning fiber. Depending on the medium and the scale at which one works, task-specific gross motor skills and overall strength may also be a factor (Minar 2001).

Hypothetically, almost any individual is capable of gaining motor skills for any manner of media through continued practice. There are some individual limitations, however. A child might lack the physical maturity to develop the needed coordination or strength, while a person who is sick, elderly, or disabled might have difficulty with particular motor skills (Kamp 2001:428). Even among those with the necessary potential, variability in aptitude and opportunity means that not all individuals reach the same level in development (Crown 2007:683). True mastery of a medium requires constant practice until the necessary motor skills become engrained in muscle memory, or in more colloquial terms, until the individual gets "the 'feel' of things" (Ingold 2001:22). When authors praise Mimbres pottery for its fine lines and precise painting, they are actually admiring the painters' exceptional fine motor skills, polished through long practice.

Cognitive Skills

In addition to motor skills, individual artists need the cognitive skills, or mental ability, to conceptualize and create a successful work of art. Cognitive skills include visualizing the final product, understanding the steps required to make that product, and knowing how to adapt one's actions dynamically during the process of handling the materials and producing an object (Ingold 2001:24; Kamp 2001:428; Keller 2001). Mental skills are often less immediately obvious to viewers of art, ancient or modern. It is easy to overlook the conceptual abilities required to translate a three-dimensional object into a two-dimensional image (see chapter 5) or to lay out a ceramic design efficiently (figure 3.2) (Brody 2005:129; Van Keuren 2006). However, a simple attempt to reproduce the design from a given work of art with pencil and paper readily highlights the required mental skills. Untrained individuals often struggle greatly even when provided an original to copy (Washburn 2001). As with motor skills, cognitive abilities require a certain level of maturity before children are able to reach full competence (Crown 2007). An adult who is impaired in some way or who has lost some cognitive function with age might also be disadvantaged.

Opportunity and Social Constraints

Developing the required motor skills and cognitive abilities to create works of art in any medium requires an extended learning period (Crown 1999, 2001; Minar and Crown 2001), coupled with consistent practice to maintain those skills (Wright 2005:299). Although motor skills and cognitive abilities are both necessary to produce art, an individual's level of skill in one arena does not necessarily correspond to the other. An individual with extraordinary motor control over the weaving process might not have the knowledge needed to create complex symmetrical designs. In contrast, someone who understands the layout of complex geometric designs in one medium may not have had sufficient opportunities to practice and therefore might lack the motor skills to reproduce the designs in another medium.

Learning and practice also require access to necessary raw materials, to technology (such as a kiln to fire pots), and to instruction, whether direct or indirect. Opportunities to master different media therefore vary not only due to the presence or absence of suitable raw materials in the environment, but also to social factors of access, such as the acceptability of different media based on an individual's gender, age, or status. Brody (2005:100) highlights some of these factors in discussing Mimbres pots that

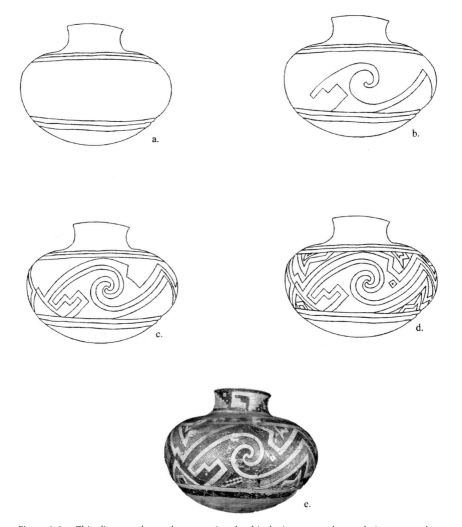

Figure 3.2.   This diagram shows the stages involved in laying out and completing a complex geometric design on a Pinedale black-on-white jar from the Mogollon Rim region. From Van Keuren (1999:fig. 4.11), courtesy of Scott Van Keuren.

have clumsy but "iconographically knowledgeable" images or scenes. He suggests that the images were painted by someone with knowledge but little skill, an "adult other than the potter, possibly a male but in any event relatively unskilled as a pottery painter." The difficulties of beginners struggling to master a new medium are addressed in recent work focusing on the learning process and socialization in the Southwest, discussed below.

An Archaeology of Artistry

Archaeological studies of artistry rely primarily on the identification of consistencies and idiosyncrasies in artists' motor skills and cognitive abilities. Identifying variation in skill level involves evaluating the quality of a work of art, an idea that may cause some archaeologists discomfort given its associations with connoisseurship, monetary value, class, and taste. However, the notion of quality should not be tied to the modern viewers' judgment of whether something is made well; instead, quality should be assessed relative to similar items in the context within which the item was produced (Smith 1994:261). In this sense, then, quality can be thought of as referring to "a combination of technical execution and standard of representation in relation to the prevailing norms of its times" (Smith 1994:260).

The best methods for assessing the relative quality of an individual object are those that archaeologists typically use to evaluate standardization. In general, greater motor skills are reflected in the most effective and efficient use of tools and manipulation of the medium (Spielmann 1998a). In most media, this implies that the highly skilled artist makes consistent and repeated motions, resulting in a regular and uniform appearance of the final product. For ceramics, strong motor skills are reflected in variables such as consistent control over the thickness of vessel walls and effective and efficient use of the brush and pigment in creating painted lines (see figure 1.1) (Crown 1999, 2001; Hagstrum 1985; Stark 1995). Quantification of standardization or skill is relatively rare for media other than ceramics (see Eerkens and Bettinger 2001), but similar measures may be applied. Skill in painting is reflected in the ability to create clear colors, to control the density of pigment and produce a clean edge, and to create paint that will adhere well to the substrate (Odegaard and Hays-Gilpin 2002:307–8). Skill in producing rock art may be reflected in even line width, distinct edges of forms, and consistent density of paint or pecking. In weaving, physical control over the material may be indicated by the thickness and consistency of the thread, the even appearance of warp and weft, and the tightness of the weave.

Quality relative to cognitive abilities, or mental skills, is reflected in factors such as the ability to replicate shapes, to reproduce appropriate symmetries, to create culturally appropriate design layouts, and to fit designs to the space available (figure 3.3) (Crown 1999, 2001; Washburn 1995). All artists, even those who are highly proficient, occasionally make errors in the layout or symmetry of their designs (e.g., Kent 1983a:9). Noticeable

Figure 3.3.   The person who painted this Mimbres bowl had fairly good motor skills, but the geometric design in the center is quite unusual in its layout and use of space. This suggests that the painter may not have had a full understanding of Mimbres conventions. Courtesy of the Peabody Museum of Archaeology and Ethnology, Harvard University, 24-15-10/94646.

mistakes may reflect problems of memory, the effects of elapsed time, and faulty mental templates (Eerkens 2000). Error rates are higher in technically demanding media, such as flaked stone, than in malleable media like clay or textiles, which can be reworked and modified to correct mistakes (Eerkens and Bettinger 2001).

Complex design styles, like the Sikyatki-style designs on Hopi yellow-ware ceramics from the late prehistoric period (Hays-Gilpin and LeBlanc 2007), are particularly difficult to generate. In Sikyatki-style ceramics, the designs are often dynamic and asymmetrical, leaving considerable freedom for a painter to construct a unique design (figure 3.4)—as well as greater opportunities to fail. A comparison of Sikyatki-style designs across different media and through space provides a good example of how different artists master complex styles. Kelley Hays-Gilpin and Steven LeBlanc (2007:120) have suggested that Sikyatki-style designs on contemporaneous pottery and kiva murals "shared a vocabulary" but that the pottery "lacked the overall grammars and narratives of murals." Presumably, this reflects the work of different artists in different media. In addition, Helen Crotty (2007) compared the layout and structure of Sikyatki-style murals from the Hopi area to Sikyatki-like murals from Pottery Mound, in the Rio Grande Valley (see figure 2.1). She notes differences between the two locations that reflect varying degrees of understanding of the Sikyatki style. The relative lack of fluency in the Pottery Mound murals, she argues, suggests that they were likely painted by locals who were imitating Sikyatki style, as opposed to artists from the Hopi area.

Figure 3.4. The complex, dynamic Sikyatki style would have been difficult to master. Drawing by Marit K. Munson, based on a bowl in the collections of the National Museum of Natural History (A155479).

The Individual and Collaboration

Studying artistic practice through the lens of skill makes it possible to examine a variety of topics relevant to artists and their work, from the actions of individual artists to the structure of the learning process and the goals of teaching (LeBlanc and Henderson 2009:27). In this chapter, I present two particular applications of archaeological study of artistry, or artistic practice.

First, I highlight studies centered on attribution of works to individual artists. Such attribution is a typically art historical goal, and one that relies mostly on art historical methods. Studies of the individual typically focus on consistencies across objects, such as multiple pots, that show repeated motor habits or consistent cognitive skills. Identifying the "hand" of the artist is useful archaeologically because it can provide insight into the relationship of individual artists to broader society.

Second, I discuss recent work focused on art as a collaborative process—that is, the important notion that more than one individual may be (and in fact often is) involved in producing a work of art. Learning and collaboration are most readily visible as inconsistencies within a single object that show different levels of cognition and of motor skills (Crown 2007:680). Although the idea of collaboration runs counter to Western stereotypes of the solitary artist, it is in fact central to understanding social organization, scheduling, and learning in the past. Collaboration also has implications for ownership of objects and associated knowledge, which is in turn tied to status and power (Brandt 1977; Lewis 2002; Mills 2004a).

The Individual Artist

There has been periodic interest in identifying individual artists archaeologically (Hill and Gunn 1977; Huse 1976; Van Keuren 2001), prompted in part by studies focusing on individuals' uses of style for communication (see Conkey and Hastorf 1990; Hegmon 1992). Discussions of individual artists in the prehistoric Southwest often rely on impressions of differential levels of skill. J. J. Brody acknowledges that some Mimbres painters seem to have been "more gifted than others" (Brody 2005:102), noting that paintings that show poor motor skills likely reflect the work of children or novices (Brody 2005:100). Richard Wright (2005:298–99), in turn, has said of White Mountain redware ceramics that "it is easy to sense the presence of individuals—of real masters at work, along with less talented or apprentice artists whose efforts appear more derivative and tentative." Watson Smith (1962:1175), for his part, provided a reminder that ceramics include the work of masters but also the work of "the students, the ateliers of the masters, the anonymous hacks, experimenters, and imitators"—all presumably separated by varying levels of talent and skill.

Some researchers have tried to move beyond such impressions by attempting to identify the specific objects made by individual artists. Most of this work is based in a connoisseurship approach adapted from art history (e.g., Beazley 1964, 1989; Donnan and McClelland 1999; Morris 1993; Reentz-Budet et al. 1994). Such studies typically focus on identifying individual quirks in the rendering of specific details of complex imagery. Artist Tony Berlant (1983:17) first suggested that he could recognize specific painters of Mimbres pottery based on "extended contact and connoisseurship." In art historical fashion, he referred to the artists by their most recognizable works, calling them the Rabbit Master and the Polychrome Priest Painter (Berlant 1983:17, 20).

More archaeological studies have drawn on a wider range of traits, including overall style, handling of space and color, and motifs. Kelley Hays-Gilpin and Steven LeBlanc (2007:122), for example, have used this combination of traits to suggest that a single artist may have been responsible for the Sikyatki-style murals at Awat'ovi, a late prehistoric village in the Hopi area. Ceramics with complex designs have proven popular for this kind of research, with studies focusing on Hopi yellowware and on Mimbres black-on-white pottery. Hannah Huse (1976) first examined authorship in Hopi yellowware in the 1970s, sorting 115 bowls from the late prehistoric site of Kawaika-a into groups that she felt reflected the work of as many as 32 different potters. She assessed the reliability of her results by comparing her identifications to those of another researcher, as well as to the results from three early computer programs that were designed to identify clusters in the attributes that Huse recorded. She documented considerable overlap between her attributions and those of the other researcher, ultimately concluding that it was, indeed, possible to identify the products of individual artists in the archaeological record.

In more recent years, Jennifer Sigler (2000) and Steven LeBlanc and Lucia Henderson (2009) have reexamined Hopi yellowware, greatly expanding the size and scope of the sample. Sigler's study drew on about 250 bowls from five sites in the Hopi area, while LeBlanc and Henderson examined images of more than 1,900 bowls. All of the studies noted a distinct contrast between the interior and exterior designs on Hopi yellowware. Interior designs are usually more complex and make more use of polychromes and special painting techniques, such as spattering and incising, than the design painted on the exterior of the same bowl. The contrast between interior and exterior designs shows up clearly in the most flamboyant Sikyatki-style pots, which combine complex designs and multiple painting techniques on the inside of pots with monochromatic and relatively simple exterior designs (compare figure 2.2 with figure 3.5). In addition, LeBlanc and Henderson (2009:36) found multiple bowls that showed disparate skill levels on the interior versus exterior painting, suggesting either that different individuals were involved in painting a single pot or that painters in some cases placed a low priority on the quality of exterior designs.

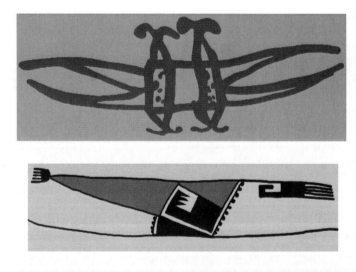

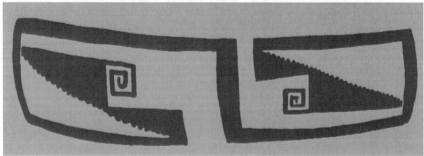

Figure 3.5.   Exterior designs on Hopi yellowware bowls are usually much simpler than interior designs. Drawings by Marit K. Munson, based on bowls in the collections of the Arizona State Museum (top: 4148; bottom: 89-39-4) and the American Museum of Natural History (middle: 8460).

LeBlanc and Henderson (2009:30) found it relatively easy to sort the exterior designs on yellowware bowls into sets that they felt were related to each other, ultimately creating about 175 sets that encompassed 46 percent of their ceramic sample. The interior paintings, in contrast, resisted all attempts to sort them into distinct groups. Based on the consistency, simplicity, and legibility of the exterior painting, LeBlanc and Henderson conclude that the designs were glyphs that served as signatures for artists— in this case, probably a small group of artists working together, such as a mother-daughter pair, or related individuals from successive generations (LeBlanc and Henderson 2009:30–32).

LeBlanc (2004, 2006) also studied specialization and the hand of the artist on Mimbres black-on-white pottery. He used similar methods but began by grouping Mimbres bowls based on common motifs, such as rabbits or negative scrolls. He then asked several people to sort the bowls within each motif category based on perceived stylistic similarities and differences. Sorting the bowls by motifs made it easier to compare images, but it also meant that it was impossible to identify the work of a single artist across different motifs. Despite considerable variability among participants' groupings, LeBlanc was able to identify multiple sets of pots that he believes were painted by the same individual, or perhaps the same household or workshop.

Both of LeBlanc's studies identifying the artist's "hand" can be criticized for their methods, which rely on the opinions of the multiple participants who sorted the ceramics into groups. Recognizing the subjectivity of his methods, LeBlanc has drawn on as much corroborating evidence as possible, cross-checking the plausibility of his results with available temporal and spatial data (LeBlanc 2006; LeBlanc and Henderson 2009:97–100). Will Russell and Michelle Hegmon (in preparation) are working on developing a method of quantifying the sorting process by tallying similarities and differences among paintings that share a common motif. They then use these figures to calculate a rate of correspondence that reflects the degree to which two paintings are similar to each other. Russell and Hegmon argue that a correspondence of 70 percent among different bowls suggests that they were painted by the same individual.

All of the recent attribution studies of Southwest ceramics have included attempts to estimate the total number of potters/painters active at any given time. Each of the studies was able to attribute a large percentage of the entire ceramic assemblage in question to specific artists (or artist groups), suggesting that the majority of both Hopi yellowware and Mimbres black-on-white bowls were decorated by a relatively small number of painters. LeBlanc explores this possibility through a series of back-of-the-envelope calculations, estimating that three to six individuals in each extant village were responsible for producing Hopi yellowware at any one time—and that just one or two painters per village could have made all of the Mimbres black-on-white bowls (LeBlanc 2006).

These surprisingly small estimates of Ancestral Hopi and Mimbres pottery painters have significant implications for ceramic specialization, patterns of trade and exchange, and relationships among different villages. In terms of artistic practice, such low numbers of artists implies the potential for relatively high rates of change in pottery traditions, as well as raising questions about how the pottery painters maintained proficiency. If, as LeBlanc (2006:140) suggests, a single potter making Mimbres bowls created just 50 to 100 bowls per year, would that level of production have provided enough practice to maintain high levels of skill at painting?

Patricia Crown (2007:684) has argued that variation in opportunities to practice ceramic production might be responsible for some of the differences in early and late Ancestral Pueblo pottery. When pottery work was done infrequently and only on a few vessels, as is true with ceramics prior to about 900 CE, motor skills would have remained at a consistently low quality. The relative lack of practice meant that potters were error prone, with little difference in skill levels among potters. Later potters, who created more vessels, had more opportunities to practice and to improve their motor skills. As potters internalized the process and motions, they became less prone to errors. At the same time, the contrast between the work of learners and skilled potters would have grown, because the greater the complexity of the piece, the longer the learning process and the more skill required to produce it (Crown 2007:683; LeBlanc 2006:145). As a consequence, there are also more qualities of the piece that are liable to vary according to the individual artist's habits, ideas, or behavioral quirks. This is particularly true of challenging techniques, like throwing ceramics on a wheel, complex designs, and perhaps representational imagery (see chapter 5) (Crown 2007:683).

Taken together, these factors suggest that attribution studies are best suited to a large set of complex or highly detailed objects made over a relatively short period of time (Rubin 1977). In the Southwest, ceramics are most amenable to attribution studies. In addition to Classic Mimbres pottery and Hopi yellowware, certain elaborate polychrome ceramics are also potentially suitable for attribution studies (Russell and Hegmon in preparation). This might include Salado polychrome (Crown 1994) and White Mountain redware (see figure 2.5) (Van Keuren 1994), both from east-central Arizona, and vessels from Paquimé (see figure 1.5) (Di Peso 1974). Attributions for other potentially promising materials, such as human figurines and other related imagery, have not yet been applied in the Southwest. Kiva murals and rock art provide other tantalizing possibilities for assessing individual contributions (Hays-Gilpin and LeBlanc 2007), although factors of preservation of murals and of the number of artists may make such work difficult.

Collaboration in the Artistic Process

Several researchers have recently questioned the assumption that individual objects were created by a single person, pointing out that collaboration of multiple people was more likely the norm (Brody 2005:99). Although collaboration seems to be difficult to address archaeologically, work by Patricia Crown (2001, 2007) and others (Bagwell 2002; Kamp 2001; Kent 1983a:58, 114–15; Minar 2001) demonstrates that variation within a work of art provides insight into the roles of different individuals involved in its production. In particular, these studies highlight the collaboration of skilled adults with learners, probably children.

Ethnographic records make it clear that the production of most artwork in the historic Southwest involved a detailed sequence of tasks, performed by various individuals (e.g., Bunzel 1929; Guthe 1925). Making pottery, for example, involved choosing materials and mixing them properly, then forming vessels and drying them successfully. The pots were often finished with some combination of slipping, polishing, and painting before they were finally fired. Men and women participated in different stages of the process, contributing their knowledge, time, or skills as appropriate (Crown 2007:679). Children generally are not capable of planning, grasping complicated concepts, and applying reasoning to the process until they reach a certain level of maturity (Kamp 2001:428). As a result, children often learn through collaboration, helping with the less complex stages of the process and gaining skills slowly over time.

In Patricia Crown's (2001, 2002, 2007) studies of children learning to make pottery in the ancient Southwest, she evaluated relative skill in producing and decorating hundreds of vessels from regions across the Southwest. Examining collections of whole vessels from numerous museums, Crown identified more than 700 examples of vessels reflecting the work of unskilled novices—most likely children (Crown 2002:112–14). Crown found that children seemed to be familiar with the process of forming pots but lacked the motor skills needed to create symmetrical vessels with even wall thickness. In addition, children generally had sufficient cognitive skills to understand what designs should look like, but they lacked the necessary motor skills and coordination to apply the designs. Their work showed shaky lines, frequent lifting of the brush, numerous errors, use of wider brushes, and so on (figure 3.6).

Discrepancies within a single vessel showed various modes of learning, from children working alone to various degrees of collaboration between a skilled adult and a child. In many cases, skilled potters formed vessels that were painted by unskilled learners. Occasionally, the opposite occurred, when a novice made a rather rough vessel that was then painted by a skilled adult. Adults also provided different guidelines to help children practice painting vessels, at times decorating part of a vessel as a model for the learner to copy. In other cases, adults painted most of the design but left

Figure 3.6.   The shaky lines and uneven layout of this Mimbres bowl suggest that it was painted by a novice with relatively weak motor skills and a poor ability to create a symmetrical design. The light gray represents areas where the paint is worn. Drawing by Marit K. Munson, from a bowl in the collection of the Peabody Museum of Archaeology and Ethnology, Harvard University, 24-15-10/94525.

hatching or other details for the child to fill in. For the most part, children seem to have learned to shape pots and paint them through observation and imitation, rather than more direct forms of hands-on instruction. When adults were involved, they typically either formed a vessel for the child to paint or painted a vessel that the child made (Crown 2002). The distinction between direct and indirect teaching styles has implications for the rate of learning, the age at which an individual masters a given medium, and the rate of change in a particular art form (Minar and Crown 2001). In general, direct instruction tends to be associated with greater interaction of teacher and learner, more direct criticism, mastery at a younger age, and greater freedom to innovate. In contrast, indirect teaching methods, such as observation and imitation, lead to a longer learning process, require more time to master a medium, and tend to enforce conformity.

Crown's research on collaboration suggests that learning frameworks differed across the Southwest in both time and space. For example, she found that collaboration was particularly common in White Mountain redware and in Chihuahuan polychrome from northern Mexico (Crown 2002:120). In addition, Crown was able to examine temporal differences in two contemporaneous wares from the Reserve area, in east-central Arizona and west-central New Mexico. She found that collaboration of children and adults increased dramatically after 1100 CE for both polychrome White Mountain redware and black-on-white Cibola whiteware. Differences in the frequency of learners' vessels among the two wares suggest that children gained competency in making the simpler black-on-white ceramics through observation and imitation before receiving more direct instruction to help finish pottery made by adults. It appears that adults took a more hands-on approach to the more complicated polychrome vessels, maintaining more control as they introduced children to the different technology (Crown 2002:121–22).

The implications of different learning frameworks for an archaeology of artistic practice become clear in Crown's comparison of Hohokam and Mimbres ceramic traditions (Crown 2001). She found that collaboration was more common in Mimbres ceramics, where 18 percent of the pots showed the work of multiple individuals, while only 6 percent of the Hohokam pottery involved collaboration. Crown (2001) concluded that the artists who worked with children on Mimbres ceramics emphasized mastery of the motor skills needed for the fine lines typical of Mimbres black-on-white (see figures 1.1, 3.2). Adults provided considerable help for children, whether by making vessels for learners to paint or, more directly, by creating templates on partly finished vessels or even painting outlines for learners to trace. At the same time, Mimbres learners seemed to have had a lot of leeway in choosing designs. Hohokam potters, in contrast, used designs that required less skill than those on Mimbres pottery and seemed to have placed less emphasis on the motor skills of painting (figure 3.7). Hohokam children learned to paint "a fairly rigid, but relatively simple set of standard designs" (Crown 2001:464), with far fewer naturalistic images. Error rates in Mimbres painting suggest that the emphasis was "on creativity, rather than getting the design 'right,'" while Hohokam adults seem to have focused on "children doing only what they were capable of doing, but doing it correctly" and "completing designs in the proper manner" (Crown 2001:464). These differences in teaching suggest that there was corresponding diversity in how children were socialized, perhaps account-

Figure 3.7.   Hohokam pottery is often decorated with "wallpaper" designs that repeat across most of the vessel's surface. This bowl, dating to 700–900 CE, includes negative-painted birds just below the rim. Courtesy of the Snite Museum of Art, University of Notre Dame, 1993.092.001.

ing, in part, for the relative conservatism of Hohokam ceramics and the startling creativity of Mimbres pottery (Crown 2001:465). In E. Wesley Jernigan's (1978:119, 149) overview of Southwestern jewelry, he suggested a similar pattern of conservatism on the part of the Hohokam and creativity for the Mogollon region as a whole, including the Mimbres Valley.

Despite the promise of studies of collaboration and learning frameworks in Southwest ceramics, few archaeologists have considered how such approaches might apply to other art forms.[4] There are, however, multiple media that might reward such consideration. Pueblo IV kiva murals show considerable variation in skill levels (Crotty 1995), but they have not, to my knowledge, been examined from the standpoint of individual contributions and collaboration. Painted ritual objects from Chaco Canyon also raise intriguing possibilities regarding collaboration. Many stylistically complex objects from Chaco, such as the painted and carved wooden birds, slats, and other objects found at Chetro Ketl (Vivian et al. 1978), combine carved three-dimensional representations with painted geometrics that appear similar to the Escavada pottery style and some loom-woven textiles (Hays-Gilpin 2000:102). Likewise, a groundstone mortar recovered from Pueblo Bonito has complex geometric designs painted on its surface (Pepper 1920:264–67). The cognitive and motor skills required to carve or cut complex shapes out of wood or to form groundstone artifacts do not seem to overlap significantly with the knowledge and skills needed to paint a coherent, appropriate ceramic-style design that may initially have been learned as a pattern affiliated with the motor skills and constraints of weaving. These apparent differences in required skills and conceptual understanding suggest that some painted ritual objects from Chaco may well have been created through the collaboration of multiple artists.

Creativity and Constraints

Without artists, there is no art. In discussing artistic practice, skill, and the learning process, I have framed these individuals with an admittedly normative view of artistic production, assuming that artists seek to make items that fit into the expectations and values of their cultural and temporal context. Such views are not uncommon in studies of non-Western art, where the force of social pressure is often assumed to be overwhelmingly conservative (Biebuyck 1969; Roe 1995:45–46). J. J. Brody (2005:102) has characterized Mimbres pottery as tradition bound, proposing that "conscious striving for radical innovations or highly individualistic personal styles would have been unthinkable." Such an approach echoes outdated notions of craftspeople in "primitive" societies as timeless, unchanging, and governed by tradition (Biebuyck 1969; Errington 1998; King 1986).

At the same time, archaeologists have always acknowledged the role of creativity on the part of Southwestern potters, painters, and other artists. Charles Amsden (1936:44) wrote of the Hohokam pottery painter as "master of the extemporaneous stroke, using her brush in truly creative delineation." A. V. Kidder (in Cosgrove and Cosgrove 1932:xxi) readily evoked a creative genius as an explanation for Mimbres pottery, just as Clara Lee Tanner (1976:114) attributed developments in particular Pueblo III and Pueblo IV pottery wares to "probably, the spark of individual genius" (also see LeBlanc 2006:146; Wright 2005:301–302). Various researchers have recognized that there are circumstances that may reinforce traditions or inhibit change (e.g., Kohler et al. 2004), while other situations may encourage creativity and innovation (e.g., Hegmon and Kulow 2005). In some cases, even highly skilled artists who usually conform to tradition make odd or unusual items for special purposes in specific contexts, something that Peter Roe (1995:49) refers to as "realms of protected deviation." Finally, it is also important to recognize that even a highly conservative art style "does not necessarily preclude some invention of novel forms" (Hegmon and Kulow 2005:319). Indeed, as Brody (2005:121) has argued, the strict limitations on the layout and motifs of Mimbres pottery may have actually provided the necessary structure within which individual artists "had the freedom to manipulate, interpolate, interpret, and invent."

Regardless of Western stereotypes or cross-cultural generalization, it is perhaps most useful to think of artists—whether potters, painters, shell-workers, weavers, or something else—as individuals, with their own thoughts, goals, and understandings of their lives and of the broader world (Hagstrum 1995:283). Artists are, certainly, restrained by tradition, but they will likely feel the effects of tradition in different ways. Some individual artists may chafe under the weight of expectations, as with the stereotype of contemporary Western artists who strive to make their creative mark. Other artists may feel that tradition provides welcome guidance or a means of engaging with those who came before. As Brody (2005:79) notes, even as the style of Classic Mimbres black-on-white changed over time, some potters would likely have continued to make more old-fashioned vessels for any number of reasons, including "nostalgia, respect for the past, ideology, introspection, the desire to please, or even whim." Similarly, Emory Sekaquaptewa and Dorothy Washburn (2004:462) remind us that variety in art at contemporary Hopi Pueblo, whether in pottery painting or in song lyrics, "is not a reflection of an individual's desire to assert his or her individuality, but, rather, reflects the fact that everyone has his or her own ways of conceptualizing how . . . basic principles might be expressed." At Hopi, in other words, creativity is expressed through "*individual* efforts to conceptualize and represent the thoughts that are shared within a community of believers" (Sekaquaptewa and Washburn 2004:462 emphasis original). This, then, is perhaps the best model for understanding the apparent contradiction between tradition and individual creativity, for it explains how, in Brody's (2005:136) words, "Rather than inhibiting [Mimbres] artists, tradition provided them with a framework within which each one could build with confidence to the full limits of individual creative ability."

Audiences

4

WITHOUT AN AUDIENCE, COULD THERE BE ART? Audiences are a definitive part of the triad of artist, art object, audience and are key to most Western definitions of art. In definitions of art by institution, an audience of curators, critics, and collectors is empowered to determine what is and is not art through the process of accepting objects as part of the art world. The audience is also given a defining role when art is characterized by attributes that include the effect of the art on the audience, such as its ability to evoke an aesthetic response or to communicate between artist and audience (see discussion in Zangwill 1999:315).

Despite audiences' relevance to art, researchers have something of a mixed record in studying them. Art historians have traditionally been more focused on artists and specific art objects, while scholars in fields such as cultural studies and visual studies tend to ignore art in favor of popular culture and mass media. Whether or not their theories of visuality, spectatorship, and the gaze are relevant cross-culturally is up for debate; nevertheless, theoretical contributions from these disciplines draw attention to the diversity among and within different audiences. They also call attention to the importance of social contexts and space in shaping audience behavior and interpretation of images.

Archaeologists, in turn, have the tools for analyzing space but seldom apply them systematically to the physical contexts within which audiences experience artwork. Indeed, just as other disciplines have largely assumed the presence of audiences, archaeology has tended to evoke a vague sense of the audience as recipients of messages communicated through style, images, or symbolic forms. Archaeologists in the Southwest have begun to pay more explicit attention to audiences, considering the implications of the physical contexts of art such as kiva murals, rock art, and ceramics used in public feasts. Nevertheless, many researchers continue to imply that audiences were passive recipients of messages, whether about religious affiliation, identity, or the location of granaries. This chapter examines the insights gained by considering differing degrees of public and private space, the social composition of audiences, and the implications of differential access to art. It also describes some provocative work on visuality and performance that may suggest more nuanced understandings of audiences in the past.

Art and the Audience

Despite the close ties between audience and art, art historical research has tended to focus on form and content of art, to the relative neglect of audiences. Traditional art historical research often focused narrowly on just a few specific works of art, which created the rather contrary effect of implying that audiences' reception of artwork was unchanging and universal. For example, art historian Erwin Panofsky's influential work on iconography and levels of meaning (discussed further in chapter 5) was based on assumptions about the uniformity of "high" culture and shared knowledge of classic texts that underlie images (Silver 1986). Art historian Michael Baxandall (1972) first challenged this understanding of the universal audience in his well-known work on 15th-century Italian painting. Working from contemporaneous documents, Baxandall tried to understand 15th-century ways of viewing, which he referred to as the "period eye"—the "habits of vision and modes of cognitive perception as they are related to pictorial styles" (Dikovitskaya 2005:9) in a particular time and place. Baxandall was able to demonstrate that Italian audiences 500 years ago saw works of art in ways that differ significantly from modern viewers' experiences of the same pieces. In this way, his work was synchronic and culture specific— an unusual innovation that was valuable in counterbalancing art history's tendency to see broad evolutionary progress in art. Ironically, Baxandall's focus on the audience, rather than the artist, has been characterized as "treating the process of viewing from the outside, like an anthropologist" (Silver 1986:519).

Since Baxandall's work on the period eye, art historians have extended the concept of different ways of seeing, arguing that there is no singular audience for any given work of art, but instead many different audiences, each with its own ways of viewing and understanding art. Indeed, social factors such as class, age, gender, knowledge, education, and religion all influence the ways in which individuals encounter a work (Bryson 1992; see Dikovitskaya 2005:9). Art historian Jas Elsner (1995), for example, has examined how different conceptual frameworks of Roman versus early Christian audiences affected their interpretations of art from the 1st to the 6th centuries CE. Other art historians have argued that changing ways of seeing had a profound effect on broader historical transformations, such as the transitions from Late Antiquity to the Middle Ages, from the Renaissance to the Baroque period, and more recently with the turn of the 20th century (Sturken and Cartwright 2001:113). These researchers were able to use written documents to reconstruct attitudes and practices of long-gone audiences; it is difficult to conceive of archaeologists accomplishing something similar. Nevertheless, the concept of different ways of seeing serves as a valuable reminder that contemporary ways of viewing the world may not be a good model for past viewers' experiences, knowledge, and worldview.

Viewing, Visuality, and Spectatorship

Research on ways of seeing has highlighted a distinction between the physiological processes of seeing and the mental processes of interpreting what is seen. Some art historians refer to the latter experience as viewing: "a dual process of interpretation in which what is seen becomes fitted into the already existent framework of the viewer's knowledge and thereby . . . changes both the content of what the viewer knows (because something new has been added) and the meaning of what is seen (because it is now framed by the viewer's knowledge)" (Elsner 1995:4). With time, it has become more typical to refer to the physiological processes as vision and the interpretation of that vision as visuality (Elsner 2007; also see Rose 2001:6). Visuality implies a more active role on the part of the audience, highlighting each individual's role in constituting that which he or she sees. Considering visuality requires a researcher to take into account "not only . . . how images look, but how they are looked at" (Rose 2001:11). There is an interaction between viewer and image, such that "taking an image seriously . . . also involves thinking about how it positions . . . its viewer, in relation to it" (Rose 2001:12).

In her textbook *Visual Methodologies*, Gillian Rose (2001:188–90) poses a series of questions relating to images, including a provocative list about audiences themselves. The questions are a useful starting point, as they prompt consideration of all potentially relevant aspects of the relationships among audiences, art, and artists. In particular, Rose's overview highlights the importance of both the literal, physical position of the viewer in space and the social context within which he or she sees the image; each affects how the audience responds to and makes sense of images (Rose 2001:25–26). Different spaces demand certain kinds of attention of an audience—quiet, thoughtful contemplation of an altarpiece in a church, for example, compared to raucous participation and socializing from fans watching the big game on TV.

In fact, the television example is an appropriate one, for recognition of the plurality of audiences and the subjectivity of viewing/visuality has resulted in something of a backlash against the study of art. Researchers in several new fields have shifted their focus away from art, which they see as an expression of elitist "high culture" (Dikovitskaya 2005), to the image as a form of popular culture and everyday experience. As a result, new disciplines or subdisciplines have arisen, including visual studies, visual culture, and media studies. These fields focus primarily on contemporary mass media such as television, advertising, the Internet, and film. They are characterized more by a multitude of different approaches to the visual, from psychoanalysis to semiotics to discourse analysis, than by any coherent agenda (Dikovitskaya 2005:29).

But what do television audiences, studies of advertisements, and visuality have to do with archaeology? To a great extent, the applicability of these approaches cross-culturally is still not clear (Newsome and Hays-Gilpin in press). Perhaps the gulf between globalized digital mass media and handmade clay bowls is too broad to find any meaningful common ground. Still, contemporary theories of audiences do provide provocative new avenues of exploration that hold some promise of expanding the models that archaeologists use in research on audiences.

According to sociologists Nicholas Abercrombie and Brian Longhurst (1998), research on audiences relies broadly on three different kinds of models. The first, the behavioral approach, sees an audience as the recipients of a fairly simple and straightforward message. Research in this vein focuses on the functions (or dysfunctions) of communication, whether in the form of propaganda posters, the influence of television violence on viewers, or the effects of an advertising campaign. Another variation on the behavioral approach considers how individuals use media for their own purposes, emphasizing the mental state and the goals of different viewers. As discussed below, behavioral approaches are typical of most archaeological research on audiences.

The behavioral approach has been criticized for treating an audience as a fairly passive and uniform group (Abercrombie and Longhurst 1998). Just as Baxandall's period eye assumes unity within a culture, behavioral approaches to visual culture tend to ignore class structures and power relations, failing to recognize ways in which images can be part of an effort to impose values on society. In response to this critique, researchers in media studies, communications, and sociology have adopted perspectives that stress the social construction of audiences and their dynamic nature.

The second model, the incorporation/resistance approach, emphasizes the audience as varied and active, structured through categories such as race, class, and gender. Research on incorporation and resistance focuses on the ways in which the dominant ideology is encoded in the visual, which is then decoded by the audience. Viewers may buy into the ideas expressed through visual material, a process of incorporation, or they may resist it. Although it would be difficult to track such processes archaeologically, some researchers have been able to adopt this approach in studies of relationships among the Pueblo people and the Spanish in the protohistoric period (Liebmann 2002; Mobley-Tanaka 2002; Spielmann et al. 2006; also see chapter 5). Overall, the incorporation/resistance approach provides an important reminder of the social divisions or distinctions that exist within even the most apparently egalitarian group.

Finally, audience studies also offers a spectacle/performance model of audiences (Abercrombie and Longhurst 1998; Schechner 2003). This approach also emphasizes the social construction (and reconstruction) of the audience, although in this case the focus is more on the formation of identity. Consideration of performance encompasses the interaction of actors (performers), the audience, the space in which the performance occurs, and the script, or mechanisms of drama. All of these factors have potential political implications, as the individuals involved negotiate and renegotiate identities and relationships. At first blush, "performance" may seem overblown; it conjures up images of heavy curtains rising as actors take the floodlit stage, or costumed rock stars launching into the latest pop number. The concept of performance, though, covers a wide range of situations, from the high drama of religious rites to the exchange of greetings when powerful leaders meet (Schechner 2003). Indeed, performance is construed as formalized or "scripted" interactions that involve physical and social distance among performers and audiences.

Performance theory may be valuable in the way that it calls attention to different aspects of the relationship between performer and audience

(Beeman 1993). It also provides a means of considering art within its context of use, rather than treating it as a special separate case of detached aesthetic contemplation. Archaeologically speaking, the physical distance of performance is the most straightforward. Architectural space such as plazas, ballcourts, and kivas may imply the effects of literal physical distance between performers and audiences. Social distance lacks the concrete manifestation of physical space, but performance theory may help archaeologists explore the implications of different kinds or degrees of social distance in different settings. Matthew Chamberlin (in press) and Daniela Triadan (2006) have begun to explore the possibilities of performance theory for studies of plaza-oriented villages in the Pueblo IV period (1325–1600 CE).

Audiences in the Ancient Southwest

Archaeologists in the Southwest have rarely engaged with the literature on audiences from other disciplines (cf. Inomata and Coben 2006). As a result, most archaeological studies fail to address the composition or actions of the audience directly, instead evoking a generic and rather passive group of potential viewers (e.g., Meyers 2007). Drawing on a behavioral model, many Southwestern archaeologists have focused on the effects of a general message, such as declarations of religious affiliation (Crown 1994; Hays-Gilpin and LeBlanc 2007:122) or of group identity (Hyder 1997). Such studies are most common for art that is fixed in space, usually in the form of rock art or mural paintings. This makes sense, as fixed works of art are the main case where both the art and its original context are known, making it possible to infer audiences through the spaces in which they gathered (Bradley 2009:42). Southwestern archaeologists have also considered the probable contexts of display for portable art, such as painted ceramic bowls, as discussed shortly.

For researchers interested in how space affects potential audiences, the contrast between art in private contexts and more public displays is important (Brody 1991; Lindauer and Zaslow 1994:326–27; Newsome and Hays-Gilpin in press; Wright 2005). Various authors have noted that the relatively small size of most Pueblo IV kivas with murals reflects controlled access to the paintings (e.g., Crotty 1995). In terms of rock art research, Polly Schaafsma (1990) suggests that some enclosed rock art sites in the Galisteo Basin were private, or perhaps even secret, shrines with a limited audience. J. J. Brody (1989) has made a similar observation for other Rio Grande rock art sites, comparing the use of space in open boulderfield sites and in rockshelters (I will return to this theme later). Despite the frequent references to limited space, however, systematic evaluation of space relative to the size of audiences is rare in these studies.

Studies of more open rock art sites often focus on the position of the images on the landscape and its implications for different audiences. Many researchers in the Southwest have tried to determine rock art's potential for communicating with individuals traveling on trails, approaching villages, or entering new territories (Schaafsma 1992a; Snead 2008:90–109; Snead and Munson 2001). Much of this work is based on the idea that the artists created petroglyphs and pictographs in order to communicate with others, whether from within or outside their own group (Munson 2002; Robins 2002:396). Ralph Hartley's (1992; Hartley and Vawser 1998) work, for example, uses geographic information systems (GIS) and measures of information potential to examine how the placement of rock art on the southern Colorado Plateau of Utah might have disseminated information about the social and physical environment.

Archaeologists also evoke audiences for performance in public spaces, such as plazas or ballcourts. As in the examples cited earlier, architectural space is relatively permanent and was used in place, so the spatial context is known. In this case, however, the art that was used or displayed—or the performance that took place—is less certain, leaving the researcher to extrapolate both art and audience from various sources of information. Considerable attention has been devoted to the context of public performances, especially in the plazas of Pueblo IV villages, ca. 1275–1600 (Chamberlin in press; Ruscavage-Barz and Bagwell 2006; Triadan 2006). These occasions are thought to have involved dancing, music, and other performing arts. Visual arts such as jewelry, textiles, and various accoutrements were surely used or displayed as part of these events as well.

Studies of ceramics and public feasting offer a good example of how archaeologists have combined known physical spaces with studies of artifact assemblages to infer the context of use for certain kinds of pottery (Mills 2004b; Potter 2000). During the Pueblo I period (700–900 CE), the distribution of large cooking jars and imported redware bowl shards in sites from the northern Southwest suggests that feasts were held by the inhabitants of particular room blocks (Blinman 1989; Potter 2000); studies of faunal remains provide another line of evidence for these early feasts. The relatively small size of the Pueblo I villages, along with the limited architectural space available for such feasts, suggests that perhaps the audience/participants were also restricted. Similarly, the architectural contexts of Pueblo II (900–1100) feasting at Pueblo Alto, in Chaco Canyon, and Pueblo III (1100–1325) feasting at Sand Canyon Pueblo, in the Four

Corners area, also have implications for the size and composition of the audience (see Potter 2000:477–79). In particular, variation in artifacts in 11th- and early 12th-century trash mounds at Pueblo Alto implies that the audience for ceramics and any other art used in these gatherings may have included a diverse group from different regions (Toll 2001).

Most dramatically, feasting appears to have shifted into the large central spaces of plaza-oriented villages during the Pueblo IV period (1325–1600). These villages, found primarily in the Rio Grande Valley and east-central and northeastern Arizona, typically take the form of multiple room blocks arranged around one or more open plazas (Rautman 2000; Ruscavage-Barz and Bagwell 2006), which would have accommodated a sizable audience who could view the ceramics as they received food. The size, color, contrast, and other attributes of the bowls have a significant impact on their degree of visibility (Graves and Eckert 1998; Graves and Spielmann 2000; Spielmann 1998b; Van Keuren 2004, in press).

Proxemics and Accessibility

Proxemics offers a model for considering the interaction of space, a potential audience, and the effects of distance on perception of artwork. Developed by anthropologist Edward Hall (1966, 1968) in the late 1960s, proxemics originated in studies of personal space in various cultures around the world. Hall (1966) defined four general spatial categories, each with different implications for the kinds of information available to a viewer or audience member. The closest range, which Hall called intimate space, is defined as less than a half-meter separating individuals. Personal space, from about one-half to 1 meter, provides a little more breathing room. In this range, the viewer can observe a great deal of subtle detail, such as facial expressions, but is too close to perceive the entire body of the individual at whom they are directing attention. The shift to social space, between 1 and 3.5 meters, marks a changing relationship between individuals. Direct physical contact is no longer possible, so at this distance interaction relies more on input from vision and hearing; fine detail begins to be lost. Public distance, which includes any interaction farther than 3.5 meters away, entirely precludes views of fine details, instead placing the emphasis on broad movements of the entire body. Each of the distances that Hall defined emphasizes different modes of communication, with greater distances necessitating more conventional or stereotyped movements and vocalizations if an individual is to be able to communicate with his or her audience.

Archaeologically, applications of proxemics usually center on an audience's visual access to an individual or group, such as performers, a speaker, or a religious leader. However, the concept can usefully be extended to encompass accessibility in terms of multiple senses and any manner of objects, including artwork. Visual access encompasses the qualities and characteristics of a work of art that are visible at different distances or from different locations. How visible is a work of rock art from different places on the landscape (Bradley 2002)? When are actual images visible, as opposed to the general location of the site (Munson and Head in press)? How does the visibility of designs inside painted bowls compare to those outside (Brody 2005; Van Keuren 2004)? How close would viewers need to be in order to observe the differences between pseudo-cloisonné and mosaic ornaments? Visual access is critical when one is concerned with art as communication, whether in the form of Salado polychrome motifs indicating religious affiliation (Crown 1994) or Basketmaker bags and baskets indicating social relationships (Webster and Hays-Gilpin 1994).

In addition to visibility, physical access to artwork is also important, for it addresses the size of the audience and their potential activities (Bradley 2009:45–47). Physical accessibility is related to the ways in which the configuration of space either facilitates or limits one's ability to engage the body in interacting with art. In the case of art that is fixed in space, physical accessibility relates to movement into and around the location of artwork. Different landscape qualities and features have varying implications for access to art that is fixed in space. The relative physical access for artists at a rock art site might depend on the size of a platform to stand on while producing petroglyphs. For an audience, physical accessibility might relate to the amount of open space below or near the panels where people can gather. Characteristics such as elevation relative to the surrounding landscape, contours of cliff faces, the height of buildings, the size and configuration of rooms, and the available lighting all have an impact on visual access (Bradley and Phillips 2008).

For portable art, physical access relates to handling objects directly. It is generally more difficult to assess, as the use of ceramics, jewelry, carved and painted wood, and similar objects must be inferred rather than observed directly. Still, use wear analysis has the potential to provide a picture of regular use of items, including works of art. Physical accessibility has important implications for a viewer's experience. As Brody (2005:122) has pointed out, handling Mimbres bowls has a dramatic effect on their appearance, depending on the angle from which one examines them (also see

Bradley 2009:45). Observing subtle details, such as fugitive paint on bowl exteriors, might also require physical access to the vessel.

Measures of access are not absolutes; they are meaningful only in a relative sense, and at the appropriate spatial scale. Depending on the questions of interest, the relevant scale could range from the placement of a single petroglyph on a boulder to the setting of an entire rock art site within the broader physical and cultural landscape (Bradley 2002; Chippindale 2004).

Locating Audiences

Locating audiences for a work of art requires examining various factors of space and form in order to determine what could have been visible and to whom. The physical characteristics of the object help determine which qualities of the work of art are most accessible to potential audiences at different distances. Ideally, this information can be combined with the physical and temporal context within which the art was encountered, providing additional information that may be used to infer the size and perhaps the composition of the audience.

Physical Characteristics

A consideration of the physical characteristics of objects helps to determine what aspects of artwork, portable or fixed in place, might be visible to an audience. Visibility is affected by numerous factors, including the size and shape of the item, the use of color, the degree of contrast between figure and ground, repetition of motifs or designs, the clarity or comprehensibility of design or shape, and so on (Voss and Young 1995). Pueblo IV polychrome ceramics may well have caught on in the early 1300s in part because their bright colors created an eye-catching, instantly recognizable statement about the individuals who owned or used them (see chapter 6). Even in areas where Pueblo IV glazeware and polychromes were never fully embraced, such as the northern reaches of the Northern Rio Grande Valley, potters may have sought to make a statement with their black-on-cream biscuitware ceramics. Severin Fowles has suggested that biscuitware potters may have chosen a whiteware clay that was difficult to work with but resulted in a "vibrantly dark painted design" (Fowles 2004:22). In other words, bichrome biscuitware pottery, so often thought of as a conservative holdover from the pre-glazeware past, may have been consciously crafted in order to create "high visual impact" (Fowles 2004:22).

As Christopher Carr (1995) points out, there is a hierarchy of attributes within a single artifact that reflects a general order of visibility. First-order attributes include the overall size, form, color, texture, and movement of an object. Finer-scale aspects of composition and layout, an object's second-order attributes, may be less immediately obvious. Third-order details, such as infill of partitions within the overall design, require the most careful study and the closest range in order to be perceived. The famous Holy Ghost pictograph panel of the Great Gallery (ca. 400 BCE–500 CE) in southeast Utah provides a good example of the hierarchy of attribute visibility (figure 4.1). The overall form of the large ghostly figures that give the site its name are obvious from a distance, yet the figures include extensive details that are difficult to see unless one is standing immediately in front of the panel. Additional images of people and animals, in a dramatically different style, are also present but are too small to be seen readily from afar. These kinds of differences in visibility have implications for communication potential and for interactions of artists, works of art, and audiences (Carr 1995; Voss and Young 1995).

Physical and Temporal Context

Studying the characteristics of the artwork itself provides information about potential accessibility, but to make the leap from the object to the audience requires additional information about the spatial context within

Figure 4.1.   The Great Gallery, a pictograph panel in Canyonlands National Park, includes the famous Holy Ghost panel (far left and inset). Photographs by Marit K. Munson.

which the art was used or displayed. Evaluation of the size and configuration of the art's context makes it possible to speculate about the potential size and composition of an audience (Carr 1995). Even large objects with highly visible attributes may have a limited audience if they are used within small or restricted spaces, such as inside a building or in a "socially closed context" (Carr 1995:195). Figurines and effigies from Chaco Canyon (Vivian et al. 1978), for example, are brightly painted and have high potential visibility. The pieces are small, though, suggesting that they would have been seen at close quarters (Hays-Gilpin 2000:101) by a correspondingly small audience.

As mentioned earlier, inferring audiences is most straightforward for artwork with a permanent orientation in space (Schiffer and Miller 1999), such as murals and other wall paintings that are fixed and that have a specific orientation and formal boundaries in the form of enclosing architecture (Brody 1989). Rock art is similar in its "placedness," although the layout of the site may not be as formal as that of buildings (Bradley 2009; Chippindale and Nash 2004). The physical dimensions of any enclosed spaces with art place upper limits on the size of the potential audience at any one time—the size of kivas limits access to murals painted on their walls, the walls of room blocks restrict the visibility of painted interior walls, and the dimensions of rockshelters limit the number of audience members.

In addition to the size of the space, its configuration is equally important. While the painted band above Moon House, a small Pueblo III (1100–1325 CE) cliff dwelling in southeast Utah, is often referred to as an exterior painting, this characterization fails to capture the whole story. The painting is indeed on an exterior wall of a structure, but it is also behind—inside—a stone wall that was built to enclose the rockshelter and that prevents any view of the painting from beyond the confines of the shelter itself (see Brody 1991:plate 10). Even expansive, open settings may impose limitations on the size and location of an audience. On the Pajarito Plateau, in the Northern Rio Grande Valley, the local topography of rock art panels high on cliff faces or on canyon edges effectively restricts the view of petroglyphs. The view *from* the site of Crane Kiva, for example, is a breathtaking panorama over Alamo Canyon and down toward the Rio Grande. The view *to* the site is nearly nonexistent, and the crane petroglyph that gives the site its name is only visible when one is standing in or immediately adjacent to the kiva itself (figure 4.2).

Readily portable artwork presents a more difficult challenge, for the context of its use is less obvious—and much more varied than that of fixed

Figure 4.2. A view from above shows the outline of a kiva perched on the lip of a deep canyon on the Pajarito Plateau. The petroglyph (inset) that gives the site its name, Crane Kiva, is just out of the photo to the right; it can only be seen from within the site. Photographs by Marit K. Munson.

objects. Formal architectural spaces such as plazas, ballcourts, and platform mounds provide space for audiences of differing sizes (Chamberlin in press; Crown and Fish 1996; Harmon 2006:204–6; Ruscavage-Barz and Bagwell 2006), but it is not always clear exactly what art might have been involved in dances, games, ceremonies, or other performances staged in these spaces. In some cases, however, contexts of use can be inferred through indirect means from the properties of the objects themselves. Studies of ceramics used for feasting infer the size of the audience/participants based on the size of bowls used for serving and eating (e.g., Spielmann 1998b). In other cases, display of bowls, figurines, or carved wooden objects is implied through use wear (e.g., Van Keuren 2001:170–71). The form of the objects themselves also provides clues, as in the case of a stone effigy of a shell trumpet in archaeologist Nels Nelson's collections from the Galisteo Basin, which has a hole for mounting on a staff or pole (also see Mills and Ferguson 2008).

The temporal context of use is also important in considering audiences, as the experience of art is not limited to a single time or event (Morphy and Perkins 2005b:16). Some works of art are quite permanent, while others last for weeks, days, or just hours. These differences in the uselife or durability of an object have important implications for its potential visibility (Nanoglou 2009; Renfrew 1994:266; Voss and Young 1995). Some extraordinarily durable works of art, such as Archaic period (5500 BCE–200 CE) petroglyphs, exist well beyond a single individual's life span to encompass multiple audiences stretching over hundreds of years or more. At the other end of the spectrum, many kiva walls were replastered so frequently that painted murals were effectively erased from view after a relatively short period of time (see chapter 6)—if not necessarily from memory (see Mills and Walker 2008).

Public Participation

Barbara Mills's (2007) work on public feasting from the Pueblo III to Pueblo IV period is an excellent example of addressing audiences in differing public settings. Focusing on pueblos from the Mogollon Rim area of east-central Arizona, Mills examined the relationship among the size of audience, the spatial organization of feasting, and the designs and colors of the bowls used to serve food between 1000 and 1400 CE. Drawing on work relating to the visual characteristics of objects and their social context, she highlighted qualities that "enhance the visibility of serving bowls" (Mills 2007:213), including vessel size, size and form of exterior designs, and the colors and contrast of slip and painted designs.

Mills (2007) was able to trace changes in the physical characteristics of bowl exteriors over time, showing varying degrees of potential visibility in different circumstances. Prior to 1100 CE, bowls were seldom painted, or even slipped, on the exterior, leaving surface color as the only prominent attribute for visibility. Between 1100–1200, however, Pueblo III potters began to use bold exterior designs on bowls, as well as polychrome designs, which stood out in comparison to other contemporaneous ceramics. In fact, bold exterior designs were ubiquitous across the northern Southwest in the 1200s, often on the largest bowls in a given area. These two factors suggest that Pueblo III ceramics were used by relatively large groups of people engaged in public feasts. On the other hand, bowls from the Pueblo III to Pueblo IV transition, around 1275–1325, tended to be smaller and had less contrast, so that they were only visible "from certain angles or at closer distances" (Mills 2007:220). Curiously enough, the decreased visibility of serving bowls coincides with evidence from faunal remains of *increased* feasting at the same time.

Drawing on ceramic data from three Mogollon Rim villages, Mills (2007) argued that the decrease in the visibility of bowl designs in the early Pueblo IV period reflects changes in the proxemics of ritual feasting. In particular, she was able to link the varied size of plazas in different villages to the relative visibility of serving bowls, showing that potters used more visible designs in settings with more expansive spaces for feasting. When larger plazas came into use in the mid-to-late 1300s, the bowls showed correspondingly more visible designs. Diversity in decorated wares was correspondingly greater, including both late Salado polychromes with "vivid exterior designs with high iconographic content" (Mills 2007:233) and contemporaneous White Mountain redware, such as Fourmile polychrome, with "highly homogenous exterior designs" (Mills 2007:233) and more diverse interior designs.

Overall, the great variety of slip, paint, and exterior designs along the Mogollon Rim, and in the Upper Little Colorado and Zuni areas, suggests diversification in ritual feasting practices in the 1300–1400s, with the scale of feasts ranging from large outdoor events to smaller indoor gatherings of members of specific ritual societies. Ancestral Pueblo potters, it appears, intentionally "manipulated the designs on the exterior of their bowls to communicate to different audiences" (Mills 2007:234).

Ways of Seeing

Archaeological studies of visibility, such as the considerable body of work on ceramics and feasting, tend to focus on *what* an audience saw. A recent paper by art historian Elizabeth Newsome and archaeologist Kelley Hays-Gilpin (in press), though, pushes the boundaries a bit, considering *how* audiences saw. In particular, they argue that Ancestral Pueblo ways of seeing changed in the late 1200s or early 1300s, as reflected by differences in wall murals from the Pueblo III and Pueblo IV periods.

Pueblo III murals (1000–1325) from across the Chaco and San Juan/Mesa Verde regions typically consist of a bicolor banded pattern or of "blended" designs (figure 4.3) combining bands with geometric designs derived from textiles and pottery (Ortman 2008). Several authors have argued that the banded designs represent landscapes, with a dark (usually red) lower register marking the horizon and a white upper register as the sky (Brody 1991:57–68; Cole 2006; Newsome and Hays-Gilpin in press). These landscapes are sometimes modified with triangular "mountain" shapes that jut up from the red band into the upper register, triangular

Figure 4.3.   This Pueblo III mural from Cliff Palace, Mesa Verde, combines a red dado, tri-angles, and dots with a textile-type design "floating" above. Photograph by Kay Barnett.

"cracks" into the lower band, or lines of dots. The repetition in these patterns suggests that time was important in Pueblo III murals, with the various dots, triangles, and other marks possibly relating to astronomical observations (Malville and Putnam 1993) or to leaders' responsibilities for scheduling rituals based on observations of sun and sky. Newsome and Hays-Gilpin (in press) argued that the position of the observer was critical to the meaning of Pueblo III murals, for the configuration of the rooms in which they are found would have situated the viewer within the landscape and the calendrical cycles defined by the paintings. They also suggested that the murals might be an early reflection of the process of linking Ancestral Pueblo people to space in a meaningful way by establishing the Center Place.

Newsome and Hays-Gilpin (in press) contrasted viewership of the earlier wall paintings with that of kiva murals of the Pueblo IV period (1325–1600 CE), which are found mostly in the Hopi area and along the Rio Grande Valley. As many researchers have noted, the Pueblo IV period was characterized by an expansion and diversification of art and iconography in many media, from ceramics and kiva murals to rock art and possibly textiles (Brody 1991:81–113; Schaafsma 1980:243–289; Webster 2007). These changes "mark a major shift in the scale and composition of Pueblo visual culture" (Newsome and Hays-Gilpin in press), as illustrated through a comparison of Sikyatki polychrome ceramics and Pueblo IV kiva murals.

Sikyatki polychromes were the first ceramics in the Hopi area to include clear images of masked figures and images of beings that resemble historic katsinas, or ancestral beings (see chapter 5). The presence of religious imagery on vessels that would have been circulated to the public through trade and ceremonial exchange suggests that the images were suitable for a broad audience (Newsome and Hays-Gilpin in press). Indeed, potters may have used these images in part to communicate religious ideals or other messages with diverse audiences, much as Katherine Spielmann and colleagues (2006) have suggested for protohistoric ceramics from the Salinas district of the Rio Grande Valley.

At the same time that ceramics incorporated identifiable religious images, some kiva murals included much more elaborate scenes of dancers and other performers, as well as ceremonial objects, plants, and animals. These seem to be related to the kinds of dances and performances that the public viewed in plazas, but the audience for the paintings was more limited, due to the physical structure of the kivas (Newsome and Hays-Gilpin in press)—and, I would add, due to the limited time that the murals were visible before being covered with a fresh coat of plaster (Smith 1952). The distinction between esoteric contexts inside kivas and public space in plazas probably helped to reinforce a distinction between members of religious societies and others (Newsome and Hays–Gilpin in press).

Even though the audiences for Pueblo III and Pueblo IV murals were equally restricted, Newsome and Hays–Gilpin (in press) suggested that the relationship of that select audience to the paintings themselves differed, based in part on the content of the art. In Pueblo III murals, they argued, the viewer was literally in the Center Place, looking out to the painted landscape of earth and sky, marked by the cyclical progression of time (figure 4.4). With the Pueblo IV murals, the visual focus was inward, with figures circling the viewer's space and creating an interactive relationship among audience and image. This, they suggested, reflects a shift in ceremonial focus, in the foundations of leadership, and in the relationship of an esoteric audience to the broader community. It is this final point, the social implications of inclusive and exclusive audiences, to which I turn next.

Figure 4.4. A close-up of a mural from Painted Kiva, in Mesa Verde, shows the dark red baseline, topped with triangular "mountains" and dots, typical of Pueblo III wall paintings. Photograph by Kay Barnett.

Social Implications of Access

The composition of an audience hinges on a wide range of social factors, including age, gender, status, and knowledge. If the audience is limited, as it is for the wall paintings and kiva murals that Newsome and Hays-Gilpin (in press) addressed, who has access and who does not? What are the social implications of differential access among community members? These questions are especially important given the various arguments for control of knowledge as a fundamental source of power among the Pueblos (Brandt 1977, 1994). Even when artwork is public and the audience includes everyone, it is useful to ask who "everyone" is. An entire village? The village plus visitors from neighboring sites?

My research on rock art in the Northern Rio Grande Valley addresses some of these questions by considering the implications of site configuration for the size and composition of audiences for Pueblo IV rock art (Munson in press-a, b). As with wall paintings and murals, Pueblo IV rock art sites in the Northern Rio Grande differ considerably from their Pueblo III counterparts. The locations and spatial organization of Pueblo IV rock art sites are much more diverse than those for earlier counterparts, suggesting increasing differentiation in the practices that led to the creation of the sites (also see Brody 1989; Munson in press-b).

The great diversity in Pueblo IV rock art sites reflects a changing relationship among their artists and audiences. Some sites appear to have been created in order to maximize visibility of petroglyphs. For example, the Creston dike (sometimes called Comanche Gap) in the Galisteo Basin includes numerous life-sized human figures with shields, perhaps aimed at outsiders from the Plains entering the Pueblo world (Schaafsma 1992a). Some of the major Pueblo IV villages in the Galisteo Basin and on the Pajarito Plateau also have large-scale images posted in locations visible to anyone entering the pueblo (figure 4.5). At the same time, other contemporaneous rock art sites are carefully structured to limit visual and physical access. Las Estrellas, a late prehistoric or protohistoric rock art site on the Pajarito Plateau, is adjacent to a large late Ancestral Pueblo village, yet its location, tucked below the edge of a canyon rim, prevents visual access and restricts physical access to a single line of approach (Munson 2003). The structure of the site therefore places strict limits on the size of the audience. Repeated images along the entry to the site suggest that individuals without required knowledge were barred from the site entirely.

Figure 4.5.   An enormous Awanyu, or horned serpent, petroglyph appears to guard the entrance to the Pueblo IV village of Tsirege, on the Pajarito Plateau. A prehistoric stairway leads visitors through the boulders (left of center) and past the petroglyph, located on the vertical cliff face in the upper center of the photograph. Photographs by Marit K. Munson; inset photograph digitally enhanced.

The rock art at the large protohistoric village of San Cristobal (1325–1690s), in the Galisteo Basin, is similarly situated (Munson in press-a). Although the rock art site is located immediately adjacent to the pueblo, access is nevertheless restricted by the local topography, a complicated maze of enormous boulders and cliff faces on the edge of a mesa to the north of the pueblo (figure 4.6). Physical access to the mesa slope itself is not difficult, given its location next to the village. Within the rock art site, however, the space is highly structured in terms of movement and access to the core areas. Giant boulders and steep cliff faces effectively divide the mesa slope into several dozen activity areas or locales, which form outdoor "rooms" open to the sky. Entry into the rock art locales is channeled through a limited number of paths, created by gaps between boulders. The space within the locales could accommodate gatherings of many individuals, suggesting that the pool of potential artists and audience members is relatively large. At the same time, none of the locales would accommodate a gathering of all of the village's inhabitants simultaneously. Only a subset

Figure 4.6. Petroglyphs at San Cristobal Pueblo are concentrated in locales bounded by cliff faces and enormous boulders. One locale is in the shadows at the lower right. Photograph by Marit K. Munson.

of the local population was involved at any given time in producing or using the rock art.

The content of the San Cristobal rock art additionally suggests that there were multiple different groups of artists and/or audiences for the talus slope rock art. Although full analysis is not yet complete, it appears that artists emphasized different icons in different locales. One locale contains most of the rare images of owls at the site, while another includes all of the known depictions of cranes or herons. The presence of superpositioning on many panels creates a picture of small groups of individuals using and reusing these semi-enclosed "rooms" for repeated ritual activity.

Taken together, the restricted audiences, repeated images, and superpositioning suggest an increasing specialization in ritual practice, with multiple sodalities or religious societies within the community taking responsibility for different rituals (Munson in press-b). Although such practices would, on one level, differentiate the active participants from the greater audience of the community as a whole, all of the villagers would have recognized the importance of the events taking place on the talus slope. After all, the rock art's proximity to the village suggests that those who were not themselves participants had ample opportunity to see the artists leave the pueblo, climb the slope, and disappear among the giant boulders. Shortly after, villagers would likely have heard some of the activities taking place at the rock art site, whether the sounds of pecking or of associated music or speech.

An even more exclusive group of artists/audience is implied by several painted rockshelters in the vicinity of San Cristobal. These shelters and overhangs, located in side canyons away from the main village, are far more restricted and private than the talus slope rock art (Munson in press-a). Unless participants carried obvious ritual paraphernalia or announced their intentions, most villagers would have had little to no idea of the activities taking place at the rockshelter sites, nor would they necessarily know who was involved. The enclosed space of the rockshelter sites also has profound implications for the size and composition of the audience, which would have been limited by knowledge of the site's location and by the physical dimensions of the enclosing cliffs. One such site, the Pine Tree site, consists of two painted shelters. One is a fairly generous 10 meters long and 4 meters deep, while the other is a cramped overhang about 1 meter high, 3 to 4 meters long, and less than a meter deep (Schaafsma 1990). Making and using rock art within the shelters would have been an intensely personal experience, one in which the artist and the audience is one and the same.

Supernatural Audiences

What was the point of returning to such isolated locations to mark the rocks? Why would a tiny group of artists return to specific spaces, time after time, to repeat the same icons or renew those that were already present? In the Northern Rio Grande Valley, the most intensely worked, most repetitive, longest-lived rock art panels are those in the most physically restricted spaces, such as the rockshelter sites near San Cristobal, or the Pajarito Plateau site, Las Estrellas, that is perched below the edge of a high cliff. These are highly structured, secluded sites, with strictly limited access and few opportunities for nonparticipants to gain knowledge about activities at these sites. Just a few individuals participated in producing, reworking, and refreshing the pictographs and petroglyphs, blurring the distinction between artists and audience. In fact, one could argue that the process of producing and working with the rock art was far more important than the images themselves. Sheltered from prying eyes, highly restricted in participation, the art-like portions of these sites were part of a larger whole, a series of actions aimed at an audience that was not human, but beyond human experience. Perhaps some art was aimed at the ultimate esoteric audience, the world of spirits.

Why Audiences?

Audiences are important to artwork. Depending on one's position on art versus artifact, the audience experience may be seen as the crucial factor in defining art or as a more passive presence receiving messages from the artist. Although art always implies an audience in some form, researchers in many fields have tended to ignore the presence of individuals who interpret and interact with art. Ironically, the greatest value in studying audiences archaeologically is that it turns attention away from the content of the artwork and instead focuses it on the physical contexts and the material properties of art and on the relationships that it implies among individuals. A plea to ignore content may seem odd in a book advocating the study of art, yet I believe that consideration of audiences is particularly helpful for objects that have too often been treated as art and art alone—the rock art that gets interpreted as meaningful pictures, with no consideration whatsoever of its material existence, or the kiva murals that get reproduced as decontextualized illustrations of headdresses, textiles, and shields. It is not that studies of, say, textiles as pictured in kiva murals (e.g., Webster 2007) are worthless—far from it—but that the study of objects labeled as art must not stop with images and icons. Instead, archaeologists should draw on other disciplines' insights in order to consider more fully the relationships among artists, works of art, and their audiences.

Images

5

> [T]he finest Mimbres paintings are at once simple and complex, clear and obscure, easily perceived and impossible to read. (Brody 2005:xxiv)

> [I]mages found on archaeological sites are artefacts, like pots or weapons. . . . [T]hey should occupy a central, culturally and archaeologically grounded position rather than hover on the margins. (Aldhouse-Green 2004:xvi)

IMAGES ARE INTRIGUING. From the appealingly cartoonish figures on Mimbres ceramics to the engaging, lively dogs and coyotes of Ancestral Pueblo rock art (figure 5.1), recognizable pictures draw us in. Representational images are far more likely than geometric designs to be treated as art (Bradley 2009; Errington 1994:210), perhaps because they "carry more emotional weight and power" (Brody 1991:33). Humans may, in fact, be hard-wired to find representational imagery appealing, particularly if it depicts humans and other animals (Davis 1995:93). Indeed, our brains seem so eager to interpret pattern as image that we often create images even when they do not exist, as anyone who has spotted elephants or rabbits in the clouds can attest. When pictures take on the patina of time, they become even more tantalizing. It is, as Stephen Lekson (1992:112) has put it, "our easy entry into the idiom—our ability to read some of the message, but not all—that fascinates us. We want to know what's going on in these pictures." Indeed, we tend to treat images as if they are completely different from other artifacts, simply because they appear to represent something or someone (Hamilton 1996).

Figure 5.1. A small, carefully pecked petroglyph of a canid, perhaps a dog or coyote, at Petroglyph Hill, in the Galisteo Basin. Photograph by Marit K. Munson.

This chapter addresses the promise and the perils of identifying and interpreting representational images from the ancient Southwest. The promise, as expressed frequently, is that images seem familiar and easy to recognize, even as they appear intriguingly alien. We feel that they will offer rare glimpses into the minds of people long gone (Berlant 1983:13; Brody 1983:74). Archaeologists tend to privilege representations in their discussions and presentation of artifacts or objects. There are countless studies that briefly acknowledge geometric designs, then set them aside in favor of discussing images.

As satisfying as it is to identify representational imagery, few archaeologists acknowledge that images are much more complicated than they appear at first glance. It may seem simple to identify images of humans or to distinguish between pictures of birds and deer, but it is equally easy to jump from some curving lines to the identification of a rainbow or from three blotches to Mickey Mouse. This happens through such a fundamental mental process that it occurs almost without our awareness of the leap that such identifications entail (Malafouris 2007:288). Patterns may be identified as almost anything that a viewer can imagine, whether a mountain lion, a teepee, Kokopelli, or an alien. Indeed, most identifications of images in the Southwest rest on a shaky foundation of assumptions and common sense, supplemented with ethnographic data from the historic Pueblos. Some images are even referred to with labels drawn directly from specific languages or traditions that may or may not have anything to do with the image in question. Kokopelli, a name drawn from the Hopi language, is one classic example of this problem; it has been applied to flute players and to phallic human images from across the Southwest, and even beyond (Aron 1981; Lambert 1946; Tisdale 1993).

In place of this ad hoc approach, I argue that identifying images should be based on understanding of theoretical and empirical aspects of representation. This chapter provides an overview of the literature on representational images from psychology and art history, considering how artists choose which characteristics or attributes to include in their pictures. Thinking of images as reflecting a process of representation will help in making more explicit and less value-laden identifications of images—something critical in studies of ancient iconography

The Nature of the Image

What, exactly, is an image? In its simplest sense, an image is something—marks, an object—produced by human beings that looks like or resembles something in the world. There are two contrasting kinds of theories about the way in which something resembles the world: perceptual theories and social theories (Costall 1985, 1997; Hagen 1986:86–87).

Perceptual theories of pictorial meaning are "based on the idea of resemblance" (Costall 1997:49), that pictures look like the thing they represent. This view, which echoes the Peircean view of icons as based on visual resemblance, implies that pictorial meaning is intrinsic to the image and universally shared. In this sense, a picture is like an open window, with images created by replicating the pattern of light that the eye receives from a given scene. Social theories of pictorial meaning, in contrast, center on "shared practice and convention" (Costall 1997:49), where artists create pictures that have meaning only within the rules of a particular time and place. This implies that pictorial meaning is arbitrary or, in the Peircean sense, that images are symbols whose meaning relies upon convention. In short, pictorial meaning is specific and culturally relative (Costall 1997; also see Malafouris 2007). From this perspective, pictures are about conveying information about what is represented, which may or may not involve depicting light.

The implications of perceptual versus social theories of images become clear if one returns to the controversy over what appear to be birth scenes painted on Mimbres pottery, described in chapter 3. All of the authors in the debate implicitly accepted a pictorial theory of representation, assuming that the paintings were intended to represent optical reality. Because the images were implausible from the perspective of actual human birth, Michelle Hegmon and Wenda Trevathan (1996) argued that they were painted by individuals who were not familiar with birthing. Subsequent debate largely centered on what the paintings on various bowls actually showed (Espenshade 1997; LeBlanc 1997; Shaffer et al. 1997)—without consideration of *how* they showed it. A social theory of pictorial meaning, however, would suggest that an artist might have been trying to convey a birth by representing information rather than an optically correct depiction. In other words, an artist might need to include facial details and limbs in order to make it clear that the image showed an infant between a woman's legs, regardless of whether or not the scene was strictly accurate.

Social and pictorial theories of representation complement each other nicely, for all images simultaneously reference universals and express conventions relevant to a particular time and place. As psychologist Alan Costall (1997:59) expresses it, "pictures do more or less look like what they depict," and yet social practices are clearly relevant. This is true because images are not just a pattern or form that resembles something else; images must evoke that other object for the viewer (Deregowski 1980:97). Indeed, the interpretation of marks or forms as resembling objects is inherently "quite special and contingent—context-bound" (Davis 1995:74).

Pictures in the Western tradition are often assumed to resemble what they depict through "optically naturalistic copies of 'reality'" (Errington 1994:209; also see Costall 1985). This notion can, like so much of the baggage surrounding art, be traced to Renaissance Europe, when artists began to codify linear perspective as the ultimate in realistic depiction (Hagen 1986). Renaissance painters were fascinated by the challenge of transforming three dimensions into intelligible two-dimensional form through mechanical means, a process that reflected more general merger of art and science in the 16th century (Sturken and Cartwright 2001:111–15). While Classical Greeks had debated realism in art and ultimately rejected perspective as "a form of trickery" (Sturken and Cartwright 2001:114), Renaissance painters thought of themselves as god-like in their ability to "deceive . . . both men and beasts" (Leonardo da Vinci, quoted in Sturken and Cartwright 2001:114). Indeed, Vasari's (1991 [1550]) biographies of artists included apocryphal stories of artists who were so skilled that they essentially created reality. Giotto reportedly painted a fly on one of his master's canvases that was so realistic that the elder artist kept trying to brush the insect off the surface.

The dominance of realism as the foundation of Western art shows through clearly in the influential work of art historian Erwin Panofsky (1955), whose discussion of the interpretation of Renaissance images is now a classic text. Panofsky described multiple levels of interpretation, each building upon the previous level or levels. One begins, according to Panofsky, with basic description of the primary or natural meaning of an image. In his terms, this meant examining the configuration of lines, colors, and shapes in order to decide what object (person, animal, or thing) is represented, and perhaps what events or expressive qualities they imply.

Panofsky's secondary level of meaning, conventional meaning, is determined through iconographic analysis, which involves making connections between what is depicted and the various themes that it reflects. In other words, iconographic analysis seeks the "intrinsic content of a work of art" (Panofsky 1955:32) by drawing connections between known stories, characters, or themes. A painting by Leonardo da Vinci might be described as showing 13 men sitting at a long table. Iconographic analysis relies on the viewers' knowledge of biblical stories to suggest that this is a depiction of the Last Supper, with Christ seated at the center of the table.

Panofsky's final level of meaning centers on intrinsic meaning of a work of art. This stage, which Panofsky referred to as iconology, involves interpreting the significance of what is depicted. One might move beyond iconographic analysis of the Last Supper in the da Vinci painting in order to try to understand what the painting says about da Vinci's personality, about the mores of the Italian Renaissance, or about religious attitudes of the time (Panofsky 1955:31).

For the most part, Panofsky assumed that artists intend to create recognizable images, implying that the realism in Renaissance art makes identification of images simple. Indeed, he asserted that recognizing images was simply a matter of drawing on "our practical experience" (Panofsky 1955:33) with the world. However, Panofsky also recognized that contextual information is required in order to recognize and analyze images. He admitted that one might need to consult published sources in order to identify objects from Renaissance paintings that were no longer in use or otherwise not immediately familiar. He also acknowledged that the problem extends beyond unfamiliar subjects, for one must also have an understanding of the stylistic conventions of a given time and place in order to correctly identify an image at the descriptive level. And, in fact, assessing the iconography of a work of art requires a thorough knowledge of the literature, whether written or oral, that is relevant to the specific time and place. Panofsky (1955:28–29) himself inadvertently drove home the need for specific contextual information in iconographic analysis when he blithely referred to "realising that a male figure with a knife is St. Bartholomew, [or] that a female figure with a peach in her hand is a personification of veracity." In 1955, these identifications may have been obvious; today, they require specialized knowledge.

The variability of the knowledge needed to understand images in Western art extends beyond the Renaissance, for ideas of what constitutes realism have shifted considerably over time. Impressionist painters re-created the effects of shifting light on a single object (Sturken and Cartwright 2001:118), like French artist Claude Monet's haystacks, declaring through their paintings that reality was more about changing light than individual wisps of hay. Cubists, likewise, broke from the single viewpoint of linear perspective to depict, instead, the constant movement of the eye across a surface (Sturken and Cartwright 2001:119–20).

Even as more recent movements in the art world have strongly challenged the central importance of representation (Sturken and Cartwright 2001:120), one need only look at the praise that is still heaped upon the invention of the vanishing point and the illusion of three-dimensional space in Renaissance painting to see its importance for Western culture (Costall 1985:18; Deregowski 1980; Gombrich 1969). The idea that art "is made meaningful by resembling something in the world and that it strives to do so in a way as optically realistic as possible" (Errington 1994:209) is still quite strong in popular opinion in the West (Anderson 2004:202–4).

Beyond Western Iconography

The need for context-specific knowledge was brought home to art historians and other researchers in the first half of the 20th century, as they struggled to understand the different modes of representation that they encountered in non-Western art (Kim 2004). Practical experience suddenly seemed insufficient when faced with art that did not follow the rules of Renaissance Europe. Why did Egyptian artists show people with legs in profile and the shoulders facing forward? How to make sense of schematic or "distorted" Iron Age and Roman images from Europe? For a long time, researchers saw such images as "'bad art,' childlike, naive, and incompetent attempts at naturalistic representation" (Aldhouse-Green 2004:13).

As researchers carefully documented representational art from Egypt, Japan, and other countries, they realized that artists in some cultures used systems of perspective that were alternatives to the linear perspective and vanishing point of the Western canon (Costall 1997:52; Davis 1989; Hagen 1986; Sturken and Cartwright 2001:111–14). In fact, alternative forms of perspective, such as relative size, vertical position in different registers, and other conventions, are relatively common ways to portray depth in art around the world. Researchers began to recognize that there is no need for perspective in order to create a realistic and recognizable image—and that, in fact, a vast array of pictures "never aspired to be in perspective" (Costall 1997:50; also see Davis 1995:93).

For archaeologists, problems arise when the mode of representation and the context of images differ greatly from their own understanding or practice (Baxandall 1972:29ff), leaving much open to interpretation. In Mimbres ceramics, for example, art historian J. J. Brody (2005:145–46) has suggested that the differential size of figures depicted on one Mimbres bowl may be a form of perspective, showing distance. In my research on Mimbres imagery, however, I interpreted the same picture as showing individuals who actually differed in size, such as an adult with a child (Munson 2000). This kind of disagreement in how different observers interpret a single image is rampant in Southwestern archaeology, as a brief look at archaeological work on images will show.

The Archaeology of Images in the Southwest

In the Southwest, as elsewhere, archaeologists have focused considerable attention on describing recognizable images (Brody 1991:16; Errington 1994:210; Munson 2008a). Representations are common in Southwestern rock art, kiva murals, some specific pottery types, carved stone or wooden figures, and some jewelry (Brody 1991; Jernigan 1978; Kent 1983a; Tanner 1976). For the most part, though, such representational imagery is relatively rare in the Southwest. Most media were dominated by geometric designs, including textiles, basketry and sandals, some murals, and most pottery types. Regardless of their ubiquity, it is images that draw our attention.

When one examines archaeological work on images, a few common features emerge. First, most researchers begin by dividing images into distinct classes, such as anthropomorphs (human figures), animals, plants, objects, and geometrics (figure 5.2) (e.g., Crotty 1995; Duran and Crotty

Figure 5.2.   An illustration from E. B. Renaud's survey of rock art from the Northern Rio Grande Valley shows his classification of these images as "fairly realistic human figures." From Renaud (1938b:Plate 4).

1994; Munson 2002). These classes are often implicitly ranked, with human figures treated as the most interesting, informative, or perhaps just plain appealing (e.g., Creel 1989; Munson 2000; Vivian 1994). The broad initial classes are usually subdivided into more specific categories, identifying various kinds of birds, distinguishing among different horned ungulates, and so on (e.g., Bostwick 1998; Short 1998; Smith 2000; Steed 1986). Such specific identifications are often presented with a rather giddy tone (e.g., Tanner 1976:141, 144), reflecting the inherent satisfaction in recognizing a 1,000-year-old picture of a mountain sheep or a coyote.

Nonetheless, identifying specific animals, or any other subject, can be surprisingly tricky. Curiously enough, depictions of corn and of lizards seem to overlap greatly in the historic rock art of the Hopi region, as Wesley Bernardini (2005:105–6) points out. This makes it surprisingly difficult to distinguish subjects that otherwise seem to differ in obvious ways. The most notoriously problematic image is probably that of "lizard men," those figures that might represent men with long penises or perhaps lizards with short tails (Hays-Gilpin 2004:25–26; also see Young 1988:122–25).

Many images seem to combine traits of multiple different subjects. When people today try to identify Mimbres pictures of animals, some rely on "features that they take to be diagnostic, ignoring those that are anomalous or conflicting, whereas others, less tolerant of anomalies, refuse to identify ambiguously drawn life-forms" (Brody 2005:152). The end result is that one ichthyologist might call a fish a saltwater species from the Gulf of California while another interprets the same image as a local, freshwater fish with idiosyncratic features (Bettison et al. 1999; Jett and Moyle 1986). Similar problems crop up in identifications of quadrupeds as dogs versus coyotes and of atlatls versus yucca pods.

More detailed identifications begin to edge into interpretations of action or of entire scenes. In one Mimbres example, Clara Lee Tanner (1976:49) describes a bowl depicting two people and a large square as showing "a man and a woman dancing behind a blanket decorated with allover, diagonal, criss-crossing lines" (figure 5.3). Brody (1983:121) interpreted a similar image as showing Hero Twins (both male) behind a shield, while I have assumed that these images depict a man and a woman lying under a blanket, perhaps having sex (Munson 2000). A similar petroglyph in the Rio Grande Valley has been described as showing people behind a blanket (Schaafsma 1975b:66; Webster et al. 2006:335). Although these interpretations share a few characteristics—the identification of people behind something—their specific details differ widely.

Figure 5.3. Images from Mimbres pottery of human figures and decorated rectangles have been interpreted in many different ways. The gray and black blotch in the middle represents a hole in the vessel. Drawing by Marit K. Munson, from Brody, Scott, and LeBlanc (1983:fig. 125).

Identifications of images also shift considerably as our understanding of the past changes. As the degree of influence attributed to Mesoamerica has waxed and waned, interpretations of imagery from across the Southwest have changed in concert (e.g., Farmer 2001; see Shaffer 2002:75–166). In one case, a single figure on a Mimbres bowl has morphed from a Meso-american Death's Head (Brody 1977:207, 209) to a female figure possibly related to corn (Hays-Gilpin and Hegmon 2005:106). The well-known "beheading" scene depicted on one or two Mimbres bowls has also been interpreted in varying lights, depending on whether researchers looked to Paquimé, in northern Chihuahua, or to Mesoamerica proper as a source of influence for the Mimbres (Brody 1983:115).

Identifications of images as supernaturals or deities are especially tempting, given the rich ethnographic and historic information available for the Pueblo people and for Mesoamerican groups. At the simplest level, many researchers readily identify images as katsinas, or ancestral spirits (e.g., Adams 1991:23–77; Cole 1984, 1989, 1992; Ferg 1982; Hays 1989, 1994; Saville 2001, 2003; Schaafsma 1994, 1999; Schaafsma and Schaafsma 1974; Wright 2005:270). Many of these identifications are not based on clear criteria, with some researchers implying that any depiction of a head with eyes and mouth is a representation of a katsina mask (Hays 1989; Rohn 1989; Saville 2002; Schaafsma and Schaafsma 1974; Schaafsma and Young 1983; H. D. Smith 1998). More conservative approaches restrict identification of katsinas only to figures with masks (e.g., Adams 1991:15–16; Brody 1991:109; Cole 1989), though they often fail to specify how one might identify a mask.

Most troubling, researchers often leap from pictures directly to identifications of specific figures named in the ethnographic record of the Pueblos, including Kokopelli (Aron 1981; Tisdale 1993), Shalako (Hays 1992; but see Hays-Gilpin 2006:71–72), Ogre katsinas (Brody 1991:127–28), and so on (Schaafsma 2000). These labels are often drawn directly from languages or traditions that may or may not have anything to do with the image in question (Hays-Gilpin 2004:141–45). They also imply a link, direct or indirect, to the specific deity or being whose name is used. When the name becomes adopted as a generic descriptive label, the problem is exacerbated. Declaring that "Tlaloc" is a meaning-neutral descriptive term is not sufficient to prevent one's mind from making the association with the Mesoamerican deity of the same name (see Creel 1989; Crotty 1990; Schaafsma 1975a:5, 1999). By the time a researcher identifies an image by name as Awanyu or Quetzalcoatl, she or he is making an interpretive leap from describing an image as a snake to discerning iconographic meaning—and often iconological significance—as a Pueblo or Mesoamerican horned or feathered serpent.

Although I would be pleased to abolish specific names entirely, I recognize that different researchers have varying degrees of tolerance for interpretive leaps of faith. Nevertheless, it is critical for archaeologists to recognize that "the pictorial nature of a stimulus, just like beauty, lies in the eye of the beholder" (Deregowski 1980:97). Archaeologists must be aware of the role of interpretation in identifying pictures and should strive to be methodical in describing images, so that readers are able to judge the evidence that one uses to move from snake to horned serpent to plumed serpent to Awanyu, Palülükon, or Quetzalcoatl (Cobb et al. 1999; Fewkes 1892; Packard and Packard 1974; Phillips et al. 2006; Renaud 1938a; Schaafsma and Wiseman 1992; Slifer 2000; Wilson 1918). To do so, it helps to understand some of the regularities based in the commonalities of human perception that account for the choices that artists make in creating pictures and that viewers use to interpret those images.

The Picture Problem

The choices that artists must make in translating an object, animal, or person into a representation have been called the picture problem (Chippindale 1992, 2001). Although making a picture seems quite straightforward, it actually involves many different decisions on the part of the artist (Malafouris 2007:291; B. Smith 1998; Washburn 1983:2). Some of these decisions involve explicit choices, such as what subject matter to depict and what degree of realism or abstraction is desired. Other decisions are contingent upon earlier choices. Once the artist chooses to use paint as his or her medium, the pigments must be collected, prepared, and so on (B. Smith 1998). If the artist wishes to represent something specific, he or she is constrained by the need to mimic the subject in a manner that is readily interpretable by viewers (B. Smith 1998)—providing, of course, that an unambiguous image is part of the artist's goal, an assumption that will be addressed later. The picture problem is most challenging when translating from three dimensions to a two-dimensional medium, such as trying to depict a mountain lion in a wall painting. Nevertheless, the problem still exists when working in three-dimensional (sculptural) form as well, when the artist must decide what to include or exclude.

Solving the picture problem requires the artist to extract the essential features of the subject while discarding other features that are not relevant to depiction (Davis 1995:74; Deregowski 2005:132; Washburn 2001). For simple geometric shapes, the essential features are unambiguous: They are the "points and lines . . . at which great changes occur" (Deregowski 1980:165), such as the corners or edges of a square or triangle. For more complicated forms, such as humans or animals, the process of discerning and portraying the essential features is considerably more tricky (Deregowski 1980:165–67, 2005). Studies of depictions from many different times and places show that figures are generally depicted in "certain 'typical' orientations" (Deregowski 1980:173; also Brody 2005:152–54; B. Smith 1998; Washburn 1995:115–16) that allow the artist to highlight the key features of the figure. This orientation is referred to as canonical perspective, the angle from which one sees the "most canonical and diagnostic features necessary for the recognition of this object" (Malafouris 2007:295).

Canonical perspective is most readily evoked by using a silhouette of the object that traces the contour that provides the most information. The typical contour for most animals is on a vertical plane going through the animal's spine when it is standing upright (Deregowski 2005). A side view of a quadruped, for example, allows the artist to show the position and relative size of the animal's four legs compared to the shape and size of the body, head, or tail. These details are the ones needed to distinguish, say, a mountain lion from a monkey, or a horse from a hamster. Lizards and turtles, on the other hand, are frequently shown from above, a perspective that allows the artist to show their salient features—how their legs, head, and tail radiate out from the central axis of the body (B. Smith 1998).

Humans are more complicated to represent, as we have potentially significant features that fall into multiple different planes (Deregowski 2005). Frontal views create an instantly recognizable silhouette of the arms and legs relative to the body and head. This works well for static depictions but is less satisfactory for depicting motion. Side views, on the other hand, are better able to indicate movement. In some cases, the most readily recognizable image requires depictions of the elements of a single person or animal from multiple points of view simultaneously (Deregowski 2005). A frontal view of a person's face, which works well for depicting eyes and mouth, might also include the person's nose in profile, a more readily recognizable view. Views that combine different planes also work well for images of elk or deer, where the antlers are most recognizable in frontal view, even when the rest of the animal is in profile.

The Importance of Conventions

Although variation in depiction may seem to be limited only by the artist's imagination (Costall 1997:58), coherent solutions to the picture problem—those that produce readily recognizable images—"turn out to be manageably small in number" (Chippindale 1992:271; also B. Smith 1998). Moreover, even within the small number of satisfactory solutions to the picture problem, artists and viewers are additionally constrained by the artistic and social conventions of their time and place (Deregowski 2005). In the Southwest, potters and painters from the Mimbres region and from Paquimé used conventions of hairstyles, clothing, posture, and the like to depict men and women (Munson 2000; VanPool and Van-Pool 2006).

Once pictorial conventions are widely accepted, they create limits on depiction (Costall 1997:58). Egyptian artists, having settled upon the convention of using the size of figures to indicate their relative status, could not readily have used size to show distance from the viewer. Or, as Scott Ortman (2000:632) has pointed out, if early Southwestern pottery designs were based on textiles, then the technical limitations inherent in weaving would also limit design possibilities for painted ceramics.

Why is the picture problem important? For one thing, it provides a means of addressing the constraints and the possibilities for representations in a given context. This makes it possible to identify images in a more systematic way, as opposed to relying on individual researchers' perceptions. It also helps to highlight when and why the norms of depiction are broken. This can be valuable in understanding why a picture was created and perhaps aid in discussing its meaning. It is also useful to know which decisions were chosen rather than forced and why the choices were made (B. Smith 1998). Finally, psychological research suggests that understanding conventions of representation actually affects one's fundamental perception of an image (figure 5.4), as the brain processes familiar images more readily than novel images (Deregowski 1980:194–95). Internalizing pictorial conventions is likely to shape our own interpretations of images, for better or for worse, by creating "perceptual expectations" (Morley 2007:71). In order to identify images systematically, archaeologists need to learn the relevant conventions yet still remain consciously aware of the process of identification in order to be able to explain it convincingly to others. In other words, "one has to learn what to look for and how to look" (Deregowski 1980:195).

Figure 5.4. A student with the University of New Mexico field schools at Pottery Mound works on a drawing of a mural from the west wall of Kiva 2. Such fragmentary images are difficult to comprehend until one has internalized the appropriate conventions. Courtesy of the Maxwell Museum of Anthropology, University of New Mexico, PM38_0070. Photographer unknown.

Identifying Images

The first step in identifying images should always be to create a solid foundation based on clear and detailed evaluation of constituent parts. This initial description of images, akin to determining Panofsky's natural meaning, should be as neutral as possible, to avoid snap decisions that will shape future assessments. Thus, one might identify basic forms like a body, limbs, and a head, as well as details such as facial features, projecting lines that might be ears or horns, a tail, and the like. More interpretive labels, such as mask or dancer or shield, should be avoided until later in the process, when one has reasons to argue for more specific iconographic interpretations. The second step consists of comparing these constituent parts to the range of known objects, animals, or humans, given what one knows about the time and place. For example, several authors have drawn upon their knowledge of textile production to identify specific techniques of dyeing or weaving cloth that are represented in Pueblo IV kiva murals (Tanner 1976:84; Teague 2000; Webster 2007).

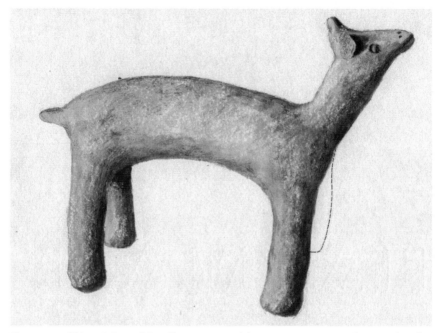

Figure 5.5.   This artist's rendition illustrates one of the ceramic "guanaco" figurines found at the Hohokam site of Los Guanacos. Courtesy of the Peabody Museum of Archaeology and Ethnology, Harvard University, 46-73-10/89421.

Ceramic "guanaco" figurines from the Hohokam region provide a good example of the potential pitfalls in identifying images (figure 5.5). In 1887, Frank Hamilton Cushing discovered two dozen of the figurines at the Pre-classic Hohokam site of Pueblo del Camino, in the Salt Valley of southern Arizona. Cushing (1890) called the figures guanacos, after a South American member of the camel family, renaming the site Los Guanacos in honor of the find. Additional figurines have since been recovered from other Hohokam sites (see Foster and James 2004:169–72). Although Cushing apparently hoped to find actual guanaco remains in the Southwest, this never panned out, leaving Hohokam archaeology with a nonsensical term and numerous competing ideas about what the figurines actually represent. Several researchers have recently tackled the most likely possibilities: mountain sheep, deer, or dogs (Chenault and Lindly 2006:117; Foster and James 2004). The authors of both studies describe the range of variation in the size and details of the figurines, but they draw on different lines of evidence and ultimately reach different conclusions.

Mark Chenault and John Lindly (2006:117) draw on effigies and images from across North America as examples of how each of the three potential subjects are typically represented. As they point out, both mountain sheep and deer are usually shown with their respective horns or antlers.[1] The lack of these features therefore suggests that the guanaco figurines are not male mountain sheep or deer but might be females of either species. Chenault and Lindly bolster their conclusions by comparing the figurines to other Hohokam representations that they believe clearly show dogs or coyotes, male mountain sheep, or deer.

Michael Foster and Steven James (2004), on the other hand, highlight similarities between indigenous dogs and the erect ears and postures of the figurines. In addition to the appearance of the figurines, they also note that dogs were important animals throughout the Americas. Foster and James discuss archaeological examples of dog burials in the Southwest, including numerous such burials at Pueblo Grande and other Hohokam sites. They argue that this archaeological evidence, combined with ethnographic information, supports the identification of the guanacos as dogs.

Both of the studies trying to identify Hohokam guanaco figurines should be commended for being clear in their description of the figures and specific in explaining the lines of reasoning that they used in arriving at their identifications. The fact that they reached different conclusions highlights some of the challenges inherent in working with imagery. Foster and James described the ways that the figurines resembled dogs but did not directly compare them to mountain sheep or deer. Chenault and Lindly attempted a more complete comparison, trying to understand the different conventions used to depict mountain sheep, deer, and dogs. The main flaw in their work, though, is that they assumed that pictures of these animals are simple to recognize, whether across North America or within the Hohokam region. Although they acknowledged the difficulties posed by ambiguous imagery, they never explained how they determined that images used for comparison were dogs, as opposed to coyotes or even female mountain sheep.

This problem is simple to rectify, as it requires nothing more than an explicit discussion of the researchers' implicit criteria. Stuart Baldwin's (1986) work on mountain lion depictions from the Tompiro region of the Rio Grande Valley is a good example. Throughout his paper, Baldwin discusses the criteria that he uses in making his identifications, such as the length and position of the tail and the size and position of the claws. One might question some of his criteria on technical grounds, but it is abundantly clear what criteria he used, making it possible for others to agree or to question specific details rather than assumptions.

Finally, reliable and valid identifications of images require far more than cautious description and careful comparison. It is also critical to examine the context of the images in time and space (e.g., see Baxandall 1972:29–32). Context is especially important as one moves beyond descriptive identifications—this is a human figure, that is a dog—and into iconographic analysis, which increasingly moves into the realm of interpretation of meaning. The more specific the identification, the more detail and context are required. Interpretations of human figures as supernaturals may be possible, but if one wishes to identify specific beings, narratives, or rituals known in the ethnographic record, context becomes absolutely critical (Brody 1991:109).

Kelley Hays-Gilpin and Michelle Hegmon's (2005) work provides good example of cautious and context-sensitive identification of images of plants in a variety of media from Mimbres and Ancestral Pueblo contexts. They identified pictures of plants in a generic sense but also suggested that specific images may represent sunflowers or corn. They made a strong argument that certain geometric patterns, such as a dot-in-square design, may be an abstract representation of corn kernels. At the same time, they acknowledged that the use of the dot-in-square to depict corn probably changed over time. In their study, Hays-Gilpin and Hegmon examined the context and distribution of various patterns, suggesting that the dot-in-square "may only have taken on the meaning of corn late in the sequence" (Hays-Gilpin and Hegmon 2005:101) of mural paintings, even though the pattern was used on earlier textiles and pottery (Webster et al. 2006). Hays-Gilpin and Steven LeBlanc (2007:119–22) take a similarly contextual approach to identifying Sikyatki-style textiles depicted in kiva murals at Pottery Mound.

As these examples show, description of images and comparison to the range of possibilities does not happen in a linear fashion. Instead, one moves constantly back and forth between image and potential subjects, without distinguishing the two processes. Nevertheless, the end result of this work should be clear and conservative identifications of images, with explicit details and descriptions to ensure that others can understand the reasoning behind the label (e.g., Bernardini 2005:105–6). As Panofsky (1955:32) notes, an error in the initial description means that the interpretations that follow are meaningless.

Degrees of Representation and Ambiguity

Throughout this discussion, I have assumed that artists intend to create clear, easily understood representational images. Clearly, this is not always the case. As J. J. Brody (2005:137) reminds us, "'Realism' in art is only one way of projecting images of phenomena as one imagines or wishes them to be." A perusal of Archaic petroglyphs, Sikyatki-style paintings of butterflies, or designs on White Mountain redware shows that artists make use of the entire continuum of representation, from "perceived reality" on one end to complete abstraction at the other (Brody 2005:137). It is important to consider when artists create realistic images or abstract designs, as well as why they might choose to create ambiguous imagery.

Representation

Assessments of realism versus abstraction vary considerably; there is no clear line between the two modes of representation (contra Herman 1978). In addition, our perception of abstraction may vary depending on the subject matter. Iain Morley (2007:71) has suggested that people may have an inherent tendency to see images of humans as more abstract than similarly detailed images of animals. When faced with a silhouette of an ibex with ears, antlers, and hooves, we might tend to find it "a 'remarkably lifelike' and 'anatomically accurate' representation of an ibex" (Morley 2007:71). In contrast, a similarly detailed outline of a human with ears, hair, and feet may be seen as "an 'abstract' and 'stylized' representation of a human" (Morley 2007:71). The degree of realism has a direct influence on how much interpretation is needed in identifying marks as images. Images that conform to canonical perspective may be simple but readily recognizable (Washburn 1983:3). Abstraction, however, "forces the viewer beyond the information that is provided" and "demands that the spectator draws inferences" (Bailey 2007:112). There has been relatively little work focusing on realism and abstraction in the Southwest, but I believe that the distinction has important ramifications for the production, use, and meanings of artwork.

In rock art from the Rio Grande Valley, there are numerous fairly naturalistic images of birds. Attributes such as the size of the head and body, the relative length of the legs and the neck, and the size and shape of the beak help to create distinct images that resemble different birds, from long-necked cranes or herons (see figure 4.2) to macaws or other parrots with stout hooked beaks. Frontal views with hourglass or triangular bodies and spread wings suggest a bird of prey, while side views showing a prominent spread tail resemble turkeys. In other cases, though, traits such as wings and beaks create a generic image of a bird, without enough details for more specific identification. By the Pueblo IV period (1325–1600 CE), Rio Grande rock art includes other images that are bird-like but much less obvious. How is one to interpret a series of horizontal lines of differing lengths with a sharp point at one end (figure 5.6)? Is this an abstract image of a macaw, a terraced shape, a collection of lines—or something else entirely?

Identifying this type of abstract figure is somewhat simplified by comparing the entire continuum of representation, recognizing that "some abstract designs could be stylized or conventionalized equivalents of designs rendered in representational form elsewhere" (Stewart et al. 1990:315). Pueblo IV glazeware ceramics contain bird images that fall along a recognizable sequence from clear representations to abstractions that are vaguely reminiscent of tails and/or feathers (Barnett 1968; Chapman 1916). That these images are of birds is widely accepted by Southwestern archaeolo-

Figure 5.6.   A petroglyph from the site of Tsankawi, on the Pajarito Plateau, is probably an abstract image of a macaw or other parrot. Photograph, digitally enhanced, by Marit K. Munson.

gists. Indeed, it is common for archaeologists to refer to considerable over-lap in subject matter between rock art and ceramic imagery in the Pueblo IV period (e.g., Graves and Eckert 1998). However, when I show bird images from Rio Grande glazeware and petroglyphs (figure 5.7) to unsus-pecting undergraduates or, in one case, to archaeologists working on the Iberian Peninsula, the identification is generally met with confused silence or howls of protest (Munson in press-a). The ceramic imagery is so much more abstract than the rock art that they appear completely unrelated.

While some of the differences in degrees of realism reflect artists' choices, some are due to the technical constraints of different media. While painting is relatively free, media with strong directional elements are much more limited (Kent 1983a:40, 201–7; Ortman 2000:620; Tanner 1976:92–94). This effect is most readily visible in textiles and basketry, where the

Figure 5.7.   Bird imagery is common on Rio Grande glazeware ceramics (above) and in Classic Rio Grande rock art (b). Drawings by Marit K. Munson, from bowl in collection of Bandelier National Monument (a, 1581) and from petroglyphs at San Cristobal Pueblo (below).

warp and weft arrangement best lends itself to geometric designs, with different plaiting and weaving techniques also influencing the pattern (Kent 1983b:119–20). Representational images that do occur in these media tend to be more schematic and abstract in comparison to painted designs (figure 5.8).[2] In some cases, artists may have used painted or tie-dyed cloth in order to have more flexibility in the design (Tanner 1976:92; Webster et al. 2006:318, 328; but see Robins and Hays-Gilpin 2000:244).

Technical limitations may apply even to media that seem relatively unconstrained. Although clay and paint lack the limitations of basketry (Tanner 1976:93–94), there are still potentially significant differences in how these materials are applied for different art forms. Petroglyphs and ceramics are relatively restricted in color (Plog 2003). Petroglyphs also tend to have less detail than pictographs or kiva murals, as the medium "generally forbids precision" (Brody 1991:122; also Schaafsma 2007). These material factors, too, have implications for representation. In Stuart Baldwin's (1986) description of mountain lion depictions from the Pueblo IV Rio

Figure 5.8.   A globular basket from Broken Flute Cave, dating to the Basketmaker III period, is decorated with birds woven in red and black elements. Drawing by Marit K. Munson, after Morris and Burgh (1941:fig. 30d).

Grande Valley, he noted that the animals are depicted in a different manner in different media. Stone effigies are carved with the mountain lion's tail extended across the top of the back, while rock art usually depicts the tail extending straight out from the body. These conventions are probably related to the limitations of stone as a medium for freestanding carving, as a long extended tail would be too difficult to produce.

Ambiguity

Artists may deliberately court ambiguity in their images, playing with abstraction or combining anomalous traits in ways that make images difficult or impossible to identify with any confidence (see figure 2.2a) (Brody 2005:136, 152). Why might an artist choose to create an image that is not clear? Ethnographic studies from around the world show that artists create ambiguous images when depiction is not their primary concern (B. Smith 1998). In some cases, artists may embrace ambiguity in order to create images that are more open to interpretation. This flexibility in terms of meaning can be a considerable asset when the artist wishes to evoke multiple meanings simultaneously (Mobley-Tanaka 2002; Schaafsma 2002:62), or, conversely, when the use of the object requires flexibility in its meaning (McLennan and Duffek 2000:141). In other cases, artists may deliberately use ambiguity to disguise their subject matter. This often occurs when the artist has access to knowledge that others lack, especially when the subject is chosen for a symbolic or mnemonic purpose (B. Smith 1998). It may also be useful in situations where the artist wishes to manipulate or hide meanings (e.g., Phillips 1989).

Jeannette Mobley-Tanaka (2002) has argued that Ancestral Pueblo people embraced ambiguity in the early historic period in response to Spanish suppression of traditional religious symbolism. She notes that Pueblo artists used a cross or X in multiple contexts prior to the arrival of the Spanish, including on glazeware pottery, in kiva murals from Pottery Mound, and in Rio Grande rock art. Depending on context, this simple shape might have represented a star, a bird, or a dragonfly. After the arrival of the Spanish in the mid-16th century, potters increasingly substituted crosses or Xs for overt bird imagery on glazeware vessels from the Rio Grande and in the Zuni area (Mobley-Tanaka 2002:80–81). "The replacement of 'idolatrous' images with crosses would have satisfied Spanish friars, while retaining a reference to those same images, allowing Pueblo people to maintain the meaning of native imagery" (Mobley-Tanaka 2002:81).

When faced with ambiguous images, it is important to consider the degree to which the ambiguity was deliberate. Although this may seem difficult to determine, a thorough consideration of pictorial conventions makes it possible to identify when specific images are more ambiguous than one would expect (Clegg 1986). Mobley-Tanaka's (2002) argument about ambiguity in early historic imagery is strengthened and extended in a recent paper comparing images across different ceramic wares (Spielmann et al. 2006). Katherine Spielmann and her colleagues documented changes over time in glazeware from the Salinas area, in the central Rio Grande Valley. In comparison to late prehistoric vessels, bowls from the early historic period showed a "sudden decrease in polychromes, the appearance of abbreviated designs, and the marked increase in runny glaze" (Spielmann et al. 2006:631). The authors were not able to explain these changes through shifting technology or materials, as sources of lead and the glaze paint recipes themselves were unchanged through the colonial period. In addition, when they compared the runny, abstract designs on glazeware to whiteware from the same time period, they found that Tabira black-on-white pottery included a range of clear and detailed images, from birds and feathers to masked beings and possible corn fetishes (figure 5.9). In fact, Tabira iconography resembles that of Pueblo IV/protohistoric kiva murals from the Rio Grande sites of Pottery Mound and Kuaua. The specificity in these images indicates that realistic representation was definitely part of the pictorial conventions of the Salinas area. Why, then, were the glazewares so unclear in their representations?

Spielmann and her colleagues (2006) argued that the context of production and use explains the contrast between these different wares. They pointed out that the glazewares were produced by potters from villages with direct Spanish presence, suggesting that women intentionally manipulated designs in order to obscure religious content in a manner that meant "the viewer who knew the meanings of the designs could still discern them" (Spielmann et al. 2006:633). The more straightforward designs on Tabira black-on-white, in contrast, were created in order to display religious iconography openly in villages without resident Spanish priests, probably to reinforce ritual knowledge for the Pueblo people.

The contrast between open and concealed religious iconography has been proposed for other areas that had heavy Spanish presence in the early historic period, mostly in the Rio Grande Valley. For example, visitors to San Cristobal Pueblo, in the Galisteo Basin, have often suggested that the rock art site adjacent to the village might have served as ritual space, away from the church.[3] Similarly, J. J. Brody (personal communication 2008) has suggested that small-scale, finely scratched petroglyph images along the Galisteo dike might have been created in order to continue ritual practices in the historic period without drawing undue attention from the Spanish at the nearby Galisteo Pueblo.

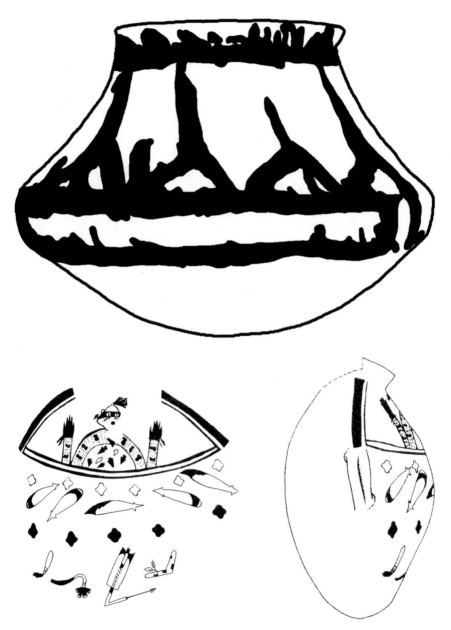

Figure 5.9.   The lead-based paints used on late glazeware ceramics (above) tend to be drippy, sometimes even obscuring the original design. Contemporaneous Tabira black-on-white ceramics (below), in contrast, include detailed images and complex iconography. Drawings by Marit K. Munson, based on Hayes, Young, and Warren (1981:figs. 124c and 115g).

Aniconicity

The motivations behind intentionally ambiguous or cryptic imagery also raise questions about the *lack* of images. Are there, in fact, situations in which artists refrain from creating an image at all? Both Severin Fowles (2008) and Richard Wright (2005) have argued that aniconicity, or the lack of images, may have been characteristic of the Ancestral Pueblo katsina religion. Wright discusses style and the individual artists of White Mountain redware from the Western Pueblo area. Although some of his claims are speculative, he quite rightly calls archaeologists to task for assuming "that thoughts about katsinas must in turn generate actual pictographic representations of them" (Wright 2005:272). Indeed, there are numerous cases from around the world in which people, places, or objects are not to be depicted (e.g., Basile 2002; Kogman-Appel 2002; Mettinger 1995; cf. Huntington 1990), often out of respect for the most holy, sacred, or mysterious religious beings.

The emergence of katsina imagery in the Ancestral Pueblo Southwest, whatever the timing, may perhaps reflect changes in the propriety of representation or the iconicity of spirits (Munson 2002:272–75). If so, this suggests that archaeologists need to be vigilant not only to the presence or absence of pictures of katsinas but also to the circumstances in which artists in different regions made explicit choices about when and how to represent katsinas at all. We should remember, above all, that art need not present a documentary catalog of real life (Aldhouse-Green 2004:8; Hays-Gilpin 2000:91). Instead, art may reflect ideas about how things *should* (and should not) be.

The Why (and How) of Images

Images seem a natural focus for studies of art. They offer potential insight into any manner of ancient activities, lives, and beliefs; they also have immense appeal to today's viewers. When it comes to images, the question is less why we study them and more *how* to study them. The direct appeal of images is part of the problem. They seem so straightforward and simple to understand that we assume identifying and comparing images will be equally easy. Nevertheless, it is critical to take the time and effort to examine images methodically, creating accounts that explain researchers' reasoning, assumptions, and interpretive leaps. Treating images as art is nothing new, but archaeologists can make a great contribution to the study of ancient pictures by incorporating systematic methods into their research, rather than assuming that a bird is always a bird.

Aesthetics   **6**

> *Archaeologists are "uncomfortable about attempting to define aesthetic behaviour, even when 'everyone agrees aesthetics permeates material culture.'" (Morphy 1994a:258, quoting Sackett 1990:35)*

I MUST ADMIT TO APPROACHING THE TOPIC of aesthetics with some trepidation, and I am not alone among archaeologists. Most of us ignore aesthetics entirely; the few who do acknowledge the topic do so primarily to dismiss it as a legitimate subject of archaeological inquiry (e.g., Lekson 1992; Smith 1994; Tomásková 1997). As Classical archaeologist R.R.R. Smith (1994:261) puts it, "Whether or not archaeologists find ancient objects beautiful or pleasing . . . seems not really relevant, except perhaps to their biographies."

There are good reasons for this discomfort (see Heyd 2005:1–2). Aesthetics is often thought of as interchangeable with notions of beauty and matters of personal taste, which are intensely individual and subjective experiences. Whether or not the aesthetic experiences of modern-day individuals are actually relevant to the past is a legitimate question. And how do we know if ancient individuals saw the world in aesthetic terms? Perhaps, as Smith (1994:260) has claimed, the question of aesthetics is "unhelpful" archaeologically because it was "not a question an ancient Roman would have posed."

Even if aesthetics is a fundamental part of all human experience, how could one hope to pursue something so ephemeral in the distant past (Heyd 2005:7; Renfrew 1994:265)? The entire notion of judgment, which is at the center of aesthetics, is also "a tricky area for archaeologists" because it "is considered to involve a certain analytical laxity" (Taylor 1994:251). To imply that an archaeologist could understand the feelings of past individuals is, in Colin Renfrew's (1994:265) words, a "rather naive view" (and one that he attributes primarily to post-processual archaeologists).

Despite these varied concerns, there has been increasing interest in aesthetics in anthropology as a whole, and even in archaeology, over the past decade or so (e.g., Gosden 2001; Heyd and Clegg 2005; Penney 2004; Taylor et al. 1994).[1] Indeed, the literature makes a strong case that researchers of all stripes need to acknowledge the importance of aesthetic values both in individuals' lived experience (Heyd 2005) and as "a potential source of evidence about two areas of culture that are otherwise hard to access: perception and feeling" (Morphy 1994a:259).

This chapter provides a brief overview of aesthetics from various perspectives, then highlights how identifying the focal points of a given culture's aesthetic attention helps guide archaeologically meaningful studies of these ephemeral experiences. I also suggest methods for doing so, first by identifying potentially relevant properties of objects, especially those chosen or enhanced by the artist, and then looking for consistent associations of properties. Ideally, one would be able to evaluate the context of those properties and associations in order to try to understand the ways that people valued them. I illustrate these suggestions with examples centered on the use of color in multiple media and on renewal in ceramics, kiva murals, and architecture. Even if we cannot hope to completely re-create the aesthetic experience of 1,000 years ago, the attempt may provide some otherwise unlikely insights.

Aesthetics

In its most general sense, aesthetics is concerned with notions of beauty and the sensory experience of the world. The term itself has its roots in the Greek *aisthetikos*, which relates to "things material and perceptible" (Taylor 1994:250), as opposed to immaterial and thinkable (Berleant 2004). The concept of aesthetics arose in its modern sense in the 18th century, grounded in the work of the European philosopher Immanuel Kant (Stecker 2005). Based on Kant's writing about aesthetic judgments, philosophers have focused on the aesthetic experience as the sensual experience of perceiving art. Kant implies that the aesthetic experience is subjective but universal. That is, aesthetics is based on a subjective feeling of pleasure (as opposed to the application of rules or guidelines) and is universal in the sense that everyone ought to have a similar judgment of or response to the same object. Kant also proposed that aesthetic judgments involve the free play of the imagination and the intellect and that such judgments are disinterested—that is, removed from any advantage or benefit one could obtain from the object (Berleant 2004; Stecker 2005). In this sense, art objects are seen as separate, discrete works, isolated from "the rest of the human world" (Berleant 2004:15). Proper appreciation of art, then, requires "disinterested pleasure," a specific attitude that rejects functionality or pragmatic matters in favor of pure, unmediated perception and appreciation (Berleant 2004). If Kant's conception of disinterested pleasure is fundamentally correct, then the vast majority of artifacts from archaeological contexts in the Southwest cannot be treated as art (see chapter 2). The functional nature of a stone palette would make it impossible for the Hohokam to see it in a disinterested light, no matter how pleasing its design.

Kantian notions of the aesthetic have been strongly challenged in the 20th and 21st centuries (e.g., Berleant 2004), as artists have increasingly pushed art beyond the pleasing and into the realm of the grotesque, the ugly, or the disturbing. As a result, there are now multiple competing conceptualizations of aesthetics within philosophy (see Stecker 2005:34–54). Philosopher Arnold Berleant has argued that there is a need to rethink aesthetics in order to encompass "many different modes of artistic activity" (Berleant 2004:3–4) and to accommodate "the crafts and all the other practices of productive making that are the locus of creative human activity, such as festivals, ceremonies, and rituals" (Berleant 2004:2). He believes that aesthetics should center on attention directed at and focused upon "the intrinsic qualities of objects and occasions" (Berleant 2004:47), but not necessarily to the extent that art objects are isolated or that practical matters are excluded. This is essentially an anthropological approach, one that is more open to different traditions and types of arts, recognizing the importance of context and cultural specifics. In fact, Berleant (2004:4) has even claimed that his approach could "help to develop an anthropology of the arts . . . to examine the profuse manifestations of artistic activity in different societies."

Aesthetics beyond the West

Even while Arnold Berleant argues that philosophy should broaden toward a more anthropological approach to aesthetics (a stand that he himself labels a "rogue" position), anthropologists are debating whether or not they can or should study aesthetics at all (Weiner et al. 1996a). As with the problem of defining art beyond the West (see chapter 2), questions of aesthetics teeter between the universal and the specific. Although most researchers seem to agree that aesthetics is relevant for all humans, few would argue for a universal aesthetic, covering all times and places (Dissanayake 1982:154; Morphy 1996:255; cf. Overing 1996:260). As Colin Renfrew (1994:265) points out, "Beauty is not a universal quality, either in time or in space"; to assume so would be naive and ethnocentric (Smith 1994:262). Even when anthropologists agree that aesthetics may be broadly relevant, many still insist upon, in Alfred Gell's (1992:42) words, "resolute indifference towards the aesthetic value of works of art." In fact, Gell (1992:41) called for strict "methodological philistinism," insisting that consideration of aesthetics should be left solely to philosophers. Anthropology, he believed, is not equipped to handle such questions (also see Gow 1996:272–73; Smith 1994:260).

Most of those who denounce aesthetics as anthropologically irrelevant adhere to a strict Kantian view, "applying a particularly narrow contemporary art world concept of aesthetics to archaeological analysis rather than seeking to define aesthetics in relation to the culture in question" (Morphy 1994a:259). Instead, anthropologist Howard Morphy has argued that aesthetics should be central to anthropologists as "a body of evidence that allows them a unique access to the sensual aspect of human experience: to how people feel in, and respond to, the world" (Morphy 1996:255). In order to accomplish this, Morphy calls for a return to the roots of aesthetics in the term's original Greek meaning as relating to the senses and perception. Sensory perception, like all other forms of human experience, is rooted in biology. This suggests that the effects of perceiving certain physical properties—form, texture, feel, smell, weight, softness, symmetry, and perhaps balance—are probably universal, even if individuals' interpretation and evaluation of that response is culturally mediated (Morphy 1994a:260). Any perceivable quality has the potential to be an aesthetic property within a given cultural context, if it is incorporated within a system of value and meaning (Morphy 1994b). That is, shininess or symmetry or any other physical property may be evaluated and experienced in ways that cause it to be viewed positively or negatively. As long as we are dealing with anatomically modern humans, then, "it must be reasonable at least to argue that we are able to put ourselves in the place of the Other and ask the question: how might they have experienced this?" (Morphy 1994a:260).

Addressing aesthetics in widely varied contexts requires a broad and cross-culturally applicable definition. Morphy's (1994a:258, also 2005:53) proposal is to define aesthetics as "the effect of the physical properties of objects on the senses and the qualitative evaluation of those properties." That is, aesthetics "involves the cultural control over, and production of, certain selected and culturally conceived properties or qualities of the natural world" (Morphy 1994b:677). This broad definition is satisfying in that it both acknowledges the biological similarities of all humans—the way that people perceive the world, broadly speaking—and addresses the culturally specific ways that individuals make sense of their perceptions.

Morphy (1994b) provides three examples that illustrate this balance between the universal, based in human physiology, and the culturally specific interpretation and experience of perception. He starts with the assumption that humans have a common physiological response to shining light, then documents the aesthetic appreciation of shimmering brilliance in three different cultures: the Yolngu of Australia, the Wahgi Valley people of Papua New Guinea, and the Mende of West Africa. Although their interest originates in the common experience of perceiving light, each group focuses on different physical properties as reflecting or representing brilliance, and each has different values associated with those properties.

The Yolngu produce shimmering brilliance by using fine white cross-hatching throughout their paintings. Adding these lines is seen as a process of transforming the painting from a dull or rough state into a shimmering, brilliant state that reflects the power of ancestral beings shining out of the painting. For the people of the Wahgi Valley, body paintings are evaluated by their shine, which is tied to health, fertility, war, and strength through analogy with the glistening pig fat used in festivals. In this case, the brilliance is important in context of rituals of competitive display, as a symbol of the wearers' relationships with fellow people from within and outside their clans. The Mende, in turn, experience brilliance in the form of burnished black wood of sowo-wui masks. The combination of shine and blackness together reflects both female beauty and the paradise towns in the depths of water, whence come dancing masked figures.

In all three cases, the creation of a particular aesthetic effect is integral to their art, but the materials differ greatly—white lines, pig fat on skin, palm oil on wood. These culturally and temporally specific aspects of aesthetics can be thought of as concrete aesthetics, or the particular ways in which a given group of people appreciates the qualities that they perceive (Heyd 2005:5). Concrete aesthetics provides an important link between the mental world of perception and the material world, as it essentially refers to the desired "look" of an object. Hence, one might speak of Yolngu aesthetics as expressed through fine white hatching, or of Wahgi Valley aesthetics as centered on glistening surfaces created with pig fat. The concrete manifestations of aesthetics not only evoke admiration but are also central to the meanings that art evokes and the ways that art is integrated into culture as a whole.

Archaeological Aesthetics in the Southwest

Southwestern archaeologists have shown considerable reluctance to consider aesthetics in the past. Although early archaeologists often referred to items as beautiful or implied that turquoise and jet ornaments and mosaics were aesthetically pleasing (e.g., Pepper 1905:197), this sense of appreciation is now rarely expressed in print. When archaeologists occasionally admit to passing judgment on specific artifacts, criticism usually follows. When Steven LeBlanc (1982:117) referred to El Paso tradition ceramics as "some of the least esthetically [sic] pleasing pottery ever produced in the Southwest," John Douglas (1992:13) criticized the statement as "weak because it is largely grounded in Western aesthetics." Stephen Lekson (1992:112), writing about Mimbres art and archaeology, echoes this concern: "It is important to remember that the Mimbres' reputation comes not from the people who made [the ceramics], but from us. We have decided that Mimbres art is good, while Reserve Black-on-white (for example) is not so good." Although he acknowledged the relevance of aesthetics for Mimbres ceramics, Lekson (1992:112) added that, as a "philistine materialist," aesthetics is "a topic beyond my competence."

When archaeologists do engage with aesthetics, it is usually in the concrete sense, focusing on the desired "look" of a given artifact class or the expression of taste on the part of producers (see Johnson 1958:130; Kamp 2001:133; Plog 2003:688; Wheat et al. 1958:36). This is particularly common with ceramics. Numerous authors have discussed the aesthetics of colorful glazeware ceramics in the Pueblo IV period (1325–1600 CE), arguing that potters sought specific clays and pigments in order to create a range of colors (see Herhahn 2006:183; Van Keuren 2006). Other researchers have compared concrete aesthetics in broader areas, comparing Hohokam and Ancestral Pueblo ceramic traditions. Art historian J. J. Brody (1991:41) wrote: "The Hohokam aesthetic goal seemed always to be the creation of open-ended harmonic compositions by the simple device of repeating design units in potentially infinite spatial situations" (see figure 3.7). These designs were made of units varied in scale to suit the available space, creating a "spontaneous and casual" appearance in Hohokam pottery (Brody 1991:41). In contrast, early Ancestral Pueblo pottery depended "on the systematic patterning of design zones, each of which was filled with several small-scale design units" (Brody 1991:41). The result was "studied and controlled" designs that are "visually complex but closed" (Brody 1991:41). Clara Lee Tanner (1976:6, 113) called early Ancestral Pueblo black-on-white pottery "precise," and "restricted." Charles Amsden (1936:44) called it "prim" in comparison to Hohokam ceramics, which he felt were "unschooled" and "free and joyous."

The most precise and controlled painting in the Southwest was probably on Classic Mimbres black-on-white ceramics, and there has been considerable discussion of the "perfection" of their painting (Brody 2005:112; also Tanner 1976:141).[2] Brody (2005:xxiii) describes it as "a type of pottery on which a certain set of visual ideals and values was pushed to its ultimate limits." Curiously enough, the potters who made Mimbres ceramics may have been less concerned about controlling the firing process than their neighbors elsewhere. Many Mimbres vessels have paint that is partly oxidized, leaving a vessel that is technically more reddish-orange-on-white than black-on-white. Brody (2005:112) has even argued that Mimbres potters allowed pots to oxidize during firing as part of "a deliberate aesthetic choice," proposing that they "courted certain kinds of accidents and imperfections" in firing as a "counterbalance to the perfection . . . that they usually sought . . . in their paintings." To me, this seems somewhat unlikely, given the difficulties of controlling relatively simple prehistoric kilns, but Brody is not the first to have commented on the contrast between perfection and creativity in Mimbres painting and carelessness in firing (Tanner 1976:141).

Billy Graves's (2002) work on late prehistoric glazeware in the Rio Grande Valley is a rare exception to archaeologists' reluctance to discuss aesthetics. Late glazewares are notorious for the drippy quality of their lead-based glaze paints (see figure 5.9a), which often ran so heavily during firing that the drips obscured the designs entirely. Although this is sometimes cited as relating to a degeneration in quality control, Graves has suggested instead that it reflects a loosening of aesthetic standards in the late 1400s through the 1500s (also see chapter 5).

Characterizations of concrete aesthetics are intriguing on one level, for they reflect differences in the ceramic traditions that appear to correspond to the preferences of the potters and painters who created the vessels. At the same time, the terms used in these descriptions are difficult to quantify— one person's "expressive" might be another's "sloppy" or "careless." What does it mean to call Hohokam pottery "free and joyous"? Or Mimbres painting "restricted but creative"? And why, of all of the potential arts of the ancient Southwest, the focus on ceramics?

The Aesthetic Locus

The broad definition of aesthetics that I have championed is potentially problematic, as it implies that anything and everything that human beings perceive may be aesthetically experienced or valued. Hypothetically speaking, this is true. Humans apparently have a knack for finding aesthetic value in any number of objects and experiences: a properly served cup of tea (D. C. Graves 2002), a painting of shipwrecked men dying as sharks circle (Gericault's *Raft of the Medusa*), the voice of a castrato (André 2006), the pain of extensive body piercings (Pitts 2003), a gift of papayas (d'Azevedo 1958:704–7), and on and on.[3] However, it is critical to note that in any given temporal and spatial context, not all sensual experiences are equally charged aesthetically. In anthropologist Jacques Maquet's (1986:30) words, no culture "maintains an equally intense aesthetic interest in all things within its borders. There are certain privileged fields where awareness and performance are high, where expectations and efforts converge."

Maquet (1986:69) refers to the fields upon which a group focuses their "aesthetic expectations and performances" as an aesthetic locus. In the West, at least since the Renaissance, the aesthetic locus has been centered largely on visual art as created by artists and displayed for viewers' visual consumption in gallery or museum spaces (Maquet 1986:69). In contemporary Western contexts, researchers have increasingly recognized more varied popular aesthetics, ranging from pop culture to muscle cars to gardening (Anderson 1999). In other parts of the world, as many classic anthropological studies show, the aesthetic locus varies from something that most Westerners would likely consider art, such as Yoruba sculpture from West Africa (Lawal 1974; Thompson 2005), to concerns with aesthetics in areas that seem quite unlike art, such as cattle coat patterns for Nilotic speakers in the Sudan (Coote 1992).

It is intriguing to consider the aesthetic loci of the peoples of the ancient Southwest, who surely found any number of phenomena aesthetically pleasing. It is hard to imagine anyone who would fail to be captivated by the watermelon-pink glow that the setting sun casts over the Sandia Mountains in the central Rio Grande Valley. And what about the veils of rain that sweep down from storm clouds (figure 6.1)? Or perhaps the darting flight of swallows catching insects? The problem is that these experiences, aesthetically pleasing as they may have been, do not leave material traces. Nor do they relate to items produced by human hands; they are therefore not art, at least in my understanding of the term.

Figure 6.1.   A cloudburst darkens the sky over Chaco Canyon. Photograph by Marit K. Munson.

To bring the problem to a more concrete level, it seems likely that ritual performance was an aesthetic locus in many different times and places across the Southwest (Neitzel in press). The aesthetic aspects of these performances probably included ephemeral or temporally limited art forms such as dance, singing and other forms of music, recitations or storytelling, and the like (Triadan 2006). Ceramics, too, were probably a typical aesthetic locus across much of the Southwest, with considerable attention paid to the apparent desired look of pottery, as described earlier. In addition, researchers' repeated references to a "fluorescence" in Pueblo IV (1325–1600 CE) visual expression suggests that mural painting, rock art, cotton textiles, and probably the construction of altars were all significant centers of energy and aesthetic attention (Brody 1991:81–114; Kent 1983a:119ff; Schaafsma 1980:243–99). Basketry during Basketmaker II and III periods (50–750 CE) suggests a similar care and attentiveness (Guernsey and Kidder 1921), as do jewelry at Chaco Canyon and shell work among the Hohokam (Jernigan 1978).

An Archaeology of Aesthetics

Identifying the aesthetic in the past is no short order, but archaeologists may be able to understand something of the concrete aesthetics of a given time and place, as reflected in material culture. Examining concrete aesthetics requires identifying all of the potentially relevant properties of objects, and in particular those chosen or enhanced by the artist. In addition, it is useful to look for patterning in the associations of properties with each other. Finally, evaluating the context in which people encountered those properties and associations may make it possible to understand the ways in which people valued them. In the end, focusing on understanding concrete aesthetics may open the door to reasonable speculation about aesthetic experiences in the more general sense.

First, archaeologists should begin by seeking aesthetics in the realm of intentions, the choices that artists and craftspeople made in selecting or highlighting specific qualities of materials. In other words, we need to look for the perceptual values of the producers (Morphy 1994a:259, 2005:56). What properties of raw materials did they choose? What perceptual qualities do they seem to have appreciated? There is a huge range of possible qualities that people might have valued, chosen, and enhanced—color, texture, sheen, and so on.

One might begin by considering properties that are known or assumed to have a strong effect on perception and the brain. Brilliance and clarity of color were probably highly valued in a time without synthetic dyes (Neitzel in press; Saunders 2004; also see Ball 2001). The bright red of macaw feathers would have been striking (Odegaard and Hays-Gilpin 2002:325), and colors such as blues and greens were rare and appear to have been highly valued across the Southwest (Lewis 2002; Tanner 1976:163; Windes 1992). Other substances, like jet, shell, and copper, may have been appreciated for their sheen and highly saturated color as much as for the color itself (Saunders 1999, 2002). In Nancy Odegaard and Kelley Hays-Gilpin's (2002:325) overview of rare clay-coated painted baskets from across the Southwest, they noted several technological and stylistic factors that "gives them a brilliance and clarity seldom seen" prehistorically. The combination of careful preparation of the clay surface, the generally high quality of painting, and fine outlines in contrasting colors all suggest that the artists worked to highlight the brilliant colors, making the baskets "an unusual and impressive sight" (Odegaard and Hays-Gilpin 2002:325).

Of course, there is an equally great range of qualities that were incidental to the material or otherwise not of interest to anyone making an item.

When I first saw a photograph of a Pueblo III (1100–1325) basket found cached outside Grants, New Mexico, I was struck immediately by the rotating motion of the design, the bright colors, the rhythm of the pattern around the still center, and the regular spiral of the coils (figure 6.2). How do we know whether Ancestral Pueblo people saw any of these properties in a similar aesthetic manner? These determinations are best made by considering the manufacturing process, looking for evidence that the artist intended to increase or highlight the effect of certain properties.

Judgments of the artists' intentions are obviously subjective, but they can be made stronger by documenting the context within which these properties occur (Morphy 2005:56). Are there relationships between certain properties and specific categories of objects? Are there consistent associations of particular qualities with each other? For example, Hohokam shell ornaments often use images of frogs and tadpoles (Jernigan

Figure 6.2.   This Pueblo III basket was found in a cave near Grants, New Mexico. Courtesy of Grants/Cibola County Chamber of Commerce.

1978:27–90). James Bayman (2002:82–83) has suggested that white marine shell and frogs might be linked together through common themes of water and fertility. If so, it might be worthwhile to consider whether the potential aesthetic properties of shells contributed to this connection, perhaps by referencing water through their bright white color and shiny surfaces. Ornaments from Chaco Canyon suggest that the association may have been quite different, as frogs were usually made of jet (Plog 2003:689).

Studying aesthetics should go beyond identification of the concrete aesthetic preferences of a particular time and place. Ideally, it involves "reconstruct[ing] the context of seeing the object: how the object was approached, in what light it was seen, what the emotional state of the viewer was and so on" (Morphy 2005:55). As with intention, this is largely subjective but may be worth pursuing for new ideas or approaches that might arise. For example, the context of some Pueblo IV to early historic (1325–1700s) petroglyphs in the Galisteo Basin hints at a highly evocative sensory experience. At San Cristobal Pueblo, there are multiple large images of water birds (probably cranes or perhaps herons) that stand about 80 centimeters tall. These bird petroglyphs were created with an unusual technique, more abrading than pecking, that produced a faint "ghostly" image with vague boundaries, quite different in appearance from the solid pecking and clear edges of most petroglyphs at the site. The main panel of these images consists of four birds in a line, moving across the sunlit cliff face into a dark, shadowy crevice before emerging again into the light on the far side of the crack (figure 6.3). The contrast of sunlight and shadow, combined with the faintness of the images, gives the appearance of cranes melting away into the crevice, disappearing beyond the cliff itself. The effect seems quite intentional, using layout and technique to create an aesthetic experience for the viewer that would not exist otherwise. I hesitate to speculate about the meanings of this panel, as I am skeptical about our ability to do more than tell stories about meaning in the deep past. At the same time, the associations and the viewing context of such art should be noted, as they may enable archaeologists to associate particular qualities with "dimensions of value—high status, low status, spiritual power and so on" (Morphy 2005:56).

Pigments and Color

Dimensions of value are strongly suggested in combinations of multiple bright colors in the Pueblo IV period (1325–1600), when pigments themselves may have been associated with spiritual power. Many researchers

Figure 6.3.   Four ghost-like cranes process across a rock face, disappearing into a dark crevice, at San Cristobal Pueblo. Photograph, digitally enhanced, by Marit K. Munson.

have discussed the color and new painting techniques of glazeware ceramics in the Pueblo IV period (see papers in Habicht-Mauche et al. 2006), which appear to mark a new aesthetic sense on the part of potters and audiences (Habicht-Mauche 2006:3, 5). In fact, it appears that color was a major factor in encouraging the spread of glazeware technology, whether signaling group identity, participation in new religious movements, or both (Eckert 2007:63; Graves and Eckert 1998; Huntley 2006:121–22; cf., Eckert 2006). The frequency of polychrome pictographs also seems to increase dramatically after about 1300, as seen at the Abo rockshelter in the Salinas Pueblo district (figure 6.4) (Cole 1984; H. D. Smith 1998:98), in various painted sites in the Galisteo Basin (Schaafsma 1990), and on the Pajarito Plateau (Munson 2002:214, 2003). Kiva murals, too, combine multiple colors of paint, with rainbows often shown arched over niches in murals from Picuris Pueblo and from Pottery Mound (Crotty 2007:97).

In addition to using multiple colors, many Pueblo IV artists created objects colored with spots or speckles. The spatter-painting techniques sometimes used on Sikyatki polychrome vessels from the Hopi area result in a spotted or speckled appearance (see figure 2.2a) (Hays-Gilpin and LeBlanc 2007:111), as do some painting techniques for pictographs. In addition, human effigies that Nels Nelson obtained from late prehistoric to protohistoric sites in the Galisteo Basin show similarly intriguing color combinations. One of the figures, a long human form without arms or legs, has a red-painted face and a body that appears to be painted blue-green. Both colors were apparently mixed with ground mica or another mineral,

Figure 6.4.   A pictograph from a rockshelter near Abo Pueblo, in the Salinas district of New Mexico, includes red, yellow, and greenish-white pigments. Photograph by Marit K. Munson.

giving the paint a glittering quality. In addition, the body is covered with short dashes of red and yellow pigment over the blue-green background. The significance of multiple colors and of sparkling pigment is well documented in the ethnographic record of the Southwest (see Lewis 2002). Combined with the archaeological examples, this suggests that speckled and glittering things might have been an important part of Ancestral Pueblo aesthetics in the Pueblo IV period.

Stephen Plog (2003) has considered the significance of color in his recent examination of Gallup-Dogozhi style black-on-white ceramics in the Chacoan world (figure 6.5). Gallup-Dogozhi was a widespread bichrome style that began in the 1030s–1040s CE, characterized by outlined shapes filled with fine-line hachure. The style formed a distinct contrast to contemporaneous black-on-white ceramics, which used solid design elements and were more limited in spatial distribution. Gallup-Dogozhi style vessels are particularly associated with Chaco Canyon, and especially with unusual

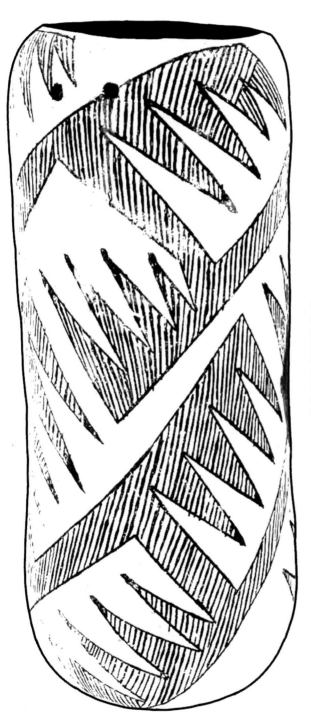

Figure 6.5. Cylinder jars from Chaco Canyon are often painted in the Gallup-Dogozhi style. Drawing by Marit K. Munson, of a vessel in the collection of the National Museum of Natural History (A336492).

cylinder jars that were used for preparing and drinking cacao (chocolate) from Mesoamerica (Crown and Hurst 2009).

Intrigued by a suggestion made by art historian J. J. Brody, Plog explored the possibility that hatched lines on Gallup-Dogozhi style black-on-white pottery served as a proxy for the color blue-green. The symbolic—and perhaps aesthetic—importance of blue-green for Chacoans is suggested by countless turquoise beads and pendants from Chaco Canyon, as well as painted wooden and stone artifacts. However, the technology of the time made it impossible to create blues or greens on fired pottery. In a few cases, potters seem to have added blue-green to ceramics after firing, in the form of fugitive (unfired) pigments (Crown and Wills 2003:517). Brody wondered if Chacoan potters might have adapted the Gallup-Dogozhi style to create a black-and-white substitute for the desired blue-green on pottery. Plog examined the possibility by comparing the use of color and hatching at Chaco across multiple media. He examined various cases in which decorated wood, textiles, or sandals used designs similar to those on ceramics, but "with different colors painted in the same position as the hachured designs on black-and-white pottery" (Plog 2003:673). When comparing the Gallup-Dogozhi style to other media, plog also noted that the juxtaposition of solid and hatched elements on a single pot seemed similar to the alternation of black jet with blue-green turquoise in mosaic and inlay. Finally, Plog (2003:689) highlighted a potential area of future research, noting that "while blue-green is frequent on prayer sticks and other ritual items, yellow and red seem more frequent on hunting-related items." Exploring such associations may provide insight into the effects that the artists sought, and therefore to their aesthetic and symbolic preferences—even when technological limitations constrained their use of a specific color.

The Aesthetics of Renewal

One of the most intriguing archaeological examples of Southwestern aesthetics is suggested by the renewal of objects. There are numerous examples of artists renewing designs in multiple media, many of which may have been aesthetically motivated. However, there are also some important differences in context that point out that the value of renewing objects was not always the same. For example, artists sometimes renewed designs because previous patterns had faded or worn to the point where they were no longer visible. Clara Lee Tanner (1976:42–43; also see Brody 1991:fig. 29) describes a repainted Pueblo III (1100–1325 CE) decorated burden basket from Painted Cave, in northeast Arizona (figure 6.6). The initial design was woven into it using colored elements. At a later time, someone painted over the designs on the outside of the basket, following the same pattern but smoothing out the edges of the lines. In the Painted Cave basket, the painter seems to have kept the original colors. In other examples, the artist changed colors to create a new combination, or even painted a completely different design (Odegaard and Hays-Gilpin 2002:310). This repainting probably reflects the concrete aesthetics of the Pueblo III people, although determining whether the preference is for decoration, for bright colors, for clean lines, or for some other look would require additional information. Renewal and reworking of objects at Chaco Canyon and in the Northern Rio Grande Valley seem to have been more significant and may, in fact, reflect an aesthetic of renewal for religious reasons.

The first example, from Chaco Canyon, draws on the work of Patricia Crown and W. H. Wills (2003; also Crown 2007) on cylinder jars and kivas at Chaco during the Bonito Phase (900–1140 CE) (figure 6.7). While studying ceramic vessels in museum collections, Crown noticed that some of the Chacoan cylinder jars in her small sample showed signs of modifica-

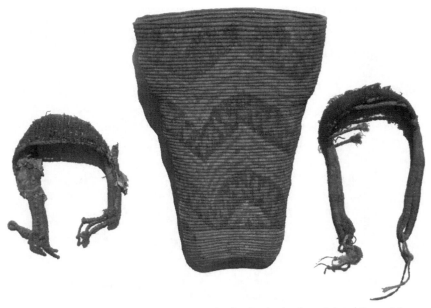

Figure 6.6.   The design that was woven into this burden basket from Painted Cave, Arizona, was later repainted on the exterior. Courtesy of the Amerind Foundation, Inc., Dragoon, Arizona. Catalog Number PC/28/01. Photographer unknown.

Figure 6.7.   A group of black-on-white cylinder jars from Chaco Canyon are displayed as part of a museum exhibit. Courtesy of the Maxwell Museum of Anthropology, University of New Mexico, 92_1_1252. Photographer unknown.

tion. Some of the changes appeared to reflect corrections, when potters scraped off mistakes and repainted to create the desired design (Crown 2007). In other cases, though, it appeared that artists intentionally obscured earlier designs in order to repaint the vessels. Sometimes they covered the earlier design with a new layer of slip, which was left as plain white or repainted with a new design. Cylinder jars with typical black-on-white designs sometimes had previous designs showing in places where the last layer of slip had flaked off or in patches where the slip was too thin to hide earlier lines. In one case, a cylinder jar that appeared to be plain white showed ghost designs under its slip. Crown also noted that artists could have obscured previous designs by refiring in an oxidizing atmosphere to burn out organic paint. There is also some evidence that the jars may have been covered with a plaster coating and painted with fugitive paints (Patricia Crown personal communication 2009). If so, they could have been cleaned and repainted by simply scrubbing the surface to remove the plaster and paint. Regardless of how the designs were obscured, the treatment of "plain" white cylinder jars and their context of discovery suggest that cylinder jars at Chaco were "cleansed of their designs" (Crown and Wills 2003:524) and then put in storage until their next use. These vessels were probably reworked and renewed on multiple occasions, a process that Crown and Wills (2003) have referred to as collaboration over time.

Although the reworking of cylinder jars is intriguing, it is not necessarily enough to postulate a widespread aesthetic of renewal in Chaco Canyon. It is the second line of evidence, however, that suggests aesthetic appreciation of renewal was more widespread, occurring in different media. As Crown and Wills (2003) document, kivas in Chaco Canyon were renewed over time. Kivas at Chaco are usually circular subterranean rooms that were built with a cribbed roof at or slightly above the level of the surrounding ground or plaza surface. Some of the kivas were rebuilt multiple times by first leveling the upper walls of the existing kiva to the level of a low bench that circled the interior, then building a new structure, overlapping but slightly offset from the earlier one. In a few cases, a new kiva was constructed directly on top of the earlier structure but was elevated by filling in the old floor and bench, then replastering and rebuilding to create an entirely new floor and new bench above the old. The destruction and rebuilding of kivas seem to have happened roughly two to four times per kiva during Chaco's peak (the Bonito Phase, 900–1140), suggesting that individual renewal events happened within a single generation.

Modification and reworking of pottery and kivas at Chaco might, of course, have been for practical reasons, such as correcting mistakes or refurbishing worn-out vessels or structures. Still, as Crown and Wills (2003) point out, these were rather inefficient ways to correct errors. Why would potters wait until after firing to fix a mistake? They had other methods of correction available, either by scraping off errors prior to firing or by reslipping part of a jar and repainting it prior to firing. Why would those building a kiva not correct problems during construction, instead of finishing the structure and rebuilding it shortly thereafter? Why reconstruct a complicated masonry structure in a slightly different orientation, as opposed to shoring up sagging walls or replastering worn surfaces?

Although renewing cylinder jars and kivas probably happened on quite different time frames, the two processes share a fundamental similarity. As Crown and Wills (2003:523) characterize the renewal of the jars, "The process of keeping while covering, rather than simply discarding the vessels and their designs and beginning anew, must have had significance." Indeed, the renewal of slip and paint "created layers, some hidden, some visible, on the pottery, preserving the past while covering and obscuring it" (Crown and Wills 2003:523). A similar process, they proposed, was probably reflected in the rebuilding of kivas at Chaco, with "repeated acts of reproducing a similar pattern, or adherence to form" (Crown and Wills 2003:525).

Crown and Wills do not discuss aesthetics in their article, but I argue that we should entertain the possibility that these two forms of ritual renewal reflect an aesthetic choice, one grounded in both the concrete aesthetics of the Chacoan people and in their perceptual experiences of cylinder jars and kivas. It appears likely that Chacoan potters preferred, at least in the specific case of the cylinder jars, to "maintain the continuity of materials and form of the object, while renewing the designs" (Crown and Wills 2003:523–24). This also suggests that the perceptual experience of an individual who saw the jars—their audience, as it were—was probably made meaningful in part by the knowledge that "the new image may have gained potency in part from the earlier image" (Crown and Wills 2003:524). The likelihood that renewal had religious significance does not negate its aesthetic potential, as awe, transcendence, and the aesthetic experience may be intertwined.

A second example of an aesthetic of renewal may be reflected in the replastering and repainting of Pueblo IV kivas (1325–1600 CE) (see figure 2.1). At most sites, kiva murals are separated by multiple layers of plaster, of which most are unpainted. At the Hopi area sites of Awat'ovi and Kawaika-a, Watson Smith (1952) noted as many as 100 plaster layers in a single room. In Rio Grande sites like Kuaua, as many as 18 out of 85 plaster layers in a single kiva were painted. At Pottery Mound Pueblo, also in the Rio Grande Valley, excavators reported so many thin layers of plaster and of paint that it was extremely difficult to tell them apart (Vivian 2007) (see figure 5.4).

There are various possible explanations for the replastering, including repairs, refurbishing dirty walls, spring cleaning, and ritual destruction of paintings (Smith 1952:19–20). Given the frequency of replastering and the number of unpainted layers, most researchers have accepted that the act of plastering itself had ritual significance, beyond the painted murals (Crotty 1995:89–91). Julia Meyers (2007) recently examined this idea by comparing the number of plaster layers at mural sites across the Southwest through time. She found that murals dating from before about 1300 CE tended to be relatively long lived, with an average of between three and eight plaster layers per painted room, depending on the time period. In contrast, Pueblo IV murals, after about 1300, were in rooms that averaged more than 29 layers of plaster, most of which were neither painted nor sooted and dirty. In fact, the rooms with the most elaborate murals, such as the famous paintings at Awat'ovi, Kawaika-a, Pottery Mound, and Kuaua, have the most layers of plaster. Less complicated wall paintings from the Pueblo IV period are in rooms that usually have just one or two layers of plaster. It seems that the most complex murals from after 1300 "exemplify . . . short use-life, in which paintings were regularly 'destroyed' by covering them with new painted images or plaster layers" (Meyers 2007:180). This, I think, represents an aesthetic of renewal, where the process of creating a clean, fresh plaster surface was a significant aesthetic experience.

An aesthetic of renewal shows up in Pueblo IV rock art as well, although in a somewhat different form. In a few cases, pictographs were, like kiva murals, covered with layers of solid pigment (usually white) to create a clean surface for additional painting (Cole 1984:24; H. D. Smith 1998:95). More commonly, painted rockshelters often include multiple layers of superimposed paintings. This differs from kiva murals in that the previous images show through in places and are obscured in others. Nevertheless, the effect of renewing by layering new upon old may have been analogous to the plastering and repainting in kivas. With petroglyphs, which cannot be covered easily, extensive reworking may also reflect a similar concern with renewal. At the protohistoric rock art site of Las Estrellas (post-1325), on the southern Pajarito Plateau, the labor-intensive images that form the core of the site were created and then reworked over a considerable period of time (Munson 2003). One large human figure was initially pecked and incised, probably using a different tool for each technique. One of its legs was then heavily ground, producing a smooth, solidly worked area that contrasts with the cliff background.

A similar example comes from Pueblo Largo, in the Galisteo Basin. During fieldwork, Nels Nelson removed a large stone slab with a human figure lightly incised on it from a shrine near the pueblo (Nelson 1914:70–71). On the chest of the figure is a single short vertical groove, rubbed and reworked by so many different hands over time that it glistens with a high polish. Sites with such intensively reworked images, which appear to be relatively rare, probably constitute sacred spaces, with restricted access that blurs the line between artist and audience (see chapter 4; and Munson 2003, 2008b, in press-b). The repetitive motions of pecking, grinding, and reworking petroglyphs or of repainting rockshelters with overlapping layers of pigment were aesthetically and spiritually charged experiences that brought power to these special places.

Beyond the Visual

The aesthetic experience of reworking and renewal, in this conception, extends far beyond the visual. It is, I suggest, more about the integration of all of the senses with ritual knowledge, so that the artist/audience is immersed in meaningful perception—the cool, dark interior of a rockshelter, the repetitive motions of grinding, the sound of music, chanting, or prayer. Such experiences are admittedly ephemeral, lasting only as long as the individual is present, participating, and perceiving the world around himself or herself. Yet we know, from shared human experience, that sound is evocative (Hedges 1993; H. D. Smith 1998), that scent can conjure up entire worlds, and that shimmering water draws the eye (Morphy 1994b; Sekaquaptewa and Washburn 2004:472). Ethnographic and historic records describe how ritual performance integrates vision with other equally important senses and impressions, such as sound, scent, and kinesthetic experience (Newsome and Hays-Gilpin in press; Sekaquaptewa and Washburn 2004). And historic and contemporary songs of Hopi Pueblo attest to the ways that desert people appreciate and are attuned to the sight and sound of different kinds of rain (Sekaquaptewa and Washburn 2004:466). Perhaps, with careful use of ethnographic analogy and, especially, cultural metaphor (Ortman 2000; Sekaquaptewa and Washburn 2004), it may be possible to examine aesthetics in an archaeological context.

Why Aesthetics?

All humans have aesthetic experiences. Some are awed by the brilliant flash of lightning arcing across the evening sky; others may be stopped in their tracks by the sweet scent of mock orange flowers perfuming the air. As ephemeral and varied as such experiences are, they form an important part of every individual's life. It may be difficult to know exactly how aesthetics influenced the color choices that a carver made when painting wooden bird effigies at Chaco, or the design elements that a Sinagua weaver combined to create a shirt. As difficult as aesthetics may be to approach archaeologically, we can feel certain that it was a significant factor in ancient artwork. Even an incomplete view of aesthetics potentially opens up new avenues for exploring the perception and experiences of past peoples.

The Future of Art in Archaeology ⟶ 7

Art may be an illusion, but in exploring it we may have expanded the basis of archaeological and anthropological insight and inference. (Morphy 2005:60)

[Archaeology and art history] view . . . the same materials with somewhat differently colored lenses. (Ekholm 1959:71)

ART DOES NOT HAVE NEAT BOUNDARIES. As a category, art encompasses paintings, sculpture, and other works central to the art historical canon, but it may also spill over to encompass any manner of curious objects—sandals, stone palettes, body paint, and even found objects. As a part of lived experience, art is implicated in social life, in the form of personal, economic, and political relationships, as well as in the cultural realm of ideas and bodies of knowledge (Morphy and Perkins 2005b). The specifics of artistic expression vary greatly, just as understandings of what constitutes art are malleable, changing constantly over time and across space. Nevertheless, humans seem to have a fundamental impulse to "shap[e] and embellish . . . everyday ordinary reality so that it becomes extraordinary" (Dissanayake 1982:148). The prevalence of art worldwide seems to be rooted in people's tendency to create striking and beautiful objects, to admire them for the unusual skill in their making, to celebrate the playfulness of their creation, and to appreciate the depth of their meaning (Dissanayake 1982:149, 1999; Dutton 2009). Shaped by human hands, created within the context of a given time and place, art expresses something about the people who made and used it. To ignore the vast world of art beyond Renaissance Europe or contemporary New York galleries is to remain willfully and intentionally ignorant of the range of the human experience.

The fact that art is difficult—or perhaps impossible—to define in an ironclad fashion is no excuse for ignoring the subject. As archaeologists, we should exploit the faint and fuzzy line between artifact and art, art and artifact. Playing with the distinction between the two categories will lead us to new insights, shaping the kinds of questions that we ask on a fundamental level. Treating artifacts as art opens up a new range of possibilities, centered on Western assumptions about the nature of artists as creative geniuses, with adoring audiences contemplating their work. It raises questions about images, from how to identify a picture of a dog to the significance of realism, abstraction, and ambiguity. And perhaps most challengingly for archaeologists, to treat an artifact as art is to highlight its aesthetic properties, to call attention to the ways that ancient artists and viewers might have experienced color, sheen, and qualities of line. Applying the term "art" is "the signal for us to look at an object in its broadest context, to explore all possible dimensions of the significance of its form" (Morphy 2005:60).

Archaeologists have no reason to fear art. A work of art is, after all, just a piece of material culture, little different from the tools, containers, and buildings that are archaeology's staple subjects. Art is amenable to study with any manner of archaeological methods, and in fact, Southwestern archaeology is replete with research that pokes and prods at art-like artifacts, using methods from chemical sourcing of ceramics to GIS analyses of rock art placement. These studies lead to insights that could only be gained through careful, systematic scientific research. I would in no way suggest that we throw out or ignore such studies in favor of just-so stories of symbolism and meaning. Instead, we need to create an archaeology of art, an approach that balances archaeological rigor with the interpretive insights of allied disciplines. Doing so will require a willingness to shift our perspective, to reframe artifacts as art, and to embrace the assumptions that "art" brings to bear.

The Challenge of "Art"

The connotations of "art" are a heavy load for ancient artifacts. Wrought by the history of Western art and contemporary art worlds, this baggage includes deeply embedded stereotypes about artists, audiences, and art itself. Throughout this book, I have tried to show that harnessing these expectations may be beneficial, for they point out new ways of approaching objects created long ago. I have addressed the individual artist and varied audiences, discussed the creation of images, and toyed with the implications of aesthetics in the past. Yet several issues still remain, for the label "art" comes with additional challenges for the archaeologist.

A Fuzzy Set

The definition of art will always be at issue in archaeological contexts. The category of "art" is constantly changing, expanding at times to a maddeningly vague notion, and then contracting to exclude all but a few exalted masterpieces. Art's fuzzy boundaries and shifting definitions seem to create a serious problem for those interested in studying art, as the subject of interest is never stable and readily identified. Although this can cause a good deal of frustration, the mutability of art is not an insurmountable problem. Struggling with definitions is a useful exercise, for it requires the researcher to consider the biases and assumptions that come with a label such as "art."

Difficulties in defining subject matter are not confined to art alone. Anthropology is rife with concepts and categories that "reflect the commonsense ideas of Europe of a particular period which are then extended to apply to other contexts" (Morphy 1994a:257) with greater or lesser degrees of success. While concepts like food or shelter translate well across most contexts, researchers have spent considerable time and energy debating the meaning and applicability of concepts such as hierarchy, gender, kinship, and the like (Morphy 1994a:257). The result in most of these debates is the eventual creation of "an analytical meta-language that is used in the analysis of data and the interpretation of culture" (Morphy 2005:51; also see Coote 1996; Morphy 1996; Michael O'Hanlon in Weiner et al. 1996b:278–79). This meta-language serves as a broad umbrella concept, reflecting "universal aspects of fully modern humans" (Morphy 2005:51). As Howard Morphy (2005:51) points out, "the fact that [these concepts] *can* be applied cross-culturally becomes part of our definition of fully modern humans, even if in some cases the attributes are shared with other animals" (also see Aiken 1998).

As the focus of research narrows to a particular case, however, it is necessary to fine-tune and modify broad concepts to suit the circumstances. The concept of art in the contemporary Western world is, of necessity, different from that of art in the ancient Southwest, for the historical circumstances and the societal contexts differ so greatly. The terminology is the same, and the conceptualization of art overlaps in some ways, but they are not entirely congruent. For those of us who prefer clarity and structure, this variability is somewhat distressing. However, as I have argued throughout this volume, the flexibility of art as a concept can be seen as a strength, for it provides a means of reframing any number of objects in ways that may lead to new research questions and perhaps new insights (Morphy 2005:60).

Uniqueness and Ubiquity

"Art" presents a challenge in the way that it encompasses the rarest, most unique, most skillfully and aesthetically made objects (Bradley 2009). The singular masterpiece has been the center of art history from the early days of the discipline (Benjamin 1992 [1936]). When we admire the carefully arranged figurines, sticks, and a basket from a cache in Cliff Valley, New Mexico (figure 7.1), our appreciation and esteem are based in part on the bright colors, bold patterns, and human representations—but also on the cache's implied status as a unique and mysterious collection of objects that

Figure 7.1.   Ritual cache, 1300/1400 CE, Salado or Mogollon(?), Cliff Valley, New Mexico. Major Acquisitions Centennial Endowment, 1979.17.1-11. Photography © the Art Institute of Chicago.

expresses the ideas and beliefs of a distant past. Art historians are used to dealing with unique objects that reflect the creativity and intellect of a single artist, where the mere presence of an image, a color, or a theme in a single work of art may be highly significant. Archaeologists, on the other hand, are trained to focus on ubiquity. We examine and analyze large bodies of data (figure 7.2), making observations of multiple variables across an entire assemblages of items and looking for patterns within the whole. When we encounter strange or unusual observations or objects, we treat them as outliers. How, then, are archaeologists to handle a single image or a lone object? Is it an anomaly, to be explained away, or is there a way to understand the significance of the unique?

The problem of presence versus ubiquity is amply illustrated in studies comparing art across multiple media or among different regions of the Southwest. For example, Joe Stewart and colleagues (1990) compared Jornada Mogollon rock art and ceramics from southern New Mexico, just to the east of the Mimbres area, by matching examples of similar images from

Figure 7.2.   Archaeologists excavating the Hohokam site of Pueblo Grande between 1929 and the 1950s apparently analyzed almost 500,000 sherds of pottery in a single season. Pueblo Grande Photographs, Arizona Collection, Arizona State University Libraries, Odd Halseth Collection, CP PG 304. Photographer unknown.

each medium. On one level, this is completely appropriate; it is necessary to identify similarities in order to study them. On another level, though, it is difficult to know how to interpret or evaluate the parallels that they found. What does it mean if there is a single image of a horned serpent on one pottery vessel, when there are countless examples in rock art? Is the presence of one image on ceramics significant, or is it an anomaly? Does it reflect the transgressive behavior of a rogue potter, or could it be a sole surviving example of a small collection of specialized pottery? Sally Cole's (1994) study of similarities in Basketmaker and Ancestral Pueblo imagery raises similar questions. She identified apparently related motifs across long periods of time, proposing that the shared images reflect cultural continuity over a period of 2,000 years. But what does it mean to find an image of a bird in rock art from the 6th century BCE and another on Pueblo IV ceramics from the 15th century CE? Are they really the same thing, or are they merely reflections of the fact that birds are present across the entire Southwest?

Art Expresses Meanings

Meaning is a problem. Expression of significant meaning seems an inherent quality of art, yet attempts to decipher past meaning raise the specter of subjective interpretation, personal opinion, and rank speculation. As J. J. Brody (2005:178) has described the problem, Mimbres pots have "the power to stimulate the imagination" but end up "evoking speculation that easily degenerates into romanticism or inanity." Empirically oriented archaeologists can be quite wary of discussions of meaning, which "often amount to simple guessing" (Chippindale 1992:271). I share this fundamental skepticism about our ability to reconstruct meanings from the distant past.

My aversion is rooted in a recognition that meaning is multilayered and complex. Some general meanings may be near universal (Douglas 1996), but there is also a host of culturally and contextually specific meanings that may not be uniformly shared and understood, even within a small community. Archaeologists interested in meaning need to recognize the different challenges associated with trying to understand specific meanings as opposed to broader general meanings. On a general level, it may be possible to discuss potential meanings that are logical within certain contexts, such as symbolism of water and fertility for farmers in a desert environment (e.g., Crotty 1992; Crown 1994; Hays-Gilpin 1999; Wright 2005). At the same time, definitive demonstrations of meanings, broad or specific, are quite difficult. As Kelley Hays-Gilpin (2004:141) warns: "The important thing to remember about Puebloan iconography is that almost everything can serve as a 'fertility symbol' of some sort."

Archaeologists often assume, overtly or implicitly, that the meanings of art are strictly aligned with ideology, religion, and ritual (Hays-Gilpin 2000). The equation of art and religion is understandable, for we think of both subjects as reflecting "the cultural imagination" (Ingold 2001:19) that encodes meanings. In Tim Ingold's (2001:19) words, "technology works; art signifies." Thus, the form and function of Mimbres bowls have been interpreted as symbolizing belief in a three-tiered universe and emergence from one world into the next (Moulard 1985; Shafer 1995), and the images on the pottery are usually interpreted as depicting rituals, supernaturals, and mythological themes (Butcher 1968; Carr 1979; Kabotie 1949; Moulard 1982; Short 1998; Thompson 1999)—but they could, in fact, be anything from clan or village symbols to thoroughly secular jokes (Brody 2005:170). To assume that image equals art equals religious meaning represents "lazy thinking about linkage between images and religion. . . . [S]uch recognition must be based on specific reasoning rather than assumption" (Aldhouse-Green 2004:xvi).

Art's Potential

An art-centered approach to the past brings with it a full complement of assumptions. To apply the term "art" to something typically seen as artifact requires full consideration of the triangle of art, artist, and audience. In chapter 3, I argued that we should think of potters, painters, weavers, and others not as craftspeople or artisans, but as artists. The term may seem inappropriate, given the burden of Western expectations that artists are extraordinary, unique, and possibly troubled individuals. Indeed, contemporary notions of an artistic personality and behavior seem completely at odds with the ethnographic portrait of Southwestern craftspeople as anonymous and self-effacing. Nevertheless, an art-centered approach harnesses those assumptions, seeking to understand artists as individual actors through studies of artistic practice that consider varying actions, intentions, and ideas. Collectively, artist-focused studies may hold promise for addressing long-standing questions about individual expression and the relationship of creativity with the constraining factor of artistic tradition.

The concept of artistic tradition calls attention to the third leg of the triangle, the audience that provides the social context within which works of art are judged. Southwestern archaeologists have something of a mixed record where audiences are concerned. There have been numerous studies considering the context of artwork, using tools from GIS to the analysis of physical characteristics of objects. Researchers have recently examined the contexts of kiva murals, some rock art sites, and ceramics used in public feasting, but most studies still adopt a behavioral approach, focusing more on the messages that people send through the creation and use of art than on the audience itself. As I argued in chapter 4, such studies can be strengthened greatly by more fully considering the specifics of the audience, including which people did or did not have access, as well as the implications of differing degrees of public and private space.

The social context of art, in the form of artists and audiences, is critical but not sufficient. An art-centered approach to the past must also consider the form and content of the art itself (Morphy and Perkins 2005b), rather than treating art as if it were a sealed black box. Images are a natural starting place when considering content, for they are visually appealing and seem laden with significant meaning. As discussed in chapter 5, archaeologists have spent more than a century lauding, illustrating, and speculating over ancient pictures, a tradition that is alive and well today. Yet most of us identify images with very little deliberation, assuming that recognizing a picture is a simple process. An examination of identifications of images from nearly any archaeological context quickly gives lie to this notion, showing a surprising variability in how different researchers interpret images and scenes. However, general principles of representation, drawn from studies in psychology and art history, can make identifying pictures more systematic, whether applied to the identity of the Hohokam "guanaco" figures or to representations of corn through time and space. A systematic and explicit approach to identifying pictures is required if we are to address why artists made the choices they did. When and why might artists choose clear, unambiguous images? When might they embrace ambiguity, or even refrain from creating depictions entirely?

The term "art" has implications for aesthetics as well, whether in the concrete sense of the desired appearance of an object or in the more abstract perceptual experience (see chapter 6). Concrete aesthetics is expressed in the properties that artists seek out and enhance through their work. Although some qualities of artwork are probably incidental to the materials or techniques, repeated associations of color, sheen, texture, and other visual properties may reflect the perceptual experience and aesthetic sense of a given time and place. When choices are limited by technology and available materials, such as the difficulty of firing blue or green pigments on ceramics, artists may embrace alternate means to create similar effects. The painters of Gallup-Dogozhi style black-on-white vessels in the Chacoan era may have done just that, replacing blue-green with hatched lines or adding fugitive paints post-firing. The use of bright colors, spotted patterns, and sparkling pigment may have been similarly pleasing and effective for Ancestral Pueblo people in late prehistory. An aesthetic of renewal may have been particularly widespread in the ancient Southwest, from Chacoan reworking of cylinder jars and rebuilding of kivas to the extensive replastering of Pueblo IV kiva murals. These cases suggest that layering and repetition over time may have contributed to the power and meaning of these arts. Indeed, aesthetics is not solely about the visual but instead encompasses the entire perceptual experience of encountering art within its setting. Nonmaterial aspects of the experience may have held aesthetic significance as well.

Material and Form

Art has physical form. Although works of art may seem to "hover on the margins as special items, separate from their context" (Aldhouse-Green 2004:xvi), they are, in the end, just material culture. Art was and is created by human hands. Someone gathered clay, ground and cleaned it, and kneaded it with water and perhaps temper until it was ready to use. Someone gathered pigments, perhaps collecting beeweed to boil into a syrupy paint, or digging minerals from rare mines to be prepared for trade. Someone collected yucca or picked cotton, cleaned and processed it, and spun it into string. Someone, somewhere, traveled to the sea to obtain shells, bringing them home or trading them down the line. Someone, whether an artist, craftsperson, or something else, worked these materials. Some were talented individuals who seem to have worked magic with their medium. Others were less capable—or less concerned with the precision, colors, rhythm, and fine finishes that we find so pleasing today. Regardless of their abilities, they all had to learn their medium, practicing in order to hone their physical and mental skills.

The material record of artists' work is preserved in the brushstrokes of individual potters and revealed in the idiosyncrasies of the individual artist's hand. Artists' struggles to learn are reflected in the wobbly lines of a young painter working to master the physical coordination needed to paint on a curved surface and in the errors in symmetry that appear in baskets and complex textiles. Their thought processes are preserved, if indirectly, in the images that they created—the pictures of dogs and men, of atlatls and women and corn—and even in the ambiguity of some of their work, which seems sometimes playful and sometimes quite serious in intent. Even their understanding of beauty and what is pleasing may be recorded in material form, through the choices that artists made, in materials and techniques, to highlight blue-green or to layer images and plaster on a kiva wall.

Audiences, too, left an impression on the material world, through the configuration of space and in the objects that they viewed and handled. The built environment of the Pueblo IV world reflects audiences for kiva murals and plaza performances, just as the layout of highly structured rock art sites reflects the artist-participants who created and used the petroglyphs and pictographs. Signs of reworking and modification of rock art, murals, and ceramics all attest to the actions of artists, audiences, and participants, who observed and made use of art in ways that hint at an image's meaning or that signal changing relationships among individuals.

Working toward an Archaeology of Art

An archaeology of art must encompass both the materiality of artifacts and the expectations heaped upon art. If the study of ancient art is to be embraced by archaeologists, it must rely on standard archaeological methods and principles. If it is to provide useful insights into the past, it must also acknowledge and draw upon the assumptions that accompany the concept of "art." This means, then, that an archaeology of art needs to strike a balance between two different, and often opposing, views of the world—an archaeological perspective, with its roots in the generalizing and hypothesis-testing of the scientific method, and an art historical paradigm that values interpretation of the particular and the unique.

An archaeology of art must, first of all, be based on a willingness to play semantic games with "art" as a concept. Insisting on a conclusive definition of art and artifact means remaining bogged down in a fascinating but irresolvable debate. A greater flexibility in definitions, on the other hand, and a willingness to move artifacts and works of art from one category to another, will change perspectives and raise new questions.

In addition, any study of ancient art must be founded in archaeological methods. The documentation and analysis of material objects is one of archaeology's great strengths, from quantification of physical characteristics to usewear analyses and sourcing of materials. Yet despite decades of productive studies, these archaeological staples are rarely integrated into art-focused studies. The same pragmatism and logic that results in collecting masses of data on projectile point form and the characteristics of fill in archaeological sites should be applied to a broader range of materials, from wear on clay figurines (Stinson 2004:116–19) to reporting the presence of pigments recovered in excavations (Lewis 2002).

At the same time, an archaeological study of art will also require more interdisciplinary approaches and an increased openness to methods and perspectives from cognate disciplines. Art history provides a considerable body of literature on iconography and symbolism. Psychology, too, has the potential to contribute to our understanding of the problem of representational imagery and universals of human perception. Newer fields, such as visual studies or media studies, may highlight productive ways of understanding the social structure of audiences and their construction of meanings. Borrowing of ideas and perspectives will not always happen smoothly or easily, as disciplinary boundaries can be difficult to breach. Still, increasing crossover among allied disciplines suggests that productive interdisciplinary collaboration may be possible (Berlo 2005; Phillips 1994, 2005b; Vastokas 1986/1987).

Finally, an archaeology of art will require greater familiarity with ethnographic research on art. Although interest in art on the part of cultural anthropologists has waxed and waned over time, there is now a substantial body of work discussing and analyzing art and aesthetics worldwide (see Morphy and Perkins 2005a; Schneider and Wright 2006; Svasek 2007; Westermann 2005). These studies provide a rich source of ideas and analogues for the past. They also sound a note of caution for archaeologists, as many of these classic works document the great complexity of the relationship between art, social life, and the cultural sphere (e.g., Firth 1995 [1936]; Morphy 1991; Munn 1973).

Indeed, if there is one great problem that hampers the development of an archaeology of art, it is the difficulty of making bridging arguments between ethnographic information and archaeological patterns (Morwood 1992). Ethnoarchaeological studies of art are unfortunately rare (see DeBoer 1990; Stanislawski 1977; Wallaert-Pêtre 2001), and much of the existing ethnographic research is difficult to translate into material correlates. With a few exceptions (Carr and Neitzel 1995; DeBoer 1991; Jones and Hegmon 1991), the lack of reasonable models for relationships of art and society mean that it is often difficult to know how to interpret the social and cultural significance of different archaeological patterns.

Studies of ancient artwork, in turn, do not always facilitate discussion among archaeologists working in different regions of the world. Researchers interested in ancient art of Europe, the Near East, and Africa have focused on broad questions about the origins of art as a defining trait of modern humans (e.g., Mithen 1998; White 1992). Beyond origins research, archaeological studies of art tend to be narrowly focused on a specific time, place, and medium, which often makes it difficult to compare results or engender broader discussion. It is not always clear, for example, the extent to which discussions of shamanism in South African rock art might be relevant to Hohokam petroglyphs, or whether studies of weaving and tribute in Mesoamerica provide useful models for Pueblo IV textile production. Nevertheless, I believe it is useful to compare art cross-culturally. Although this volume focuses on studies of art from the U.S. Southwest, I hope that the theories and methods presented will be of interest to archaeologists working elsewhere.

The Future of Art in the Ancient Southwest

What is the future of art in Southwestern archaeology? There are intriguing artifacts in many different settings and contexts that cry out for an art-centered approach to research. Mogollon and Ancestral Pueblo jewelry has had surprisingly little attention beyond basic description and discussions of production locales and techniques (Jernigan 1978; Mathien 1997). Surely a study of aesthetics and images in jewelry from Chaco Canyon would be intriguing. The colors, contexts, and physical characteristics of painted arrow shafts and decorated sticks from various contexts (Cosgrove 1947) could provide interesting information about audiences and aesthetics, as would similar studies of incised bone tubes from Snaketown and other Hohokam sites (Gladwin et al. 1937), or of Hohokam jewelry that incorporates carved and painted designs (Haury 1945). Might the colors and materials of polished stone celts from the Rio Grande Valley be significant aesthetically? What about the color and sheen of bowls with smudged and polished interiors, such as Reserve Smudged from the Mogollon area? Or the elaborate textures of Tularosa patterned corrugated pottery?

All of these objects are potentially susceptible to treatment as art, yet they have had relatively little attention beyond description and, in some cases, a discussion of technology. This may be due, in part, to the problem of presence versus ubiquity. It is difficult to talk about the aesthetics of tapestry weave quivers when there are so few extant examples (Tanner 1976:88–89). Still, there are numerous examples of the insights that can come out of studies drawing on small bodies of material (Odegaard and Hays-Gilpin 2002). Cross-media studies are especially useful in examining colors, images, designs, and other themes as integrated parts of the cultural whole, regardless of the medium in which they are expressed (Christensen 1994; Hays-Gilpin 2002; Washburn and Webster 2006).

While I strongly encourage archaeological studies of art, the reverse is also necessary in some cases. A few entrenched cases of ancient art would be well served by more consideration as artifact. The stunning iconography of Pueblo IV rock art and kiva murals has been examined time and again, with numerous interpretations of symbolism and meaning. Human figures in the murals have been matched with ethnographic records of katsinas and ceremonies, identified as specific beings, and noted for their war-like or egalitarian nature—yet archaeologists have seldom examined the technical details of the murals' production (Meyers 2007; Smith 1952). Numerous authors have noted similarities between kiva murals and contemporaneous rock art (e.g., Schaafsma 2000, 2007), but there are, to my knowledge, no substantial quantitative studies comparing the images.[1] Similar problems plague the enigmatic painted figures of Barrier Canyon style rock art in the northern Southwest, the tantalizingly detailed Jornada Mogollon petroglyphs of southern New Mexico, and even the exuberant designs of Sikyatki polychrome pottery from the Hopi area (cf. LeBlanc and Henderson 2009). These items are artistically rich and aesthetically laden, to be sure, but we should not allow that to distract us from the artifact-like attributes that are also valid subjects of study: the placement of images in the landscape, the sources of the clay, the pigments and paint recipes.

In order to better understand the past, we need to wrench our eyes away from the art-like aspects of these items and ensure that we do not lose sight of the materiality of this art. The lively figures "dancing" across Mimbres pots (Short 1998) are charming, cartoon-like, and yes, informative. Still, we would do well to remember that Classic Mimbres black-on-white ceramics are vessels, with three-dimensional form. "Mimbres art" does not consist of a set of isolated pictures rendered in two dimensions, and there is every reason to believe that the hemispherical shape of most bowls was a significant aspect of their function and meaning (Moulard 1985; Shafer 1995). Why not look at pictographs and kiva murals in terms of standardization and the organization of production? Why not examine the technology of mosaics on stone and wood, or of paint recipes beyond glazeware ceramics? And what about labor investment in rock art? I know of just a single study of the tools found on petroglyph sites in the Southwest (Moore 1994), yet there are many sites that have hammerstones and other tools in great quantity.

Above all, why not integrate standard artifact-focused archaeological approaches, such as technological studies and analyses of hard data, with art-like concerns such as consideration of the artist's creativity, interpretation of form, and evaluation of aesthetic principles? To do so requires integrating multiple perspectives and disciplines, from archaeology to art history, cultural anthropology, and visual studies. It means finding a balance between art-centered approaches that celebrate the unique, the particular, and the creativity of the individual with artifact-centered approaches that focus on the ubiquitous, the general, and the weight of norms and cultural tradition. Bringing together such disparate perspectives may not be simple, but it will, I believe, reframe our view of ancient objects, generating new questions and, ultimately, providing a richer understanding of the past.

Notes

Chapter 1

1. Kivas are subterranean or semi-subterranean rooms that are typical of many Ancestral Pueblo and Mogollon villages. Based in part on ethnographic analogy with the historic pueblos, kivas are usually assumed to be ceremonial structures (see discussion in Adler 1993; papers in Lipe and Hegmon 1989; Peckham 1979; Smith 1990).

2. There are several fine summaries of prehistoric Southwestern art (Berlo and Phillips 1998:37–60; Brody 1991, 2005; Tanner 1976), as well as numerous descriptive overviews of different media, some from art history and some from within archaeology: kiva murals (Crotty 1995; Dutton 1963; Hibben 1975; Smith 1952), textiles (Kent 1983a; Teague 1998; Webster 1997), ceramics (Peckham 1990), basketry (Morris and Burgh 1941), and rock art (Schaafsma 1980, 1992b).

Chapter 2

1. In Western traditions, well-known artists were usually male from the Renaissance through the early 20th century—and, some would argue, today as well (Nochlin 1988). See chapter 3 for additional discussion.

2. Gell (1996) sees understandings of art in similar fashion, though he characterizes the three positions as (1) art exists as the creation of an artist's intent; (2) art is anything interpreted as art within a system of ideas, such as art history; (3) art may be defined through institutions, such as acceptance by an art world. Where Gell and Morphy diverge, however, is in Morphy's descriptions of art by attribute, which Gell (1998) eschews completely.

3. The notion of the aesthetic experience has been central to definitions of art since the 19th century (Stecker 2005:2), although there have been numerous attempts to "disentangle aesthetics from art" (see Coote 1992; Morphy 1994a:257; Stecker 2005).

4. There is constant debate about the propriety of the term "rock art" among researchers and aficionados (see Morales 2005). Some researchers have suggested using "rock-art" instead (e.g., Taçon and Chippindale 1998), in an attempt to create some distance from the implications of art.

5. The notion of art and science as polar opposites is long-standing but more variable over time than one might think (Jones and Galison 1998:2–6), as is even the apparently straightforward concept of objectivity in science (Galison 1998).

6. There are, however, a surprising number of contemporary art installations and performance art pieces that are inspired by archaeological excavation and make use of just such materials (Evans 2004; Mithen 2004; Renfrew 2003).

Chapter 3

1. These ideas are strong enough that they surface consistently in psychological studies of contemporary North American artists. Interestingly enough, psychologists have found that many artists emphasize these very traits in themselves, even when more objective observers might not agree to their presence (Sawyer 2006).

2. Others have pointed out the contradiction in the present day between Pueblo values of modesty and anonymity and the kind of individual attention needed to ensure success as an artist in the 20th and 21st centuries (Wade 1986).

3. As discussed later, the skill required to make baskets of any size makes this relatively unlikely.

4. Studies of cordage twist are an exception to this trend (e.g., Haas 2006). Work on collaboration in textile production in the ancient Southwest is just beginning (Jolie 2007).

Chapter 5

1. Of course, it may be that we simply do not recognize depictions of deer or mountain sheep without their antlers or horns.

2. Although basketry designs are often assumed to have provided the model for later designs on painted pottery (Breternitz et al. 1974:26; Brody 1991:27; Morris 1927; Ortman 2000; Tanner 1976), recent research suggests that this was not necessarily the case (Washburn and Webster 2006). Indeed, Washburn and Webster (2006) found little continuity in design motifs or in structure from late Basketmaker III baskets to the earliest black-on-white ceramics.

3. At the same time, the sound of pecking petroglyphs must surely have been audible to the Spanish priests in the church; one wonders just how secret the mesa slope rock art really was.

Chapter 6

1. The theme for the 2010 Visiting Scholar Conference at Southern Illinois University, Carbondale, was "Making Senses of the Past: Toward a Sensory Ar-

chaeology." The conference proceedings, to be edited by Jo Day, will likely be published in 2012.

2. It is curious that Crown's (2001) study of learning, discussed in chapter 3, seems to suggest almost the opposite result— that Mimbres children learned techniques but had more emphasis on creativity rather than doing things correctly, while Hohokam children were taught to make a limited range of designs, with emphasis on doing them right.

3. Morphy's definition obliquely raises another important issue, about the distinction between art and aesthetics. There are numerous experiences of the world that may be aesthetically pleasing, but few people would argue that they constitute art (Heyd 2005:6): sunsets, bird song, veils of rain from thunderclouds, even the spotted patterns of oxen, to the Dinka and other Nilotic speakers in the Sudan (Coote 1992).

Chapter 7

1. Helen Crotty's (1995) unpublished dissertation is an exhaustive study of kiva mural iconography, but it is primarily a catalog and art historical discussion of images.

References

Abercrombie, Nicholas, and Brian Longhurst. 1998. *Audiences*. Sage, London, UK.

Adams, E. Charles. 1991. *The Origin and Development of the Pueblo Katsina Cult*. University of Arizona Press, Tucson.

Adler, Michael. 1993. Why is a kiva? New interpretations of prehistoric social integrative architecture in the Northern Rio Grande region of New Mexico. *Journal of Anthropological Research* 49:319–46.

Aiken, Nancy E. 1998. *The Biological Origins of Art*. Praeger, Westport, CT.

Aldhouse-Green, Miranda. 2004. *An Archaeology of Images: Iconology and Cosmology in Iron Age and Roman Europe*. Routledge, New York.

Alexander, Victoria D. 2003. *Sociology of the Arts: Exploring Fine and Popular Forms*. Blackwell, Malden, MA.

Amsden, Charles Avery. 1936. *An Analysis of Hohokam Pottery Design*. Medallion Papers 23. Gila Pueblo, Globe, AZ.

Anderson, Richard L. 1989. *Art in Small-scale Societies*. Prentice Hall, Englewood Cliffs, NJ.

———. 1990. *Calliope's Sisters: A Comparative Study of Philosophies of Art*. Prentice Hall, Englewood Cliffs, NJ.

———. 1992. Do other cultures have "art"? *American Anthropologist* 94:926–29.

———. 1999. *American Muse: Anthropological Excursions into Art and Aesthetics*. Prentice Hall, Englewood Cliffs, NJ.

———. 2004. *Calliope's Sisters: A Comparative Study of Philosophies of Art*, 2nd ed. Prentice Hall, Englewood Cliffs, NJ.

André, Naomi. 2006. *Voicing Gender: Castrati, Travesti, and the Second Woman in Early-Nineteenth-Century Italian Opera*. Indiana University Press, Bloomington, IN.

Aron, Fanchon. 1981. Kokopelli: Petroglyphs on the Pajarito Plateau. *El Palacio* 87(2):13–15.

Babcock, Barbara A. 1993. Shaping selves, reshaping lives: The art and experience of Helen Cordero. In *Imagery and Creativity: Ethnoaesthetics and Art Worlds in the Americas*, edited by D. S. Whitten and N. E. Whitten Jr., pp. 205–34. University of Arizona Press, Tucson.

———. 1995. Marketing Maria: The tribal artist in the age of mechanical reproduction. In *Looking High and Low: Art and Cultural Identity*, edited by B. J. Bright and L. Bakewell, pp. 124–50. University of Arizona Press, Tucson.

Bagwell, Elizabeth A. 2002. Ceramic form and skill: Attempting to identify child producers at Pecos Pueblo, New Mexico. In *Children in the Prehistoric Puebloan Southwest*, edited by K. A. Kamp, pp. 90–107. University of Utah Press, Salt Lake City.

Bailey, Douglass W. 2007. The anti-rhetorical power of representational absence: Incomplete figurines from the Balkan Neolithic. In *Image and Imagination: A Global Prehistory of Figurative Representation*, edited by C. Renfrew and I. Morley, pp. 111–20. McDonald Institute of Archeological Research, University of Cambridge, Cambridge.

Baldwin, Stuart J. 1986. The mountain lion in Tompiro stone art. In *By Hands Unknown: Papers in Honor of James G. Bain*, edited by A. Poore, pp. 8–17. Papers of the Archaeological Society of New Mexico, vol. 12. Ancient City Press, Santa Fe, New Mexico.

Ball, Philip. 2001. *Bright Earth: Art and the Invention of Color*. Farrar, Straus & Giroux, New York.

Barker, Emma, Nick Webb, and Kim Woods. 1999. *The Changing Status of the Artist*. Yale University Press, New Haven, CT.

Barnett, F. 1968. *Birds on Rio Grande Pottery: Bird, Birdling, and Bird Tail Motifs Found on Rio Grande Glaze Pottery Vessels from Ancient Tonque Ruin in New Mexico*. Southwest Printers, Yuma, AZ.

Basile, Joseph J. 2002. Two visual languages at Petra: Aniconic and representational sculpture of the Great Temple. *Near Eastern Archaeology* 65(4):255–58.

Baxandall, Michael. 1972. *Painting and Experience in Fifteenth Century Italy: A Primer in the Social History of Pictorial Style*. Clarendon Press, Oxford, UK.

Bayman, James M. 2002. Hohokam craft economies and the materialization of power. *Journal of Archaeological Method and Theory* 9(1):69–95.

Beazley, John D. 1964. *The Development of Attic Black-Figure*. University of California Press, Berkeley.

———. 1989. *Greek Vases: Lectures*. Clarendon Press, Oxford, UK.

Becker, Howard. 1982. *Art Worlds*. University of California Press, Berkeley.

Beeman, William O. 1993. The anthropology of theater and spectacle. *Annual Review of Anthropology* 22:369–93.

Benedict, Ruth. 1961. *Patterns of Culture*. Routledge, London.

Benjamin, Walter. 1992 [1936]. The work of art in the age of mechanical reproduction. In *Illuminations*, edited by H. Arendt. Fontana Press, London.

Berlant, Tony. 1983. Mimbres painting: An artist's perspective. In *Mimbres Pottery: Ancient Art of the American Southwest*, edited by J. J. Brody, C. J. Scott, and S. A. LeBlanc, pp. 13–20. Hudson Hills Press, New York.

Berleant, Arnold. 2004. *Re-thinking Aesthetics: Rogue Essays on Aesthetics and the Arts*. Ashgate, Aldershot, Hampshire.

Berlo, Janet C. 1993. Dreaming of Double Woman: The ambivalent role of the female artist in North American Indian myth. *American Indian Quarterly* 17(1):31–43.

———. 2005. Anthropologies and histories of art: A view from the terrain of native North American art history. In *Anthropologies of Art*, edited by M. Westermann, pp. 178–92. Yale University Press, New Haven, CT.

Berlo, Janet C., and Ruth B. Phillips. 1998. *Native North American Art*. Oxford University Press, New York.

Bernardini, Wesley. 2005. *Hopi Oral Tradition and the Archaeology of Identity*. University of Arizona Press, Tucson.

Bettison, Cynthia Ann, Roland Shook, Randy Jennings, and Dennis Miller. 1999. New identifications of naturalistic motifs on a subset of Mimbres pottery. In *Sixty Years of Mogollon Archaeology: Papers from the Ninth Mogollon Conference, Silver City, New Mexico, 1996*, edited by S. M. Whittlesey, pp. 119–25. SRI Press, Tucson, AZ.

Biebuyck, Daniel (ed.). 1969. *Tradition and Creativity in Tribal Art*. University of California Press, Berkeley.

Blair, Mary Ellen, and Laurence R. Blair. 1999. *The Legacy of a Master Potter: Nampeyo and Her Descendants*. Rio Nuevo, Tucson, AZ.

Blinman, Eric. 1989. Potluck in the protokiva: Ceramics and ceremonialism in Pueblo I villages. In *The Architecture of Social Integration in Prehistoric Pueblos*, edited by W. D. Lipe and M. Hegmon, pp. 113–24. Occasional Paper, vol. 1. Crow Canyon Archaeological Center, Cortez, CO.

Blocker, H. Gene. 1994. *The Aesthetics of Primitive Art*. University Press of America, Lanham, MD.

Boas, Franz. 1955 [1927]. *Primitive Art*. 2nd ed. Dover, New York.

Boas, George. 1940. The Mona Lisa in the history of taste. *Journal of the History of Ideas* 1(2):207.

Bostwick, Todd W. 1998. Songs of the water bird: Hohokam petroglyph bird designs in the South Mountains, Phoenix, Arizona. *Rock Art Research* 13:7–20.

Bradley, Richard. 2002. Access, style, and imagery: The audience for prehistoric rock art in Atlantic Spain and Portugal, 4000–2000 BC. *Oxford Journal of Archaeology* 21(3):231–47.

———. 2009. *Image and Audience: Rethinking Prehistoric Art*. Oxford University Press, Oxford, UK.

Bradley, Richard, and T. Phillips. 2008. Display, disclosure, and concealment: The organisation of raw material in the chambered tombs of Bohuslan. *Oxford Journal of Archaeology* 27:1–13.

Brandt, Elizabeth A. 1977. The role of secrecy in a Pueblo society. In *Flowers of the Wind: Papers on Ritual, Myth, and Symbolism in California and the Southwest*, edited by T. C. Blackburn, pp. 11–28. Ballena Press, Socorro, NM.

———. 1994. Egalitarianism, hierarchy, and centralization in the Pueblos. In *The Ancient Southwestern Community: Models and Methods for the Study of Prehistoric Social Organization*, edited by W. H. Wills and R. D. Leonard, pp. 9–23. University of New Mexico Press, Albuquerque.

Breternitz, David A., Arthur Rohn, and Elizabeth Ann Morris. 1974. *Prehistoric Ceramics of the Mesa Verde Region*. Museum of Northern Arizona Ceramic Series 5. Museum of Northern Arizona, Flagstaff, AZ.

Brody, J. J. 1974. In advance of the readymade: Kiva murals and Navajo dry painting. In *Art and Environment in Native America*, edited by M. E. King and I. R. Traylor Jr., pp. 11–21. Special Publications of the Museum, Texas Tech University, vol. 7. Texas Tech Press, Lubbock.

———. 1977. *Mimbres Painted Pottery*. University of New Mexico Press, Albuquerque.

———. 1983. Mimbres painting. In *Mimbres Pottery: Ancient Art of the American Southwest*, edited by J. J. Brody, C. J. Scott, and S. A. LeBlanc, pp. 69–125. Hudson Hills Press, New York.

———. 1989. Site use, pictorial space, and subject matter in late prehistoric and early historic Rio Grande Pueblo art. *Journal of Anthropological Research* 45:15–28.

———. 1991. *Anasazi and Pueblo Painting*. University of New Mexico Press, Albuquerque.

———. 2005. *Mimbres Painted Pottery*. 2nd ed. School of American Research Press, Santa Fe, NM.

Brody, J. J., Catherine J. Scott, and Steven A. LeBlanc. 1983. *Mimbres Pottery: Ancient Art of the American Southwest*. Hudson Hills Press, New York.

Brody, J. J., and Rina Swentzell. 1996. *To Touch the Past: The Painted Pottery of the Mimbres People*. Hudson Hills Press, New York.

Bryson, Norman. 1992. Art in context. In *Studies in Historical Change*, edited by R. Cohen, pp. 18–42. University of Virginia Press, Charlottesville.

Bunzel, Ruth. 1929. *The Pueblo Potter*. Columbia University Press, New York.

Butcher, Russell D. 1968. Winged messengers. *El Palacio* 75:39–43.

Carr, Christopher. 1995. A unified middle-range theory of artifact design. In *Style, Society, and Person*, edited by C. Carr and J. E. Neitzel, pp. 171–258. Plenum Press, New York.

Carr, Christopher, and Jill E. Neitzel (eds.). 1995. *Style, Society, and Person*. Plenum Press, New York.

Carr, Patricia. 1979. *Mimbres Mythology*. Southwestern Studies 56. University of Texas, El Paso.

Carroll, Noel (ed.). 2000. *Theories of Art Today*. University of Wisconsin Press, Madison.

Chamberlin, Matthew. In press. A practical religion: Plazas and performance in the Ancestral Pueblo world. In *Gathering Ancestors: Religious Transformation in the Pueblo World*, edited by D. M. Glowacki and S. Van Keuren. University of Arizona Press, Tucson.

Chapman, Kenneth M. 1916. The evolution of the bird in decorative art. *Art and Archaeology* 4(6):307–16.

———. 1917a. The cave pictographs of the Rito de los Frijoles. *Papers of the School of American Archaeology*.

———. 1917b. Conservatism in the evolution of decorative art. *Papers of the School of American Archaeology*.

———. 1923. Casas Grandes pottery. *Art and Archaeology* 16(1–2):25–34.

Chenault, Mark L., and John M. Lindly. 2006. Guanacos, symbolism, and religion during the Hohokam Preclassic. In *Religion in the Prehispanic Southwest*, edited by C. S. VanPool, T. L. VanPool, and D. A. Phillips Jr., pp. 115–34. AltaMira Press, Lanham, MD.

Chippindale, Christopher. 1992. Grammars of archaeological design: A generative and geometrical approach to the form of artifacts. In *Representations in Archaeology*, edited by J.-C. Gardin and C. S. Peebles, pp. 251–76. Indiana University Press, Bloomington.

———. 2001. Studying ancient pictures as pictures. In *Handbook of Rock Art Research*, edited by D. S. Whitley, pp. 247–72. AltaMira, New York.

———. 2004. From millimetre up to kilometre: A framework of space and of scale for reporting and studying rock-art in its landscape. In *The Figured Landscapes of Rock-Art: Looking at Pictures in Place*, edited by C. Chippindale and G. Nash, pp. 102–17. Cambridge University Press, Cambridge.

Chippindale, Christopher, and George Nash. 2004. Pictures in place: Approaches to the figured landscapes of rock-art. In *The Figured Landscapes of Rock-Art: Looking at Pictures in Place*, edited by C. Chippindale and G. Nash, pp. 1–36. Cambridge University Press, Cambridge.

Christensen, Don D. 1994. Rock art, ceramics, and textiles: The validity of unifying art motifs. In *Rock Art Papers*, vol. 11, edited by K. Hedges, pp. 107–16. San Diego Museum of Man, San Diego, CA.

Clegg, John. 1986. Two feet on one hind leg: Ambiguity in some prehistoric pictures. In *By Hands Unknown: Papers in Honor of James G. Bain*, edited by A. Poore, pp. 86–102. Papers of the Archaeological Society of New Mexico, vol. 12. Ancient City Press, Santa Fe.

Cobb, Charles R., Jeffrey Maymon, and Randall H. McGuire. 1999. Feathered, horned, and antlered serpents: Mesoamerican connections with the Southwest and Southeast. In *Great Towns and Regional Polities in the Prehistoric American Southwest and Southeast*, edited by J. E. Neitzel, pp. 165–82. University of New Mexico Press, Albuquerque.

Cohodas, Marvin, and Barbara DeMott. 1985. Meaning of women's arts in North America. *Phoebus* 4:99–106.

Cole, Sally J. 1984. *The Abo Painted Rocks: Documentation and Analysis.* Privately printed, Grand Junction, CO.

———. 1989. Katsina iconography in Homol'ovi rock art. *Kiva* 54(3):319–29.

———. 1992. *Katsina Iconography in Homol'ovi Rock Art: Central Little Colorado River Valley, Arizona.* Arizona Archaeologist 25. Arizona Archaeological Society, Phoenix.

———. 1994. Roots of Anasazi and Pueblo imagery in Basketmaker II rock art and material culture. *Kiva* 60(2):289–311.

———. 2006. Imagery and tradition: Murals of the Mesa Verde region. In *The Mesa Verde World: Explorations in Ancestral Pueblo Archaeology*, edited by D. G. Noble, pp. 92–99. School for Advanced Research Press, Santa Fe, NM.

Colton, Mary-Russell F., and Harold S. Colton. 1943. An appreciation of the art of Nampeyo and her influence on Hopi pottery. *Plateau* 15(3):43–45.

Colwell-Chanthaphonh, Chip. 2004. Those obscure objects of desire: Collecting cultures and the archaeological landscape in the San Pedro Valley of Arizona. *Journal of Contemporary Ethnography* 10(33):571–601.

———. 2008. Artist unknown: The significance of signatures on Pueblo pottery. In *A River Apart: The Pottery of Cochiti and Santo Domingo Pueblos*, edited by V. K. Verzuh, pp. 17–31. Museum of New Mexico Press, Santa Fe.

Congdon, Kristin G. 1987. Toward a theoretical approach to teaching folk art: A definition. *Studies in Art Education* 28(2):96–104.

Conkey, Margaret W. 1987. New approaches in the search for meaning? A review of research in "Paleolithic art." *Journal of Field Archaeology* 14(4):413–30.

———. 2006. Style, design, and function. In *Handbook of Material Culture*, edited by C. Tilley, W. Keane, S. Kuchler, M. J. Rowlands, and P. Spyer, pp. 355–72. Sage, London.

Conkey, Margaret W., and Christine Hastorf (eds.). 1990. *The Uses of Style in Archaeology.* Cambridge University Press, New York.

Conkey, Margaret W., Olga Soffer, Deborah Stratmann, and Nina G. Jablonski (eds.). 1997. *Beyond Art: Pleistocene Image and Symbol.* University of California Press, San Francisco.

Coote, Jeremy. 1992. "Marvels of everyday vision": The anthropology of aesthetics and the cattle-keeping Nilotes. In *Anthropology, Art, and Aesthetics*, edited by J. Coote and A. Shelton, pp. 245–73. Oxford University Press, New York.

———. 1996. Debate: Aesthetics is a cross-cultural category: For the motion (2). In *Key Debates in Anthropology*, edited by T. Ingold, pp. 266–71. Routledge, London.

———. 2005. "Marvels of everyday vision": The anthropology of aesthetics and the cattle-keeping Nilotes. In *The Anthropology of Art: A Reader*, edited by H. Morphy and M. Perkins, pp. 281–301. Blackwell, Malden, MA.

Cordell, Linda S. 1997. *Archaeology of the Southwest.* Academic Press, San Diego, CA.

Cosgrove, C. B. 1947. *Caves of the Upper Gila and Hueco Areas in New Mexico and Texas*. Papers of the Peabody Museum of American Archaeology and Ethnology 24. Harvard University, Cambridge, MA.

Cosgrove, H. S., and C. B. Cosgrove. 1932. *The Swarts Ruin: A Typical Mimbres Site in Southwestern New Mexico*. Papers of the Peabody Museum of American Archaeology and Ethnology 15(1). Harvard University, Cambridge, MA.

Costall, Alan. 1985. How meaning covers the traces. In *Visual Order*, edited by N. H. Freeman and M. V. Cox, pp. 17–30. Cambridge University Press, Cambridge.

———. 1997. Things and things like them. In *The Cultural Life of Images: Visual Representation in Archaeology*, edited by B. L. Molyneaux, pp. 49–59. Routledge, New York.

Creel, Darrell G. 1989. Anthropomorphic rock art figures in the middle Mimbres Valley, New Mexico. *Kiva* 55:71–86.

Crotty, Helen K. 1983. *Honoring the Dead: Anasazi Ceramics from the Rainbow Bridge–Monument Valley Expedition*. UCLA Museum of Cultural History Monograph Series 22. University of California, Los Angeles.

———. 1990. Formal qualities of the Jornada style and Pueblo IV Anasazi rock art: A comparison with implications for the origins of Pueblo ceremonialism. *American Indian Rock Art* 16:147–66.

———. 1992. Protohistoric Anasazi kiva murals: Variation in imagery as a reflection of differing social contexts. In *Archaeology, Art, and Anthropology: Papers in Honor of J. J. Brody*, edited by M. S. Duran and D. T. Kirkpatrick, pp. 51–61. Papers of the Archaeological Society of New Mexico, vol. 18. Archaeological Society of New Mexico, Albuquerque.

———. 1995. Anasazi Mural Art of the Pueblo IV Period, A.D. 1300–1600: Influences, Selective Adaptation, and Cultural Diversity in the Prehistoric Southwest. Ph.D. dissertation, University of California, Los Angeles.

———. 2007. Western Pueblo influences and integration in the Pottery Mound painted kivas. In *New Perspectives on Pottery Mound Pueblo*, edited by P. Schaafsma, pp. 85–107. University of New Mexico Press, Albuquerque.

Crown, Patricia L. 1994. *Ceramics and Ideology: Salado Polychrome Pottery*. University of New Mexico Press, Albuquerque.

———. 1999. Socialization in American Southwest pottery decoration. In *Pottery and People: A Dynamic Interaction*, edited by J. M. Skibo and G. M. Feinman, pp. 25–43. University of Utah Press, Salt Lake City.

———. 2001. Learning to make pottery in the prehispanic American Southwest. *Journal of Anthropological Research* 57(4):451–70.

———. 2002. Learning and teaching in the prehispanic American Southwest. In *Children in the Prehistoric Puebloan Southwest*, edited by K. A. Kamp, pp. 108–24. University of Utah Press, Salt Lake City.

———. 2007. Life histories of pots and potters: Situating the individual in archaeology. *American Antiquity* 72(4):677–90.

Crown, Patricia L., and Suzanne K. Fish. 1996. Gender and status in the Hohokam Pre-classic to Classic transition. *American Anthropologist* 98(4):803–17.

Crown, Patricia L., and W. Jeffrey Hurst. 2009. Evidence of cacao use in the Prehispanic American Southwest. *Proceedings of the National Academy of Sciences* 106(7):2110–13.

Crown, Patricia L., and W. H. Wills. 2003. Modifying pottery and kivas at Chaco: Pentimento, restoration or renewal? *American Antiquity* 68(2):511–32.

Cumming, Elizabeth. 1991. *The Arts and Crafts Movement*. The Story of Art. Thames and Hudson, New York.

Cushing, Frank Hamilton. 1890. Preliminary notes on the origin, working hypotheses, and preliminary researches of the Hemenway Southwestern Expedition. In *Congrès International des Americanistes, Compte Rendu de la Septième Session*, pp. 151–94. W. H. Kuhl, Berlin.

Danto, Arthur C. 1964. The artworld. *Journal of Philosophy* 61(19):571–84.

———. 1988. Artifact and art. In *ART/artifact: African Art in Anthropology Collections*, edited by S. M. Vogel, pp. 18–32. Center for African Art, New York.

Dark, P.J.C. 1978. What is art for anthropologists? In *Art in Society: Studies in Style, Culture, and Aesthetics*, edited by M. Greenhalgh and V. Megaw, pp. 31–50. St. Martin's Press, New York.

David, Bruno. 2004. Intentionality, agency, and an archaeology of choice. *Cambridge Archaeological Journal* 14:67–71.

Davies, Stephen. 2000. Non-Western art and art's definition. In *Theories of Art Today*, edited by N. Carroll, pp. 199–216. University of Wisconsin Press, Madison.

Davis, Whitney. 1989. *The Canonical Tradition in Ancient Egyptian Art*. Cambridge University Press, Cambridge.

———. 1993. Beginning the history of art. *Journal of Aesthetics and Art Criticism* 51(3):327–50.

———. 1995. *Replications: Archaeology, Art History, Psychoanalysis*. Penn State University Press, University Park, PA.

d'Azevedo, Warren L. 1958. A structural approach to esthetics: Toward a definition of art in anthropology. *American Anthropologist* 60(4):702–14.

DeBoer, Warren R. 1990. Interaction, imitation, and communication as expressed in style: The Ucayali experience. In *The Uses of Style in Archaeology*, edited by M. W. Conkey and C. Hastorf, pp. 82–104. Cambridge University Press, New York.

———. 1991. The decorative burden. In *Ceramic Ethnoarchaeology*, edited by W. Longacre, pp. 144–61. University of Arizona Press, Tucson.

Deregowski, J. B. 1980. *Illusions, Patterns, and Pictures: A Cross-Cultural Perspective*. Academic Press, New York.

———. 2005. Perception and ways of drawing: Why animals are easier to draw than people. In *Aesthetics and Rock Art*, edited by T. Heyd and J. Clegg, pp. 131–42. Ashgate, Burlington, VT.

Dickie, George. 1974. *Art and the Aesthetic: An Institutional Analysis*. Cornell University Press, Ithaca, NY.

Dikovitskaya, Margaret. 2005. *Visual Culture: The Study of the Visual after the Cultural Turn*. MIT Press, Cambridge, MA.

Di Peso, Charles C. 1974. *Casas Grandes: A Fallen Trading Center of the Gran Chichimeca*. Amerind Foundation, Dragoon, AZ.

Dissanayake, Ellen. 1982. Aesthetic experience and human evolution. *Journal of Aesthetics and Art Criticism* 41(2):145–55.

———. 1999. *Homo Aestheticus: Where Art Comes From and Why*. University of Washington Press, Seattle.

Domingo Sanz, Inés, Dánae Fiore, and Sally K. May (eds.). 2008. *Archaeologies of Art: Time, Place, and Identity*. Left Coast Press, Walnut Creek, CA.

Donnan, Christopher B., and Donna McClelland. 1999. *Moche Fineline Painting: Its Evolution and Its Artists*. UCLA Fowler Museum of Cultural History, Los Angeles.

Donne, J. B. 1978. African art and Paris studios 1905–20. In *Art in Society: Studies in Style, Culture, and Aesthetics*, edited by M. Greenhalgh and V. Megaw, pp. 105–20. St. Martin's Press, New York.

Douglas, John E. 1992. Distant sources, local contexts: Interpreting nonlocal ceramics at Paquimé (Casas Grandes), Chihuahua. *Journal of Anthropological Research* 48(1):1–24.

Douglas, Mary. 1996. *Natural Symbols: Explorations in Cosmology*. Routledge, London, UK.

Driscoll-Engelstad, Bernadette. 1996. Beyond anonymity: The emergence of textile artists in the Canadian Arctic. *Museum Anthropology* 20(3):26–38.

Duran, Meliha S., and Helen K. Crotty. 1994. *Three Rivers Petroglyph Site: Results of the ASNM Rock Art Recording Field School*. Human Systems Research, Inc. HSR Report No. 9301.

Dutton, Bertha P. 1963. *Sun Father's Way*. University of New Mexico Press, Albuquerque.

Dutton, Denis. 2000. "But they don't have our concept of art." In *Theories of Art Today*, edited by N. Carroll, pp. 217–38. University of Wisconsin Press, Madison.

———. 2009. *The Art Instinct: Beauty, Pleasure, and Human Evolution*. Bloomsbury Press, New York.

Eckert, Suzanne L. 2006. Black-on-white to glaze-on-red: Migration, ritual, and exchange in the Middle Rio Grande. In *The Social Life of Pots: Glaze Wares and Cultural Dynamics in the Southwest, AD 1250–1680*, edited by J. A. Habicht-Mauche, S. L. Eckert, and D. L. Huntley, pp. 163–78. University of Arizona Press, Tucson.

———. 2007. Understanding the dynamics of segregation and incorporation at Pottery Mound through analysis of glaze-decorated bowls. In *New Perspectives on Pottery Mound Pueblo*, edited by P. Schaafsma, pp. 55–73. University of New Mexico Press, Albuquerque.

Eerkens, Jelmer W. 2000. Practice makes within 5% of perfect: Visual perception, motor skills, and memory in artifact variation. *Current Anthropology* 41(4):664–68.

Eerkens, Jelmer W., and Robert L. Bettinger. 2001. Techniques for assessing standardization in artifact assemblages: Can we scale material variability? *American Antiquity* 66(3):493–504.

Ekholm, Gordon R. 1959. Art in archaeology. In *Aspects of Primitive Art*, edited by R. Redfield, M. J. Herskovits, and G. R. Ekholm, pp. 70–88. Museum of Primitive Art, New York.

Elsner, Jas. 1995. *Art and the Roman Viewer: The Transformation of Art from the Pagan World to Christianity*. Cambridge University Press, Cambridge.

———. 2007. *Roman Eyes: Visuality and Subjectivity in Art and Text*. Princeton University Press, Princeton, NJ.

Errington, Shelly. 1994. What became authentic primitive art? *Cultural Anthropology* 9(2):201–26.

———. 1998. *The Death of Authentic Primitive Art and Other Tales of Progress*. University of California Press, Berkeley.

———. 2005. History now: Post-tribal art. In *Anthropologies of Art*, edited by M. Westermann, pp. 221–41. Yale University Press, New Haven, CT.

Espenshade, Christopher T. 1997. Mimbres pottery, births, and gender: A reconsideration. *American Antiquity* 62(4):733–36.

Evans, Christopher. 2004. Unearthing displacement: Surrealism and the "archaeology" of Paul Nash. In *Substance, Memory, Display: Archaeology and Art*, edited by C. Renfrew, C. Gosden, and E. DeMarrais, pp. 103–17. McDonald Institute for Archaeological Research, Cambridge, UK.

Ewers, John C. 1981. The emergence of the named Indian artist in the American West. *American Indian Art* 6(2):52–61, 77.

Farmer, James D. 2001. Goggle eyes and crested serpents of Barrier Canyon: Early Mesoamerican iconography and the American Southwest. In *The Road to Aztlan: Art from a Mythic Homeland*, edited by V. M. Fields and V. Zamudio-Taylor, pp. 123–37. Los Angeles County Museum of Art, Los Angeles.

Ferg, Alan. 1982. 14th century kachina depictions on ceramics. In *Collected Papers in Honor of John W. Runyan*, edited by G. X. Fitzgerald, pp. 13–29. Papers of the Archaeological Society of New Mexico, vol. 7. Archeological Society of New Mexico, Albuquerque.

Fewkes, J. Walter. 1892. A few Tusayan pictographs. *American Anthropologist* 5:9–26.

———. 1903. Hopi katcinas, drawn by native artists. In *Twenty-First Annual Report of the Bureau of American Ethnology to the Secretary of the Smithsonian Institution, 1899–1900*, edited by J. W. Powell, pp. 3–126. Government Printing Office, Washington, DC.

———. 1914. *Archaeology of the Lower Mimbres Valley, New Mexico.* Smithsonian Miscellaneous Collections 63, no. 10. Smithsonian Institution, Washington, DC.

———. 1923. *Designs on Prehistoric Pottery from the Mimbres Valley, New Mexico.* Smithsonian Miscellaneous Collections 74, no. 6. Smithsonian Institution, Washington, DC.

———. 1924. *Additional Designs on Prehistoric Mimbres Pottery.* Smithsonian Miscellaneous Collections 76, no. 8. Smithsonian Institution, Washington, DC.

Firth, Raymond. 1995 [1936]. *Art and Life in New Guinea.* AMS Press, New York.

Foster, Michael S., and Steven R. James. 2004. Dogs, deer, or guanacos: Zoomorphic figurines from Pueblo Grande, central Arizona. *Journal of Field Archaeology* 29(1–2):165–76.

Fowles, Severin M. 2004. Tewa versus Tiwa: Northern Rio Grande settlement patterns and social history, AD 1275–1540. In *The Protohistoric Pueblo World, A.D. 1275–1600,* edited by E. C. Adams and A. I. Duff, pp. 17–25. University of Arizona Press, Tucson.

———. 2008. Katsinalessness, or why the Northern Tiwa didn't make pictures of spirits. Paper presented at the 73rd Annual Meeting of the Society for American Archaeology. Vancouver, BC.

Galison, Peter. 1998. Judgment against objectivity. In *Picturing Science, Producing Art,* edited by C. A. Jones and P. Galison, pp. 327–59. Routledge, London, UK.

Gaut, Berys. 2000. "Art" as a cluster concept. In *Theories of Art Today,* edited by N. Carroll, pp. 25–44. University of Wisconsin Press, Madison.

Gedo, John E. 1996. *The Artist and the Emotional World: Creativity and Personality.* Columbia University Press, New York.

Gell, Alfred. 1992. The technology of enchantment and the enchantment of technology. In *Anthropology, Art and Aesthetics,* edited by J. Coote and A. Shelton, pp. 40–63. Oxford University Press, New York.

———. 1995. On Coote's "Marvels of everyday vision." *Social Analysis* 38:18–31.

———. 1996. Vogel's net: Traps as artworks and artworks as traps. *Journal of Material Culture* 1(1):15–38.

———. 1998. *Art and Agency: An Anthropological Theory.* Oxford University Press, Oxford, UK.

———. 2005. Vogel's net: Traps as artworks and artworks as traps. In *The Anthropology of Art: A Reader,* edited by H. Morphy and M. Perkins, pp. 219–35. Blackwell, Malden, MA.

Gerbrands, Adrian. 1969. The concept of style in non-Western art. In *Tradition and Creativity in Tribal Art,* edited by D. Biebuyck, pp. 58–70. University of California Press, Berkeley.

Gill, David W. J., and Christopher Chippindale. 1993. Material and intellectual consequences of esteem for Cycladic figures. *American Journal of Archaeology* 97:601–59.

Gilman, Patricia A., Ronald L. Bishop, and Veletta Canouts. 1994. The production and distribution of Classic Mimbres black-on-white pottery. *American Antiquity* 59(4):695–709.

Gladwin, Harold S., Emil W. Haury, E. B. Sayles, and Nora Gladwin. 1937. *Excavations at Snaketown: Material Culture.* Medallion Papers 25. Gila Pueblo, Globe, AZ.

Goldstein, Judith L. 1994. The devil and the art world: Notes on the reenchantment of art. *Visual Anthropology Review* 10(1):1–9.

Gombrich, Ernst H. 1969. *Art and Illusion: A Study in the Psychology of Pictorial Representation.* Princeton University Press, Princeton, NJ.

Gosden, Chris (ed.). 2001. *World Archaeology: Special Issue on Archaeology and Aesthetics* 33(2).

Gow, Peter. 1996. Debate: Aesthetics is a cross-cultural category: Against the motion (2). In *Key Debates in Anthropology*, edited by T. Ingold, pp. 271–75. Routledge, London.

Graburn, Nelson H. H. 1976. *Ethnic and Tourist Arts: Cultural Expressions from the Fourth World.* University of California Press, Los Angeles.

Grant, Campbell. 1978. *Canyon de Chelly.* University of Arizona Press, Tucson.

Graves, David C. 2002. Art and the Zen Master's tea pot: The role of aesthetics in the institutional theory of art. *Journal of Aesthetics and Art Criticism* 60(4):341–52.

Graves, Michael W. 1982. Breaking down ceramic variation: Testing models of White Mountain redware design style development. *Journal of Anthropological Archaeology* 1:305–54.

Graves, William. 2002. Fundamental transformations in Rio Grande glazeware aesthetics. Paper presented at the 67th Annual Meeting of the Society for American Archaeology, Denver, CO.

Graves, William M., and Suzanne L. Eckert. 1998. Decorated ceramic distributions and ideological developments in the Northern and Central Rio Grande Valley, New Mexico. In *Migration and Reorganization: The Pueblo IV Period in the American Southwest*, edited by K. A. Spielmann, pp. 263–83. Anthropological Research Papers 51, Arizona State University, Tempe.

Graves, William M., and Katherine A. Spielmann. 2000. Leadership, long distance exchange, and feasting in the protohistoric Rio Grande. In *Alternative Leadership Strategies in the Greater Southwest*, edited by B. J. Mills, pp. 45–59. University of Arizona Press, Tucson.

Greene, Candace S. 2001. Art until 1900. In *Plains*, edited by R. J. DeMallie, pp. 1039–54. Handbook of North American Indians, vol. 13. Smithsonian Institution, Washington, DC.

Guernsey, Samuel J., and A. V. Kidder. 1921. *Basket-maker Caves of Northeastern Arizona: Report on the Explorations, 1916–17.* Papers of the Peabody Museum of American Archaeology and Ethnology, Harvard University, Cambridge, MA.

Guthe, Carl Eugen. 1925. *Pueblo Pottey Making: A Study at the Village of San Ildefonso.* Yale University Press, New Haven, CT.

Haas, William Randall, Jr. 2006. The social implications of Basketmaker II cord-age design distribution. *Kiva* 71(3):275–98.

Habicht-Mauche, Judith A. 2006. The social history of Southwestern glaze wares. In *The Social Life of Pots: Glaze Wares and Cultural Dynamics in the Southwest, AD 1250–1680*, edited by J. A. Habicht-Mauche, S. L. Eckert, and D. L. Huntley, pp. 3–16. University of Arizona Press, Tucson.

Habicht-Mauche, Judith A., Suzanne L. Eckert, and Deborah L. Huntley (eds.). 2006. *The Social Life of Pots: Glaze Wares and Cultural Dynamics in the Southwest, AD 1250–1680*. University of Arizona Press, Tucson.

Hagen, Margaret A. 1986. *Varieties of Realism: Geometries of Representational Art*. Cambridge University Press, New York.

Hagstrum, Melissa B. 1985. Measuring prehistoric ceramic craft specialization: A test case in the American Southwest. *Journal of Field Archaeology* 12:65–75.

———. 1995. Creativity and craft: Household pottery traditions in the American Southwest. In *Ceramic Production in the American Southwest*, edited by B. J. Mills and P. L. Crown, pp. 281–99. University of Arizona Press, Tucson.

Hall, Edward T. 1966. *The Hidden Dimension*. Doubleday, Garden City, NY.

———. 1968. Proxemics. *Current Anthropology* 9(2–3):83–95.

Halseth, Odd. 1926. The revival of Pueblo pottery making. *El Palacio* 21(6):135–54.

Hamilton, Naomi. 1996. The personal as political. *Cambridge Archaeological Journal* 6(2):282–85.

Hardin, Kris L. 1988. Aesthetics and the cultural whole: A study of Kono dance occasions. *Empirical Studies of the Arts* 6(1):35–57.

Hardin, Margaret Ann. 1991. Sources of ceramic variability at Zuni Pueblo. In *Ceramic Ethnoarchaeology*, edited by W. Longacre, pp. 40–70. University of Arizona Press, Tucson.

Harmon, Marcel J. 2006. Religion and the Mesoamerican ball game in the Casas Grandes region of northern Mexico. In *Religion in the Prehispanic Southwest*, edited by C. S. VanPool, T. L. VanPool, and D. A. Phillips Jr., pp. 185–218. AltaMira Press, Lanham, MD.

Hartley, Ralph J. 1992. *Rock Art on the Northern Colorado Plateau: Variability in Content and Context*. Ashgate, Brookfield, VT.

Hartley, Ralph, and Anne M. Wolley Vawser. 1998. Spatial behaviour and learning in the prehistoric environment of the Colorado River drainage (south-eastern Utah), western North America. In *The Archaeology of Rock-Art*, edited by C. Chippindale and P.S.C. Taçon, pp. 185–211. Cambridge University Press, New York.

Haury, Emil W. 1934. *The Canyon Creek Ruin and the Cliff Dwellers of the Sierra Ancha*. Medallion Papers 14. Gila Pueblo, Globe, AZ.

———. 1936. *The Mogollon Culture of Southwestern New Mexico*. Medallion Papers 20. Gila Pueblo, Globe, AZ.

———. 1945. *The Excavation of Los Muertos and Neighboring Ruins in the Salt River Valley, Southern Arizona*. Papers of the Peabody Museum of American Archaeology and Ethnology 24, Harvard University, Cambridge, MA.

Hayes, Alden C., Jon Nathan Young and A. Helene Warren (editors). 1981. Excavation of Mound 7: Gran Quivira National Monument, New Mexico. Publications in Archeology 16. National Park Service, Washington, DC.

Haynes, Deborah J. 1997. *The Vocation of the Artist*. Cambridge University Press, New York.

Hays, Kelley Ann. 1989. Katsina depictions on Homol'ovi ceramics: Toward a fourteenth century Pueblo iconography. *Kiva* 54:297–311.

———. 1992. Shalako depictions on prehistoric Hopi pottery. In *Archaeology, Art, and Anthropology: Papers in Honor of J. J. Brody*, edited by M. S. Duran and D. T. Kirkpatrick, pp. 73–83. Papers of the Archaeological Society of New Mexico, vol. 18. Archaeological Society of New Mexico, Albuquerque.

———. 1994. Kachina depictions on prehistoric Pueblo pottery. In *Kachinas in the Pueblo World*, edited by P. Schaafsma, pp. 47–62. University of New Mexico Press, Albuquerque.

Hays-Gilpin, Kelley. 1995. Art and archaeology of the Puebloan region: New views from the basement. *Museum Anthropology* 19(3):47–57.

———. 1996. Commercialization before capitalists: Hopi ceramic production and trade in the fourteenth century. *Journal of the Southwest* 38(4):395–414.

———. 1999. The Flower World in material culture: An iconographic complex in the Southwest and Mesoamerica. *Journal of Anthropological Research* 55(1):1–37.

———. 2000. Gender ideology and ritual activities. In *Women and Men in the Prehispanic Southwest: Labor, Power, and Prestige*, edited by P. L. Crown, pp. 91–135. School of American Research Press, Santa Fe, NM.

———. 2002. Wearing a butterfly, coming of age: A 1500 year old Pueblo tradition. In *Children in the Prehistoric Puebloan Southwest*, edited by K. A. Kamp, pp. 196–210. University of Utah Press, Salt Lake City.

———. 2004. *Ambiguous Images: Gender and Rock Art*. AltaMira Press, New York.

———. 2006. Icons and ethnicity: Hopi painted pottery and murals. In *Religion in the Prehispanic Southwest*, edited by C. S. VanPool, T. L. VanPool, and D. A. Phillips Jr., pp. 67–80. AltaMira Press, Lanham, MD.

Hays-Gilpin, Kelley, and Michelle Hegmon. 2005. The art of ethnobotany: Depictions of maize and other plants in the prehispanic Southwest. In *Engaged Anthropology: Research Essays on North American Archaeology, Ethnobotany, and Museology*, edited by M. Hegmon and B. S. Eiselt, pp. 89–113. Anthropological Papers, University of Michigan Museum of Anthropology, vol. 94. University of Michigan, Ann Arbor.

Hays-Gilpin, Kelley, and Steven A. LeBlanc. 2007. Sikyatki style in regional context. In *New Perspectives on Pottery Mound Pueblo*, edited by P. Schaafsma, pp. 109–36. University of New Mexico Press, Albuquerque.

Hedges, Ken. 1993. Places to see and places to hear: Rock art and features of the sacred landscape. In *Time and Space: Dating and Spatial Considerations in Rock Art Research*, edited by J. Steinbring, A. Watchman, P. Faulstich, and P.S.C. Taçon, pp. 121–27. Occasional AURA Publication 8. Australian Rock Art Research Association, Melbourne.

Hegmon, Michelle. 1986. Information exchange and integration on Black Mesa, Arizona, A.D. 931–1150. In *Spatial Organization and Exchange: Archaeological Survey on Northern Black Mesa*, edited by S. Plog, pp. 256–81. Southern Illinois University Press, Carbondale.

———. 1992. Archaeological research on style. *Annual Review of Anthropology* 21:517–36.

———. 2002. Recent issues in the archaeology of the Mimbres region of the North American Southwest. *Journal of Archaeological Research* 10(4):307–57.

Hegmon, Michelle, and Stephanie Kulow. 2005. Painting as agency, style as structure: Innovations in Mimbres pottery designs from Southwest New Mexico. *Journal of Archaeological Method and Theory* 12(4):313–34.

Hegmon, Michelle, and Margaret C. Nelson. 2007. In sync, but barely in touch: Relations between the Mimbres region and the Hohokam regional system. In *Hinterlands and Regional Dynamics in the Ancient Southwest*, edited by A. P. Sullivan and J. Bayman, pp. 70–96. University of Arizona Press, Tucson.

Hegmon, Michelle, Margaret C. Nelson, and Susan M. Ruth. 1998. Abandonment and reorganization in the Mimbres region of the American Southwest. *American Anthropologist* 100:148–62.

Hegmon, Michelle, and Wenda R. Trevathan. 1996. Gender, anatomical knowledge, and pottery production: Implications of an anatomically unusual birth depicted on Mimbres pottery from southwestern New Mexico. *American Antiquity* 61(4):747–54.

———. 1997. Response to comments by LeBlanc, by Espenshade, and by Shaffer et al. *American Antiquity* 62(4):737–39.

Herhahn, Cynthia. 2006. Inferring social interactions from pottery recipes: Rio Grande glaze paint composition and cultural transmission. In *The Social Life of Pots: Glaze Wares and Cultural Dynamics in the Southwest, AD 1250–1680*, edited by J. A. Habicht-Mauche, S. L. Eckert, and D. L. Huntley, pp. 179–96. University of Arizona Press, Tucson.

Herman, Josef. 1978. The modern artist in modern society. In *Art in Society: Studies in Style, Culture, and Aesthetics*, edited by M. Greenhalgh and V. Megaw, pp. 121–30. Duckworth, London, UK.

Herr, Sarah, and Susan Stinson. 2005. A potter's assemblage from Tla Kii Pueblo, Arizona. *Kiva* 71(1):57–78.

Heyd, Thomas. 2005. Aesthetics and rock art: An introduction. In *Aesthetics and Rock Art*, edited by T. Heyd and J. Clegg, pp. 1–17. Ashgate, Burlington, VT.

Heyd, Thomas, and John Clegg (eds.). 2005. *Aesthetics and Rock Art*. Ashgate, Burlington, VT.

Hibben, Frank C. 1975. *Kiva Art of the Anasazi at Pottery Mound*. KC Publications, Las Vegas, NV.

Hill, James N. 1970. *Broken K Pueblo: Prehistoric Social Organization in the American Southwest*. Anthropological Papers of the University of Arizona 18. University of Arizona Press, Tucson.

Hill, James N., and Joel Gunn (eds.). 1977. *The Individual in Prehistory: Studies of Variability in Style in Prehistoric Technologies.* Academic Press, New York.

Hough, Walter. 1923. Casas Grandes pottery in the National Museum. *Art and Archaeology* 16(1–2):34.

Howell, Todd L. 1995. Tracking Zuni gender and leadership roles across the contact period in the Zuni region. *Journal of Anthropological Research* 51:125–47.

Hucko, Bruce. 1996. *Where There Is No Name for Art: The Art of Tewa Pueblo Children.* School of American Research Press, Santa Fe, NM.

Huntington, Susan L. 1990. Early Buddhist art and the theory of aniconism. *Art Journal* 49(4):401–8.

Huntley, Deborah L. 2006. From recipe to identity: Exploring Zuni glaze ware communities of practice. In *The Social Life of Pots: Glaze Wares and Cultural Dynamics in the Southwest, AD 1250–1680,* edited by J. A. Habicht-Mauche, S. L. Eckert, and D. L. Huntley, pp. 105–23. University of Arizona Press, Tucson.

Huse, Hannah. 1976. Identification of the Individual in Archaeology: A Case Study from the Prehistoric Hopi Site of Kawaika-a. Unpublished Ph.D. dissertation, Department of Anthropology, University of Colorado, Boulder.

Hyder, William D. 1997. Basketmaker social identity: Rock art as culture and praxis. In *Rock Art as Visual Ecology,* edited by P. Faulstich, pp. 31–42. International Rock Art Conference Proceedings, vol. 1. American Rock Art Research Association, Tucson, AZ.

Ingold, Tim. 2001. Beyond art and technology: The anthropology of skill. In *Anthropological Perspectives on Technology,* edited by M. B. Schiffer, pp. 17–31. University of New Mexico Press, Albuquerque.

Inomata, Takeshi, and Lawrence S. Coben (eds.). 2006. *The Archaeology of Performance: Theaters of Power, Community, and Politics.* AltaMira Press, Lanham, MD.

Jamison, Kay Redfield. 1996. *Touched with Fire: Manic-Depressive Illness and the Artistic Temperament.* Free Press, New York.

Jenks, Albert Ernest. 1932. Geometric designs on Mimbres bowls. *Art and Archaeology* 33(3):137–39, 158.

Jernigan, E. Wesley. 1978. *Jewelry of the Prehistoric Southwest.* School of American Research Press, Santa Fe, NM.

Jett, Stephen C., and Peter B. Moyle. 1986. The exotic origins of fishes depicted on prehistoric Mimbres pottery from New Mexico. *American Antiquity* 51:688–720.

Johnson, Ann Stofer. 1958. Similarities in Hohokam and Chalchihuites artifacts. *American Antiquity* 24(2):126–30.

Jolie, Edward A. 2007. Technology, learning, and innovation in textile arts: Integrating archaeological and ethnographic perspectives. Paper presented at Weaving Together: Archaeological Organic Artifact Analysis and Textile Arts, Red Bank, New Brunswick.

Jones, Caroline A., and Peter Galison. 1998. Introduction: Picturing science, producing art. In *Picturing Science, Producing Art,* edited by C. A. Jones and P. Galison, pp. 1–23. Routledge, London, UK.

Jones, K., and Michelle Hegmon. 1991. The medium and the message: A survey of information conveyed by material culture in middle range societies. Paper presented at the 56th Annual Meeting of the Society for American Archaeology, New Orleans, LA.

Kabotie, Fred. 1949. *Designs from the Ancient Mimbreños with a Hopi Interpretation.* Graborn Press, San Francisco, CA.

Kamp, Kathryn A. 2001. Prehistoric children working and playing: A Southwestern case study in learning ceramics. *Journal of Anthropological Research* 57(4):427–50.

Kasfir, Sidney Littlefield. 2000. Artists' reputations: Negotiating power through separation and ambiguity. *African Arts* 33(1):70–76, 96.

Keller, Charles M. 2001. Thought and production: Insights of the practitioner. In *Anthropological Perspectives on Technology*, edited by M. B. Schiffer, pp. 33–46. University of New Mexico Press, Albuquerque.

Kent, Kate Peck. 1983a. *Prehistoric Textiles of the Southwest.* University of New Mexico Press, Albuquerque.

———. 1983b. Temporal shifts in the structure of traditional Southwestern textile design. In *Structure and Cognition in Art*, edited by D. K. Washburn, pp. 113–37. Cambridge University Press, Cambridge.

Kim, Nanyoung. 2004. Ernst H. Gombrich, pictorial representation, and some issues in art education. *Journal of Aesthetic Education* 38(4):32–45.

King, J.C.H. 1986. Tradition in Native American art. In *Arts of the North American Indian: Native Traditions in Evolution*, edited by E. L. Wade, pp. 65–92. Hudson Hills Press, New York.

Kogman-Appel, Katrin. 2002. Hebrew manuscript painting in Late Medieval Spain: Signs of a culture in transition. *Art Bulletin* 84(2):246–72.

Kohler, Timothy A., Stephanie Van Buskirk, and Samantha M. Ruscavage-Barz. 2004. Vessels and villages: Evidence for conformist transmission in early village aggregations on the Pajarito Plateau, New Mexico. *Journal of Anthropological Archaeology* 23:100–18.

Kreps, Christina F. 2003. *Liberating Culture: Cross-cultural Perspectives on Museums, Curation, and Heritage Preservation.* Routledge, New York.

Kroeber, A. L. 1916. *Zuni Potsherds.* Anthropological Papers of the American Museum of Natural History 18. American Museum of Natural History, New York.

Lambert, Marjorie F. 1946. A Kokopelli effigy pitcher from northwestern New Mexico. *American Antiquity* 32(3):398–401.

Laszlo, Judith I., and Pia A. Broderick. 1985. The perceptual-motor skill of drawing. In *Visual Order*, edited by N. H. Freeman and M. V. Cox, pp. 356–73. Cambridge University Press, Cambridge.

Lawal, Babatunde. 1974. Some aspects of Yoruba aesthetics. *British Journal of Aesthetics* 14:239–49.

LeBlanc, Steven A. 1982. Temporal change in Mogollon ceramics. In *Southwestern Ceramics: A Comparative Review*, edited by A. H. Schroeder, pp. 106–27. Arizona Archaeological Society, Phoenix.

———. 1983. *The Mimbres People: Ancient Pueblo Painters of the American Southwest.* Thames and Hudson, New York.

———. 1997. A comment on Hegmon and Trevathan's "Gender, anatomical knowledge, and pottery production." *American Antiquity* 62(4):723–26.

———. 2004. *Painted by a Distant Hand: Mimbres Pottery from the American Southwest.* Harvard University Press, Cambridge, MA.

———. 2006. Who made the Mimbres bowls? Implications of recognizing individual artists for craft specialization and social networks. In *Mimbres Society*, edited by V. Powell-Marti and P. A. Gilman, pp. 109–50. University of Arizona Press, Tucson.

LeBlanc, Steven A., and Lucia R. Henderson. 2009. *Symbols in Clay: Seeking Artists' Identities in Hopi Yellow Ware Bowls.* Papers of the Peabody Museum of Archaeology and Ethnology, vol. 84. Harvard University, Cambridge, MA.

Lekson, Stephen H. 1992. Mimbres art and archaeology. In *Archaeology, Art, and Anthropology: Papers in Honor of J. J. Brody*, edited by M. S. Duran and D. T. Kirkpatrick, pp. 111–22. Papers of the Archaeological Society of New Mexico, vol. 18. Archaeological Society of New Mexico, Albuquerque.

Lewis, Candace K. 2002. Knowledge Is Power: Pigments, Painted Artifacts, and Chacoan Ritual Leaders. Unpublished M.A. thesis, Department of Anthropology, Northern Arizona University, Flagstaff.

Liebmann, Matthew. 2002. Signs of power and resistance: The (re)creation of Christian imagery and identities in the Pueblo Revolt era. In *Archaeologies of the Pueblo Revolt: Identity, Meaning, and Renewal in the Pueblo World*, edited by R. W. Preucel, pp. 132–44. University of New Mexico Press, Albuquerque.

Lindauer, Owen, and Bert Zaslow. 1994. Homologous style structures in Hohokam and Trincheras art. *Kiva* 59(3):319–44.

Linton, R. 1941. Primitive art. *Kenyon Review* 3:34–51.

Lipe, William D., and Michelle Hegmon (eds.). 1989. *The Architecture of Social Integration in Prehistoric Pueblos.* Crow Canyon Archaeological Center, Cortez, CO.

Longacre, William A. 1970. *Archaeology as Anthropology: A Case Study.* Anthropological Papers of the University of Arizona 17. University of Arizona Press, Tucson.

Malafouris, Lambros. 2007. Before and beyond representation: Towards an enactive conception of the Paleolithic image. In *Image and Imagination: A Global Prehistory of Figurative Representation*, edited by C. Renfrew and I. Morley, pp. 287–300. McDonald Institute of Archeological Research, University of Cambridge, Cambridge.

Malville, J. McKim, and Claudia Putnam. 1993. *Prehistoric Astronomy in the Southwest.* Johnson Books, Boulder, CO.

Maquet, Jacques. 1986. *The Aesthetic Experience: An Anthropologist Looks at the Visual Arts.* Yale University Press, New Haven, CT.

Marriott, Alice. 1982. The trade guild of the Southern Cheyenne women. In *Native North American Art History: Selected Readings*, edited by Z. P. Mathews and A. Jonaitis, pp. 247–55. Peek Publications, Palo Alto, CA.

Martin, Paul S. 1975. Early developments in Mogollon research. In *Archaeological Researches in Retrospect*, edited by G. R. Willey, pp. 3–29. Winthrop, Cambridge.

Mathien, Frances Joan. 1997. Ornaments of the Chaco Anasazi. In *Ceramics, Lithics, and Ornaments of Chaco Canyon: Analyses of Artifacts from the Chaco Project, 1971–1978, vol. 3, Lithics and Ornaments*, edited by F. J. Mathien, pp. 1119–1219. Publications in Archeology, Chaco Canyon Studies, vol. 18G. National Park Service, Santa Fe, NM.

McLennan, Bill, and Karen Duffek. 2000. *The Transforming Image: Painted Arts of Northwest Coast First Nations*. University of British Columbia Press, Vancouver.

Mettinger, Tryggve N. D. 1995. *No Graven Image? Israelite Aniconism in Its Ancient Near Eastern Context*. Almqvist and Wiksell, Stockholm, Sweden.

Meyers, Julia Isabell. 2007. Prehistoric Wall Decoration in the American Southwest: A Behavioral Approach. Unpublished Ph.D. dissertation, Department of Anthropology, University of Arizona, Tucson.

Miller, Daniel. 1991. Primitive art and the necessity of primitivism to art. In *Myth of Primitivism: Perspectives on Art*, edited by S. Hiller, pp. 50–71. Routledge, London, UK.

Mills, Barbara J. 2004a. The establishment and defeat of hierarchy: Inalienable possessions and the history of collective prestige structures in the Pueblo Southwest. *American Anthropologist* 106(2):238–51.

———. 2004b. *Identity, Feasting, and the Archaeology of the Greater Southwest*. University Press of Colorado, Boulder.

———. 2007. Performing the feast: Visual display and suprahousehold commensalism in the Puebloan Southwest. *American Antiquity* 72(2):210–39.

Mills, Barbara J., and Patricia L. Crown. 1995. Ceramic production in the American Southwest: An introduction. In *Ceramic Production in the American Southwest*, edited by B. J. Mills and P. L. Crown, pp. 1–29. University of Arizona Press, Tucson.

Mills, Barbara J., and T. J. Ferguson. 2008. Animate objects: Shell trumpets and ritual networks in the Greater Southwest. *Journal of Archaeological Method and Theory* 15:338–61.

Mills, Barbara J., and William H. Walker (eds.). 2008. *Memory Work: Archaeologies of Material Practices*. School for Advanced Research Press, Santa Fe, NM.

Minar, C. Jill. 2001. Motor skills and the learning process: The conservation of cordage final twist direction in communities of practice. *Journal of Anthropological Research* 57(4):381–405.

Minar, C. Jill, and Patricia L. Crown. 2001. Learning and craft production: An introduction. *Journal of Anthropological Research* 57(4):269–80.

Mithen, Steven (ed.). 1998. *Creativity in Human Evolution and Prehistory*. Routledge, London, UK.

———. 2004. Contemporary Western art and archaeology. In *Substance, Memory, Display: Archaeology and Art*, edited by C. Renfrew, C. Gosden, and E. DeMarrais, pp. 153–68. McDonald Institute for Archaeological Research, University of Cambridge, Cambridge.

Mobley-Tanaka, Jeannette L. 2002. Crossed cultures, crossed meanings: The manipulation of ritual imagery in early Historic Pueblo resistance. In *Archaeologies of the Pueblo Revolt: Identity, Meaning, and Renewal in the Pueblo World*, edited by R. W. Preucel, pp. 77–84. University of New Mexico Press, Albuquerque.

Moore, Roger A., Jr. 1994. The lithic assemblage from a Pueblo petroglyph site. In *Artifacts, Shrines, and Pueblos: Papers in Honor of Gordon Page*, edited by M. S. Duran and D. T. Kirkpatrick, pp. 167–82. Papers of the Archaeological Society of New Mexico, vol. 20. Archaeological Society of New Mexico, Albuquerque.

Morales, Reinaldo, Jr. 2005. Considerations on the art and aesthetics of rock art. In *Aesthetics and Rock Art*, edited by T. Heyd and J. Clegg, pp. 61–74. Ashgate, Burlington, VT.

Morley, Iain. 2007. New questions of old hands: Outlines of human representation in the Paleolithic. In *Image and Imagination: A Global Prehistory of Figurative Representation*, edited by C. Renfrew and I. Morley, pp. 69–82. McDonald Institute of Archeological Research, University of Cambridge, Cambridge.

Morphy, Howard. 1991. *Ancestral Connections: Art and an Aboriginal System of Knowledge*. University of Chicago Press, Chicago, IL.

———. 1994a. Aesthetics across time and place: An anthropological perspective. *Cambridge Archaeological Journal* 4(2):257–60.

———. 1994b. The anthropology of art. In *Companion Encyclopedia of Anthropology*, edited by T. Ingold, pp. 648–85. Routledge, New York.

———. 1996. Debate: Aesthetics is a cross-cultural category: For the motion (1). In *Key Debates in Anthropology*, edited by T. Ingold, pp. 255–60. Routledge, London, UK.

———. 2005. Aesthetics across time and place: An anthropological perspective on archaeology. In *Aesthetics and Rock Art*, edited by T. Heyd and J. Clegg, pp. 51–60. Ashgate, Burlington, VT.

———. 2008. *Becoming Art: Exploring Cross-Cultural Categories*. Berg, New York.

Morphy, Howard, and Morgan Perkins (eds.). 2005a. *The Anthropology of Art: A Reader*. Blackwell, Malden, MA.

———. 2005b. The anthropology of art: A reflection on its history and contemporary practice. In *The Anthropology of Art: A Reader*, edited by H. Morphy and M. Perkins, pp. 1–32. Blackwell, Malden, MA.

———. 2005c. Primitivism, art, and artifacts: Introduction. In *The Anthropology of Art: A Reader*, edited by H. Morphy and M. Perkins, pp. 125–28. Blackwell, Malden, MA.

Morris, Christine. 1993. Hands up for the individual! The role of attribution studies in Aegean prehistory. *Cambridge Archaeological Journal* 3(1):41–66.

Morris, Earl H. 1927. The beginnings of pottery making in the San Juan area: Unfired proto-types and the wares of the earliest ceramic period. *Anthropological Papers of the American Museum of Natural History* 28(2):125–98.

Morris, Earl H., and Robert F. Burgh. 1941. *Anasazi Basketry.* Carnegie Institution of Washington Publications 533. Carnegie Institution of Washington, Washington, DC.

Mortensen, Preben. 1997. *Art in the Social Order: The Making of the Modern Conception of Art.* State University of New York Press, Albany.

Morwood, M. J. 1992. Introductory essay on ethnography and the archaeological study of art. In *Rock Art and Ethnography,* edited by M. J. Morwood and D. R. Hobbs, pp. 1–6. Occasional AURA Publication 5. Archaeological Publications, Melbourne.

Moulard, Barbara L. 1982. Mimbres Iconography: A Study in Methodology and Interpretation. Unpublished M.A. thesis, Arizona State University, Tempe.

———. 1984. *Within the Underworld Sky: Mimbres Ceramic Art in Context.* Twelvetrees Press, Pasadena, CA.

———. 1985. Form, function, and interpretation of Mimbres ceramic hemispheric vessels. *Phoebus* 4:86–98.

Munn, Nancy D. 1973. *Walbiri Iconography: Graphic Representation and Cultural Symbolism in a Central Australian Society.* Cornell University Press, Ithaca, NY.

Munson, Marit K. 2000. Sex, gender, and status: Human images from the Classic Mimbres. *American Antiquity* 65:127–43.

———. 2002. On Boundaries and Beliefs: Rock Art and Identity on the Pajarito Plateau. Unpublished Ph.D. dissertation, Department of Anthropology, University of New Mexico, Albuquerque.

———. 2003. Rock art imagery and the power of place at Las Estrellas, New Mexico. In *Climbing the Rocks: Papers in Honor of Helen and Jay Crotty,* edited by R. N. Wiseman, T. C. O'Laughlin, and C. T. Snow, pp. 127–36. Archaeological Society of New Mexico, Albuquerque.

———. 2006. Creating the Codex Hopiensis: Jesse Walter Fewkes and Hopi artists, 1899–1900. *American Indian Art* 31(4):70–83, 120.

———. 2007. *Kenneth Chapman's Santa Fe: Artists and Archaeologists, 1907–1931.* School for Advanced Research Press, Santa Fe, NM.

———. 2008a. The problem of art in archaeology, as viewed from the ancient Southwest. Paper presented at the School for Advanced Research Colloquium Series, Santa Fe, NM.

———. 2008b. Rock art, ritual, and landscape in the 14th-century Galisteo Basin, New Mexico. Paper presented at the 73rd Annual Meeting of the Society for American Archaeology, Vancouver, BC.

———. In press-a. Gender, art, and ritual hierarchy in the Ancient Pueblos of the Rio Grande Valley, New Mexico. In *Comparative Archaeologies: The American Southwest (AD 900–1600) and the Iberian Peninsula (3000–1500 BC),* edited by K. T. Lillios. Cotsen Institute for Archaeology, Los Angeles, CA.

———. In press-b. Iconography, space, and practice: Rio Grande rock art, AD 1150–1600. In *Gathering Ancestors: Religious Transformation in the Pueblo World,* edited by D. M. Glowacki and S. Van Keuren. University of Arizona Press, Tucson.

Munson, Marit K., and Genevieve Head. In press. Surveying Petroglyph Hill: Cultural landscapes of the Galisteo Basin. In *Conflagration and Conflict: Burnt Corn Pueblo and the Galisteo Basin in the 14th century AD*, edited by J. E. Snead and M. Allen. University of Arizona Press, Tucson.

Myers, Fred. 2006. "Primitivism," anthropology, and the category of "primitive art." In *Handbook of Material Culture*, edited by C. Tilley, W. Keane, S. Kuchler, M. J. Rowlands, and P. Spyer, pp. 267–84. Sage, London, UK.

Nanoglou, Stratos. 2009. The materiality of representation: A preface. *Journal of Archaeological Method and Theory* 16(3):157–61.

Naumann, Francis M. 1999. *Marcel Duchamp: The Art of Making Art in the Age of Mechanical Reproduction*. Ludion Press, Ghent, Belgium.

Neitzel, Jill. 2000. Gender hierarchies: A comparative analysis of mortuary data. In *Women and Men in the Prehispanic Southwest: Labor, Power, and Prestige*, edited by P. L. Crown, pp. 137–68. School of American Research Press, Santa Fe, NM.

———. In press. Mixed messages: Art and leadership in the late prehispanic Southwest. In *Comparative Archaeologies: The American Southwest (AD 900–1600) and the Iberian Peninsula (3000–1500 BC)*, edited by K. T. Lillios. Cotsen Institute for Archaeology, Los Angeles, CA.

Nelson, Margaret C., and Michelle Hegmon. 2010. Mimbres lives and landscapes. In *Mimbres Lives and Landscapes*, edited by M. C. Nelson and M. Hegmon, pp. 1–7. School for Advanced Research Press, Santa Fe, NM.

Nelson, Nels C. 1914. *Pueblo Ruins of the Galisteo Basin*. American Museum of Natural History, New York.

Newsome, Elizabeth A., and Kelley Hays-Gilpin. In press. Spectatorship and performance in mural painting, 1250–1500: Visuality and social integration. In *Gathering Ancestors: Religious Transformation in the Pueblo World*, edited by D. M. Glowacki and S. Van Keuren. University of Arizona Press, Tucson.

Nochlin, Linda. 1988. Why have there been no great women artists? In *Women, Art, and Power and Other Essays*, edited by Linda Nochlin, pp. 145–77. Harper & Row, New York. Novitz, David. 1998. Art by another name. *British Journal of Aesthetics* 38:19–32.

Odegaard, Nancy, and Kelley Hays-Gilpin. 2002. Technology of the sacred: Painted basketry in the Southwest. In *Traditions, Transitions, and Technologies: Themes in Southwestern Archaeology*, edited by S. H. Schlanger, pp. 307–31. University Press of Colorado, Boulder.

Olsen, Nancy H. 1985. *Hovenweep Rock Art: An Anasazi Visual Communication System*. Occasional Paper 14. Institute for Archaeology, University of California, Los Angeles.

Ortman, Scott G. 2000. Conceptual metaphor in the archaeological record: Methods and an example from the American Southwest. *American Antiquity* 65(4):613–45.

———. 2008. Architectural metaphor and Chacoan influence in the Northern San Juan. In *Archaeology Without Borders: Contact, Commerce, and Change in the US Southwest and Northwestern Mexico*, edited by L. D. Webster and M. E. McBrinn, pp. 227–56. University Press of Colorado, Boulder.

Overing, Joanna. 1996. Debate: Aesthetics is a cross-cultural category: Against the motion (1). In *Key Debates in Anthropology*, edited by T. Ingold, pp. 260–66. Routledge, London, UK.

Packard, Gar, and Maggy Packard. 1974. *Suns and Serpents: The Symbolism of Indian Rock Art*. Packard Publications, Santa Fe, NM.

Panofsky, Erwin. 1955. Iconography and iconology: An introduction to the study of Renaissance art. In *Meaning in the Visual Arts*, edited by E. Panofsky, pp. 26–54. Doubleday, New York.

Peckham, Stewart. 1979. When is a Rio Grande kiva? In *Collected Papers in Honor of Bertha Pauline Dutton*, edited by A. H. Schroeder, pp. 55–86. Papers of the Archaeological Society of New Mexico, vol. 4. Archaeological Society of New Mexico, Albuquerque.

———. 1990. *From This Earth: The Ancient Art of Pueblo Pottery*. Museum of New Mexico Press, Santa Fe.

Penney, David W. 2004. The archaeology of aesthetics. In *Hero, Hawk, and Open Hand: American Indian Art of the Ancient Midwest and South*, edited by R. F. Townsend and R. V. Sharp, pp. 43–55. Yale University Press, New Haven, CT.

Pepper, George H. 1905. Ceremonial objects and ornaments from Pueblo Bonito, New Mexico. *American Anthropologist* 7(2):183–97.

———. 1920. *Pueblo Bonito*. Anthropological Papers of the American Museum of Natural History 27. American Museum of Natural History, New York.

Perkins, Morgan. 2006. "Do we still have no word for art?" A contemporary Mohawk question. In *Exploring World Art*, edited by E. Venbrux, P. S. Rosi, and R. L. Welsch, pp. 291–315. Waveland Press, Long Grove, IL.

Phillips, David A., Jr., Christine S. VanPool, and Todd L. VanPool. 2006. The horned serpent tradition in the North American Southwest. In *Religion in the Prehispanic Southwest*, edited by C. S. VanPool, T. L. VanPool, and D. A. Phillips Jr., pp. 17–30. AltaMira Press, Lanham, MD.

Phillips, Ruth B. 1989. Dreams and designs: Iconographic problems in Great Lakes twined bags. In *Great Lakes Indian Art*, edited by D. W. Penney, pp. 53–67. Wayne State University Press, Detroit, MI.

Phillips, Ruth B. 1994. Fielding culture: Dialogues between art history and anthropology. *Museum Anthropology* 18(1):39–46.

———. 2002. A proper place for art or the proper arts of place? Native North American objects and the hierarchies of art, craft, and souvenir. In *On Aboriginal Representation in the Gallery*, edited by L. Jessup and S. Bagg, pp. 45–72. Mercury Series, Canadian Ethnology Service. Canadian Museum of Civilization, Hull, Quebec.

———. 2005a. The collecting and display of souvenir arts: Authenticity and the "strictly commercial." In *The Anthropology of Art: A Reader*, edited by H. Morphy and M. Perkins, pp. 431–53. Blackwell, Malden, MA.

———. 2005b. The value of disciplinary difference: Reflections on art history and anthropology at the beginning of the twenty-first century. In *Anthropologies of Art*, edited by M. Westermann, pp. 242–59. Yale University Press, New Haven, CT.

Pitts, Victoria. 2003. *In the Flesh: The Cultural Politics of Body Modification*. Palgrave Macmillan, New York.

Plog, Stephen. 1980. *Stylistic Variation in Prehistoric Ceramics: Design Analysis in the American Southwest*. Cambridge University Press, Cambridge.

———. 1983. Analysis of style in artifacts. *Annual Review of Anthropology* 12:125–42.

———. 2003. Exploring the ubiquitous through the unusual: Color symbolism in Pueblo black-on-white pottery. *American Antiquity* 68:665–95.

Pocius, Gerald L. 1995. Art. *Journal of American Folklore* 108:413–31.

Potter, James M. 2000. Pots, parties, and politics: Communal feasting in the American Southwest. *American Antiquity* 65(3):471–92.

Powell-Marti, Valli, and Patricia A. Gilman (eds.). 2006. *Mimbres Society*. University of Arizona Press, Tucson.

Powell-Marti, Valli, and William D. James. 2006. Ceramic iconography and social asymmetry in the Classic Mimbres heartland, AD 970–1140. In *Mimbres Society*, edited by V. Powell-Marti and P. A. Gilman, pp. 151–73. University of Arizona Press, Tucson.

Price, Sally. 1989. *Primitive Art in Civilized Places*. University of Chicago Press, Chicago, IL.

Rautman, Alison E. 2000. Population aggregation, community organization, and plaza-oriented Pueblos in the American Southwest. *Journal of Field Archaeology* 27(3):271–83.

Reents-Budet, Dorie, Joseph Ball, Ronald Bishop, Virginia Fields, and Barbara MacLeod. 1994. *Painting the Maya Universe: Royal Ceramics of the Classic Period*. Duke University Press, Durham, NC.

Renaud, Etienne B. 1938a. The snake among the petroglyphs from north-central New Mexico. *Southwestern Lore* 4:42–47.

———. 1938b. *Petroglyphs of North Central New Mexico, 1938*. Archaeological Survey Series Report 11. Colorado Museum of Natural History, Denver.

Renfrew, Colin. 1994. Hypocrite voyant, mon semblable. *Cambridge Archaeological Journal* 4(2):264–69.

———. 2003. *Figuring It Out: The Parallel Visions of Artists and Archaeologists*. Thames and Hudson, London, UK.

Risatti, Howard. 2007. *A Theory of Craft: Function and Aesthetic Expression*. University of North Carolina Press, Chapel Hill.

Ritzenthaler, Robert E. 1979. From folk art to fine art : The emergence of the name artist among the Southwest Indians. In *The Visual Arts: Plastic and Graphic*, edited by J. M. Cordwell, pp. 431–38. Mouton, The Hague.

Robins, Michael R. 2002. Status and social power: Rock art as prestige technology among the San Juan Basketmakers of Southeast Utah. In *Traditions, Transitions, and Technologies: Themes in Southwestern Archaeology*, edited by S. H. Schlanger, pp. 386–400. University Press of Colorado, Boulder.

Robins, Michael R., and Kelley Hays-Gilpin. 2000. The bird in the basket: Gender and social change in Basketmaker iconography. In *Foundations of Anasazi Culture: The Basketmaker-Pueblo Transition*, edited by P. F. Reed, pp. 231–47. University of Utah Press, Salt Lake City.

Roe, Peter G. 1995. Style, society, myth, and structure. In *Style, Society, and Person*, edited by C. Carr and J. E. Neitzel, pp. 27–76. Plenum Press, New York.

Rohn, Arthur H. 1989. *The Rock Art of Bandelier National Monument*. University of New Mexico Press, Albuquerque.

Rose, Gillian. 2001. *Visual Methodologies: An Introduction to the Interpretation of Visual Materials*. Sage, London, UK.

Rubin, Arnold. 1977. The individual in prehistory: An art-historical perspective. In *The Individual in Prehistory: Studies of Variability in Style in Prehistoric Technologies*, edited by J. N. Hill and J. Gunn, pp. 247–50. Academic Press, New York.

Rubin, William (ed.). 1984. *"Primitivism" in 20th Century Art: Affinity of the Tribal and the Modern*. Museum of Modern Art, New York.

Ruscavage-Barz, Samantha M., and Elizabeth A. Bagwell. 2006. Gathering spaces and bounded places: The religious significance of plaza-oriented communities in the Northern Rio Grande, New Mexico. In *Religion in the Prehispanic Southwest*, edited by C. S. VanPool, T. L. VanPool, and D. A. Phillips Jr., pp. 81–102. AltaMira Press, Lanham, MD.

Russell, Will G., and Michelle Hegmon. Manuscript in preparation. Painted by the same hand: Identifying individual artists in Mimbres pottery from the US Southwest. Paper in possession of the author.

Sackett, James R. 1990. Style and ethnicity in archaeology: The case for isochrestism. In *The Uses of Style in Archaeology*, edited by Margaret W. Conkey and Christine Hastorf, pp. 32–43. Cambridge University Press, New York.

Saunders, Nicholas J. 1999. Biographies of brilliance: Pearls, transformations of matter and being, c. AD 1492. *World Archaeology* 31(2):243–57.

———. 2002. The colours of light: Materiality and chromatic cultures of the Americas. In *Colouring the Past: The Significance of Colour in Archaeological Research*, edited by A. Jones and G. MacGregor, pp. 209–26. Berg, Oxford.

———. 2004. The cosmic earth: Materiality and mineralogy in the Americas. In *Soils, Stones, and Symbols: Cultural Perceptions of the Mineral World*, edited by N. Boivin and M. A. Owoc, pp. 123–42. UCL Press, London, UK.

Saville, Dara. 2001. Regional Variations of Kachina Iconography in Eastern Pueblo Rock Art. Unpublished M.S. thesis, Department of Geography, University of New Mexico, Albuquerque.

———. 2002. Kachina iconography of Piedras Marcadas Canyon, Petroglyph National Monument. *American Indian Rock Art* 28:151–59.

———. 2003. Rock art, kachinas, and the landscape at Cerro Indio, New Mexico. In *Climbing the Rocks: Papers in Honor of Helen and Jay Crotty*, edited by R. N. Wiseman, T. C. O'Laughlin and C. T. Snow, pp. 177–87. Archaeological Society of New Mexico, Albuquerque.

Sawyer, R. Keith. 2006. *Explaining Creativity: The Science of Human Innovation.* Oxford University Press, Oxford.

Schaafsma, Polly. 1975a. Rock art and ideology of the Mimbres and Jornada Mogollon. *The Artifact* 13(3):1–14.

———. 1975b. *Rock Art in the Cochiti Reservoir District.* Papers in Anthropology 16. Museum of New Mexico Press, Santa Fe.

———. 1980. *Indian Rock Art of the Southwest.* University of New Mexico Press, Albuquerque.

———. 1990. The Pine Tree site: A Pueblo IV shrine in the Galisteo Basin, New Mexico. In *Clues to the Past: Papers in Honor of William M. Sundt*, edited by M. S. Duran and D. T. Kirkpatrick. Papers of the Archaeological Society of New Mexico, vol. 16. Archeological Society of New Mexico, Albuquerque.

———. 1992a. Imagery and magic: Petroglyphs at Comanche Gap, Galisteo Basin, New Mexico. In *Archaeology, Art, and Anthropology: Papers in Honor of J. J. Brody*, edited by M. S. Duran and D. T. Kirkpatrick, pp. 157–74. Archaeological Society of New Mexico, Albuquerque.

———. 1992b. *Rock Art in New Mexico.* Museum of New Mexico Press, Santa Fe.

———. 1994. *Kachinas in the Pueblo World.* University of New Mexico Press, Albuquerque.

———. 1999. Tlalocs, kachinas, sacred bundles, and related symbolism in the Southwest and Mesoamerica. In *The Casas Grandes World*, edited by C. F. Schaafsma and C. L. Riley, pp. 164–92. University of Utah Press, Salt Lake City.

———. 2000. *Warrior, Shield, and Star: Imagery and Ideology of Pueblo Warfare.* Western Edge Press, Santa Fe, NM.

———. 2002. Pottery metaphors in Pueblo and Jornada Mogollon rock art. In *Rock Art and Cultural Processes*, edited by S. A. Turpin, pp. 51–66. Special Publication 3. Rock Art Foundation, San Antonio, TX.

———. 2007. The Pottery Mound murals and rock art: Implications for regional interaction. In *New Perspectives on Pottery Mound Pueblo*, edited by P. Schaafsma, pp. 137–66. University of New Mexico Press, Albuquerque.

Schaafsma, Polly, and Curtis F. Schaafsma. 1974. Evidence for the origins of the Pueblo katchina cult as suggested by Southwestern rock art. *American Antiquity* 39:535–45.

Schaafsma, Polly, and Regge N. Wiseman. 1992. Serpents in the prehistoric Pecos Valley of southeastern New Mexico. In *Archaeology, Art, and Anthropology: Papers in Honor of J. J. Brody*, edited by M. S. Duran and D. T. Kirkpatrick, pp. 175–83. Papers of the Archaeological Society of New Mexico, vol. 18. Archaeological Society of New Mexico, Albuquerque.

Schaafsma, Polly, and M. Jane Young. 1983. Early masks and faces in Southwest rock art. In *Collected Papers in Honor of Charlie R. Steen, Jr.*, edited by N. L. Fox, pp. 11–33. Papers of the Archaeological Society of New Mexico, vol. 8. Archeological Society of New Mexico, Albuquerque.

Schechner, Richard. 2003. *Performance Theory*. Revised ed. Routledge, London, UK.

Schiffer, Michael B., and Andrea R. Miller. 1999. *The Material Life of Human Beings: Artifacts, Behavior, and Communication*. Routledge, London, UK.

Schleher, Kari L., and Marit K. Munson. 2010. Ceramics and rock art in the Northern Rio Grande: A comparison of design. Poster presented at the 75th Annual Meeting of the Society for American Archaeology, St. Louis, MO.

Schneider, Arnd, and Christopher Wright (eds.). 2006. *Contemporary Art and Anthropology*. Berg, New York.

Scott, Catherine J. 1983. The evolution of Mimbres pottery. In *Mimbres Pottery: Ancient Art of the American Southwest*, edited by J. J. Brody, C. J. Scott, and S. A. LeBlanc, pp. 39–67. Hudson Hills Press, New York.

Sekaquaptewa, Emory, and Dorothy K. Washburn. 2004. They go along singing: Reconstructing the Hopi past from ritual metaphors in song and image. *American Antiquity* 69:457–86.

Shafer, Harry J. 1985. A Mimbres potter's grave: An example of Mimbres craft-specialization? *Bulletin of the Texas Archeological Society* 56:185–200.

———. 1995. Architecture and symbolism in transitional Pueblo development in the Mimbres Valley, SW New Mexico. *Journal of Field Archaeology* 22:23–47.

Shafer, Harry J., and Robbie L. Brewington. 1995. Microstylistic changes in Mimbres black-on-white pottery: Examples from the NAN Ruin, Grant County, New Mexico. *Kiva* 61(1):5–29.

Shaffer, Brian S. 2002. The Mythology of Classic Period Mimbres Painted Pottery Iconology: Evaluation of the Iconographic Interpretations. Unpublished Ph.D. dissertation, Department of Anthropology, Texas A&M University, College Station.

Shaffer, Brian S., Karen M. Gardner, and Harry J. Shafer. 1997. An unusual birth depicted in Mimbres pottery: Not cracked up to what it is supposed to be. *American Antiquity* 62(4):727–32.

Shiner, Larry. 2001. *The Invention of Art: A Cultural History*. University of Chicago Press, Chicago, IL.

Short, Susan Alice. 1998. When the Animals Still Danced: Animal Images in Mimbres Pottery and Petroglyphs. Unpublished Ph.D. dissertation, Department of Anthropology, University of Minnesota, Minneapolis.

Shostak, M. 1993. The creative individual in the world of the !Kung San. In *Creativity/Anthropology*, edited by S. Lavie, K. Narayan, and R. Rosaldo, pp. 54–69. Cornell University Press, Ithaca, NY.

Sigler, Jennifer A. 2000. Using Exterior Designs to Identify Production Groups Among 14th-century Hopi Potters. Unpublished M.A. thesis, Department of Anthropology, University of Arizona, Tucson.

Silver, Larry. 1986. The state of research in northern Renaissance art. *Art Bulletin* 68(4):528–35.

Slifer, Dennis. 2000. *The Serpent and the Sacred Fire: Fertility Images in Southwestern Rock Art*. Museum of New Mexico Press, Santa Fe.

Smith, Alexa M. 2000. Zoomorphic iconography on preclassic Hohokam red-on-buff pottery: A whole vessel study from the Gila river basin. *Kiva* 66(2):223–47.

Smith, Benjamin. 1998. The tale of the chameleon and the platypus: Limited and likely choices in making pictures. In *The Archaeology of Rock-Art*, edited by C. Chippindale and P.S.C. Taçon, pp. 212–28. Cambridge University Press, New York.

Smith, Helene Denise. 1998. The Rock Art of Abo Pueblo: Analyzing a Cultural Palimpsest. Unpublished Ph.D. dissertation, Department of Art and Art History, University of New Mexico, Albuquerque.

Smith, R.R.R. 1994. A Greek and Roman point of view. *Cambridge Archaeological Journal* 4(2):260–64.

Smith, Watson. 1952. *Kiva Mural Decorations at Awatovi and Kawaika-a, with a Survey of Other Wall Paintings in the Pueblo Southwest*. Papers of the Peabody Museum of American Archaeology and Ethnology 37. Harvard University, Cambridge, MA.

———. 1962. Schools, pots, and potters. *American Anthropologist* 64:1165–78.

———. 1990. *When Is a Kiva? and Other Questions about Southwestern Archaeology*. University of Arizona Press, Tucson.

Snead, James E. 2001. *Ruins and Rivals: The Making of Southwest Archaeology*. University of Arizona Press, Tucson.

———. 2002. Lessons of the ages: Archaeology and the construction of cultural identity in the American Southwest. *Journal of the Southwest* 44(1):17–34.

———. 2008. *Ancestral Landscapes of the Pueblo World*. University of Arizona Press, Tucson.

Snead, James E., and Marit K. Munson. 2001. Mapping the world: Space and place in the Puebloan Southwest. Poster presented at the 67th Annual Meeting of the Society for American Archaeology, New Orleans, LA.

Soffer, Olga, and Margaret W. Conkey. 1997. Studying ancient visual cultures. In *Beyond Art: Pleistocene Image and Symbol*, edited by M. W. Conkey, O. Soffer, D. Stratmann, and N. G. Jablonski, pp. 1–16. University of California Press, San Francisco.

Sparshott, Francis. 1997. Art and anthropology. *Journal of Aesthetics and Art Criticism* 55(3):239–43.

Spielmann, Katherine A. 1998a. Ritual craft specialists in middle range societies. In *Craft and Social Identity*, edited by C. L. Costin and R. P. Wright, pp. 153–59. Archeological Papers of the American Anthropological Association, vol. 8. American Anthropological Association, Arlington, VA.

———. 1998b. Ritual influences on the development of Rio Grande Glaze A ceramics. In *Migration and Reorganization: The Pueblo IV Period in the American*

Southwest, edited by K. A. Spielmann, pp. 253–61. Anthropological Research Papers, vol. 51. Arizona State University, Tempe.

Spielmann, Katherine A., Jeannette L. Mobley-Tanaka, and James M. Potter. 2006. Style and resistance in the seventeenth century Salinas province. *American Antiquity* 71(4):621–47.

Stanislawski, Michael B. 1977. Ethnoarchaeology of Hopi and Hopi-Tewa pottery making: Styles of learning. In *Experimental Archaeology*, edited by D. Ingersoll, J. Yellen, and W. MacDonald, pp. 378–408. Columbia University Press, New York.

Stanislawski, Michael B., and B. Stanislawski. 1978. Hopi and Hopi-Tewa ceramic tradition networks. In *The Spatial Organization of Culture*, edited by I. Hodder, pp. 61–76. University of Pittsburgh Press, Pittsburgh, PA.

Stark, Barbara L. 1995. Problems in analysis of standardization and specialization in pottery. In *Ceramic Production in the American Southwest*, edited by B. J. Mills and P. L. Crown, pp. 231–67. University of Arizona Press, Tucson.

Stark, Miriam T. 2006. Glaze ware technology, the social lives of pots, and communities of practice in the late prehistoric Southwest. In *The Social Life of Pots: Glaze Wares and Cultural Dynamics in the Southwest, AD 1250–1680*, edited by J. A. Habicht-Mauche, S. L. Eckert, and D. L. Huntley, pp. 17–33. University of Arizona Press, Tucson.

Stecker, Robert. 2000. Is it reasonable to attempt to define art? In *Theories of Art Today*, edited by N. Carroll, pp. 45–64. University of Wisconsin Press, Madison.

———. 2003. Definition of art. In *The Oxford Handbook of Aesthetics*, edited by J. Levinson, pp. 136–54. Oxford University Press, Oxford.

———. 2005. *Aesthetics and the Philosophy of Art: An Introduction*. Rowman & Littlefield, Lanham, MD.

Steed, Paul P., Jr. 1986. The birds of La Cienega Mesa. In *By Hands Unknown: Papers in Honor of James G. Bain*, edited by A. Poore, pp. 5–7. Papers of the Archaeological Society of New Mexico, vol. 12. Ancient City Press, Santa Fe.

Stewart, Joe D., Paul Matousek, and Jane H. Kelley. 1990. Rock art and ceramic art in the Jornada Mogollon region. *Kiva* 55(4):301–19.

Stinson, Susan Lynne. 2004. Household Ritual, Gender, and Figurines in the Hohokam Regional System. Unpublished Ph.D. dissertation, Department of Anthropology, University of Arizona, Tucson.

Stoffel, Diane E. 1991. Classic Mimbres Iconography: An Investigation of Style, Symbol, and Meaning. Unpublished M.A. thesis, University of New York, Buffalo.

Stuhr, Joanne (ed.). 2002. *Talking Birds, Plumed Serpents, and Painted Women: The Ceramics of Casas Grandes*. Tucson Museum of Art, Tucson, AZ.

Sturken, Marita, and Lisa Cartwright. 2001. *Practices of Looking: An Introduction to Visual Culture*. Oxford University Press, Oxford.

Svasek, Maruska. 2007. *Anthropology, Art, and Cultural Production*. Pluto Press, Ann Arbor, MI.

Taçon, Paul S. C., and Christopher Chippindale. 1998. An archaeology of rock-art through informed methods and formal methods. In *The Archaeology of Rock-Art*, edited by C. Chippindale and P.S.C. Taçon, pp. 1–10. Cambridge University Press, New York.

Tanner, Clara Lee. 1976. *Prehistoric Southwestern Craft Arts*. University of Arizona Press, Tucson.

Taylor, Timothy. 1994. Excavating art: The archaeologist as analyst and audience. *Cambridge Archaeological Journal* 4(2):250–56.

Taylor, Timothy, Michael Vickers, Howard Morphy, R.R.R. Smith, and Colin Renfrew. 1994. Viewpoint: Is there a place for aesthetics in archaeology? *Cambridge Archaeological Journal* 4(2):249–69.

Taylor, Walter W. 1948. A study of archaeology. *American Anthropologist* 50(3):1–256.

Teague, Lynn S. 1998. *Textiles in Southwestern Prehistory*. University of New Mexico Press, Albuquerque.

———. 2000. Outward and visible signs: Textiles in ceremonial contexts. In *The Archaeology of Regional Interaction: Religion, Warfare, and Exchange across the American Southwest and Beyond*, edited by M. Hegmon, pp. 429–77. University of Colorado Press, Boulder.

Teilhet, Jehanne H. 1978. The equivocal role of women artists in non-literate cultures. *Heresies* 4:96–102.

Thompson, Marc. 1999. Mimbres Iconology: Analysis and Interpretation of Figurative Motifs. Unpublished Ph.D. dissertation, Department of Archaeology, University of Calgary, Calgary, AB.

Thompson, Robert Farris. 2005. Yoruba artistic criticism. In *The Anthropology of Art: A Reader*, edited by H. Morphy and M. Perkins, pp. 242–69. Blackwell, Malden, MA.

Tisdale, Shelby J. 1993. From rock art to Wal-Mart: Kokopelli representations in historical perspective. In *Why Museums Collect: Papers in Honor of Joe Ben Wheat*, edited by M. S. Duran and D. T. Kirkpatrick, pp. 213–23. Archaeological Society of New Mexico, Albuquerque, New Mexico.

Toll, H. Wolcott. 2001. Making and breaking pots in the Chaco world. *American Antiquity* 66(1):56–78.

Tomásková, Silvia. 1997. Places of art: Art and archaeology in context. In *Beyond Art: Pleistocene Image and Symbol*, edited by M. W. Conkey, O. Soffer, D. Stratmann, and N. G. Jablonski, pp. 265–87. University of California Press, San Francisco.

Triadan, Daniela. 2006. Dancing gods: Ritual, performance, and political organization in the prehistoric Southwest. In *The Archaeology of Performance: Theaters of Power, Community, and Politics*, edited by T. Inomata and L. S. Coben, pp. 159–86. AltaMira Press, Lanham, MD.

Trigger, Bruce. 2006. *A History of Archaeological Thought*. 2nd ed. Cambridge University Press, Cambridge.

Van Keuren, Scott. 1994. Judging the mark of an individual: An investigation of design variation in prehistoric pottery from Grasshopper Pueblo, Arizona. *Arizona Anthropologist* 11:31–55.

———. 1999. *Ceramic Design Structure and the Organization of Cibola White Ware Production in the Grasshopper Region, Arizona*. Arizona State Museum Archaeological Series 191. Arizona State Museum, Tucson.

———. 2001. Ceramic Style and the Reorganization of Fourteenth Century Pueblo Communities in East-Central Arizona. Unpublished Ph.D. dissertation, Department of Anthropology, University of Arizona, Tucson.

———. 2004. Crafting feasts in the prehispanic Southwest. In *Identity, Feasting, and the Archaeology of the Greater Southwest*, edited by B. J. Mills, pp. 192–209. University Press of Colorado, Boulder.

———. 2006. Decorating glaze-painted pottery in east-central Arizona. In *The Social Life of Pots: Glaze Wares and Cultural Dynamics in the Southwest, AD 1250–1680*, edited by J. A. Habicht-Mauche, S. L. Eckert, and D. L. Huntley, pp. 86–104. University of Arizona Press, Tucson.

———. In press. Polychrome bowls and the localization of regional ideologies. In *Gathering Ancestors: Religious Transformation in the Pueblo World*, edited by D. M. Glowacki and S. Van Keuren. University of Arizona Press, Tucson.

VanPool, Christine S. 2009. The signs of the sacred: Identifying shamans using archaeological evidence. *Journal of Anthropological Archaeology* 28(2):177–90.

VanPool, Christine S., and Todd L. VanPool. 2006. Gender in middle range societies: A case study in Casas Grandes iconography. *American Antiquity* 71(1):53–75.

Vasari, Giorgio. 1991 [1550]. *The Lives of the Artists*. Translated by J. C. Bondanella and P. Bondanella. Oxford University Press, Oxford.

Vastokas, Joan M. 1986/1987. Native art as art history: Meaning and time from unwritten sources. *Journal of Canadian Studies* 21(4):7–36.

Venbrux, Eric, Pamela Sheffield Rosi, and Robert L. Welsch (eds.). 2006. *Exploring World Art*. Waveland Press, Long Grove, IL.

Vincent, Gilbert T. 1995. *Masterpieces of American Indian Art: From the Eugene and Clare Thaw Collection*. Harry N. Abrams, New York.

Vivian, Patricia. 1994. Anthropomorphic figures in the Pottery Mound murals. In *Kachinas in the Pueblo World*, edited by P. Schaafsma, pp. 81–91. University of New Mexico Press, Albuquerque.

———. 2007. The kiva murals of Pottery Mound: A history of discovery and methods of study, Kivas 1–10. In *New Perspectives on Pottery Mound Pueblo*, edited by P. Schaafsma, pp. 75–83. University of New Mexico Press, Albuquerque.

Vivian, R. Gwinn, Dulce N. Dodgen, and Gayle H. Hartman. 1978. *Wooden Ritual Artifacts from Chaco Canyon, New Mexico: The Chetro Ketl Collection*. University of Arizona Press, Tucson.

Vogel, Susan Mullin (ed.). 1988a. *ART/artifact: African Art in Anthropology Collections*. Center for African Art, New York.

———. 1988b. Introduction. In *ART/artifact: African Art in Anthropology Collections*, edited by S. M. Vogel, pp. 11–17. Center for African Art, New York.

———. 1999. Known artists but anonymous works: Fieldwork and art history. *African Arts* 32(1):40–55, 93–94.

Voss, Jerome A., and Robert L. Young. 1995. Style and the self. In *Style, Society, and Person*, edited by C. Carr and J. E. Neitzel, pp. 77–99. Plenum Press, New York.

Wade, Edwin L. 1986. Straddling the cultural fence: The conflict for ethnic artists within Pueblo societies. In *Arts of the North American Indian: Native Traditions in Evolution*, edited by E. L. Wade, pp. 243–54. Hudson Hills Press, New York.

Wallaert-Pêtre, Hélène. 2001. Learning how to make the right pots: Apprenticeship strategies and material culture, a case study in handmade pottery from Cameroon. *Journal of Anthropological Research* 57(4):407–25.

Walt, Henry J. 1978. An Effigy Cache from the Cliff Valley, New Mexico. Unpublished M.A. thesis, Department of Art and Art History, University of New Mexico, Albuquerque.

Warner, John Anson. 1986. The individual in Native American art: A sociological view. In *Arts of the North American Indian: Native Traditions in Evolution*, edited by E. L. Wade, pp. 171–202. Hudson Hills Press, New York.

Washburn, Dorothy K. 1977. *A Symmetry Analysis of Upper Gila Area Ceramic Design*. Peabody Museum of Archaeology and Ethnology, Harvard University, Cambridge, MA.

———. 1978. A symmetry classification of Pueblo ceramic designs. In *Discovering Past Behavior: Experiments in the Archaeology of the Southwest*, edited by P. Grebinger, pp. 101–21. Gordon and Breach, New York.

———. 1983. Toward a theory of structural style in art. In *Structure and Cognition in Art*, edited by D. K. Washburn, pp. 1–7. Cambridge University Press, Cambridge.

———. 1995. Style, perception, and geometry. In *Style, Society, and Person*, edited by C. Carr and J. E. Neitzel, pp. 101–22. Plenum Press, New York.

———. 2001. Remembering things seen: Experimental approaches to the process of information transmittal. *Journal of Archaeological Method and Theory* 8(1):67–99.

Washburn, Dorothy K., and Laurie D. Webster. 2006. Symmetry and color perspectives on Basketmaker cultural identities: Evidence from designs on coiled baskets and ceramics. *Kiva* 71(3):235–64.

Watson, Editha Latta. 1932. The laughing artists of the Mimbres valley. *Art and Archaeology* 33:188–93, 224.

Webster, Laurie D. 1997. Effects of European Contact on Textile Production and Exchange in the North American Southwest: A Pueblo Case Study. Unpublished Ph.D. dissertation, Department of Anthropology, University of Arizona, Tucson.

———. 2007. Ritual costuming at Pottery Mound: The Pottery Mound textiles in regional perspective. In *New Perspectives on Pottery Mound Pueblo*, edited by P. Schaafsma, pp. 167–206. University of New Mexico Press, Albuquerque.

———. 2008. An initial assessment of perishable artifact relationships among Salmon, Aztec, and Chaco Canyon. In *Chaco's Northern Prodigies: Salmon, Aztec, and the Ascendency of the Middle San Juan Region After AD 1100*, edited by P. F. Reed, pp. 167–89. University of Utah Press, Salt Lake City.

Webster, Lori D., and Kelley Hays-Gilpin. 1994. New trails for old shoes: Sandals, textiles, and baskets of the Basketmaker culture. *Kiva* 60:313–18.

Webster, Lori D., Kelley Hays-Gilpin, and Polly Schaafsma. 2006. A new look at tie-dye and the dot-in-a-square motif in the Prehispanic Southwest. *Kiva* 71(3):317–48.

Weiner, James F., Howard Morphy, Joanna Overing, Jeremy Coote, and Peter Gow. 1996a. Debate: Aesthetics is a cross-cultural category. In *Key Debates in Anthropology*, edited by T. Ingold, pp. 251–93. Routledge, London, UK.

———. 1996b. Debate: Aesthetics is a cross-cultural category: The debate. In *Key Debates in Anthropology*, edited by T. Ingold, pp. 276–93. Routledge, London, UK.

Weitz, Morris. 1956. The role of theory in aesthetics. *Journal of Aesthetics and Art Criticism* 15(1):27–35.

Westermann, Mariet (ed.). 2005. *Anthropologies of Art*. Yale University Press, New Haven, CT.

Wheat, Joe Ben, James C. Gifford, and William W. Wasley. 1958. Ceramic variety, type cluster, and ceramic system in Southwestern pottery analysis. *American Antiquity* 24(1):34–47.

White, Randall. 1992. Beyond art: Toward an understanding of the origins of material representation in Europe. *Annual Review of Anthropology* 21:537–64.

Whitley, David S. 2001. Rock art and rock art research in worldwide perspective: An introduction. In *Handbook of Rock Art Research*, edited by D. S. Whitley, pp. 1–54. AltaMira Press, New York.

Wilson, Lucy L. 1918. Hand sign or Avanyu: A note on a Pajaritan biscuit-ware motif. *American Anthropologist* n.s. 20(3):310–17.

Windes, Thomas C. 1992. Blue notes: The Chacoan turquoise industry in the San Juan Basin. In *Anasazi Regional Organization and the Chaco System*, edited by D. E. Doyel, pp. 159–68. Anthropological Papers no. 5. Maxwell Museum of Anthropology, Albuquerque, New Mexico.

Wright, Richard B. 2005. Style, meaning, and the individual artist in Western Pueblo polychrome ceramics after Chaco. *Journal of the Southwest* 47(2):259–325.

Wyckoff, Lydia L. 1985. *Designs and Factions: Politics, Religion, and Ceramics on the Hopi Third Mesa*. University of New Mexico Press, Albuquerque.

Young, M. Jane. 1988. *Signs from the Ancestors: Zuni Cultural Symbolism and Perceptions of Rock Art*. University of New Mexico Press, Albuquerque.

Zangwill, Nick. 1999. Art and audience. *Journal of Aesthetics and Art Criticism* 57(3):315–32.

Index

About the Author

Marit K. Munson is associate professor in the Department of Anthropology at Trent University and director of the Trent University Archaeological Research Centre, Peterborough, Ontario, Canada.